Are You the
One Who
Is to Come?

ARE YOU THE ONE WHO IS TO COME?

The Historical Jesus
and the Messianic Question

Michael F. Bird

Foreword by Stanley E. Porter

𝕭

Baker Academic

a division of Baker Publishing Group
Grand Rapids, Michigan

Published by Baker Academic
a division of Baker Publishing Group
PO Box 6287, Grand Rapids, MI 49516-6287
www.bakeracademic.com

Printed in the United States of America

Library of Congress Cataloging-in-Publication Data
Bird, Michael F.
    Are you the One who is to come? : the historical Jesus and the messianic question / Michael F. Bird ; with a foreword by Stanley E. Porter.
        p.   cm.
    Includes bibliographical references and indexes.
    ISBN 978-0-8010-3638-5 (pbk.)
    1. Jesus Christ—Knowledge of his own divinity. 2. Jesus Christ—Messiahship. I. Title.
BT216.5.B57 2009
232′.1—dc22   2009000915

Short Scripture phrases are the author's translation. Unless otherwise indicated, longer Scripture quotations are from the New Revised Standard Version of the Bible, copyright © 1989, by the Division of Christian Education of the National Council of the Churches of Christ in the United States of America. Used by permission. All rights reserved.

Scripture quotations marked RSV are from the Revised Standard Version of the Bible, copyright 1952 [2nd edition, 1971] by the Division of Christian Education of the National Council of the Churches of Christ in the United States of America. Used by permission. All rights reserved.

Contents

Foreword

What did Jesus know, and when did he know it?[1] This is a question that has been asked not only of American presidents but also, and perhaps more importantly, of Jesus regarding his messianic awareness. It is the specific question that Michael Bird asks and answers in this important book on Jesus's messianic knowledge.

Scholars interested in the historical Jesus have for some time shied away from offering positive answers to two important questions: Can you re-create the self-consciousness of an ancient person such as Jesus so as to examine what he thought about himself? Did Jesus say or do anything of significance to indicate that he thought of himself as the Messiah?

As Bird so ably points out, scholars have been hesitant to acknowledge that Jesus may have claimed to be the Messiah or that the Gospels clearly depict him as such. The major burden of this volume is to reexamine the question of whether in fact the Gospels depict Jesus as Messiah and, more than that, whether Jesus himself may have done or said things indicating that he was the Messiah.

I find it interesting that throughout most of last century and so far into this one, much scholarship has increasingly avoided discussing the self-consciousness or self-awareness of Jesus. With the rise of form criticism and the distancing of Jesus from the literary forms that depict him,[2] there has been

1. This paraphrases the question posed by Senator Howard Baker in the Watergate hearings in the United States Senate in 1973 concerning the extent of President Nixon's involvement in the scandal.
2. I prefer to frame the situation with reference to form criticism, rather than in terms of the supposed periods of historical Jesus research, not least because I find these periods to be highly problematic and at best confined to a small segment of German historical Jesus scholarship. See S. E. Porter, *The Criteria for Authenticity in Historical-Jesus Research: Previous Discussion and New Proposals* (JSNTSup 191; Sheffield: Sheffield Academic Press, 2000; repr., London: T&T Clark, 2004), esp. 28–59.

less and less effort to attempt to discover what Jesus himself thought about a range of important topics, and especially to discover what internal consciousness or awareness he had regarding a possible messianic vocation. This is surprising in the light of other scholarship. The self-consciousness of ancient personages—even fictional ancient personages, such as Oedipus, Antigone, and Ulysses, to name only a few—have provided the basis for developing entire behavioral theories. More than that, ancient historical figures on repeated occasions have been analyzed through their actions and words to determine their inner thoughts and perceptions.[3]

If we believe that the social-scientific methods that we have developed, including psychology and sociology, have any explanatory power, and if we believe that human nature, despite its changing surroundings, has at least a minimal constant element, then there is the opportunity to ask probing and personal questions of ancient personages—including Jesus—regarding what they thought of themselves and others. These questions can be asked in such a way as to examine what they said and what they did, and, more importantly, to penetrate into the internal cognizance that must have existed behind such statements and actions. This is an area that bears renewed attention in study of the Jesus of history as we refine our methods for historical exploration under the influence of complementary models, such as those developed in the social sciences, and as we learn to benefit from the advances made in other historically based disciplines. This is not the ostensive purpose of this volume by Michael Bird, and in the light of the problematic issues this topic raises (as I have noted), it is probably better, at least for the time being, that he avoids such questions regarding Jesus's self-awareness.

Instead, Bird takes another approach in this concise volume, an approach more consistent with the general tenor of current historical Jesus research. Bird essentially makes three significant moves in his exploration of whether and how Jesus understood his ministry as messianic. The first is to examine messianic expectation in the Second Temple period. There he finds that, though the thought is not necessarily widespread or consistent, there are clear messianic themes and expectations in the Second Temple literature. The second move is to refute explanations of the messianic elements of Jesus's ministry that are predicated wholly upon early-church developments of a messianic view of Jesus. The third and most important (and longest) step is to examine the evidence, especially in the Gospels but also in related literature, regarding Jesus's possible messianism. Here Bird believes he can show certain things Jesus said and did indicating that Jesus's ministry and message were depicted and understood in messianic categories.

3. I think that the most well-known of such figures is probably Alexander the Great. Some of the questions asked about Alexander are the same ones that are asked about Jesus, especially in terms of the question of consciousness of divinity.

I do not wish to detract in any way from readers' digesting for themselves Bird's arguments or savoring his conclusions, but I do wish to note some of his wording along the way as he expounds the various parts of his positive argument in chapter 4. Regarding the use of the term "Son of man," Bird says that Jesus "can even use it to make tacit references to his divinely given regal-like authority," and as this "Son of man" Jesus "is already exercising the dominion of the Messiah." With regard to Jesus's being the anointed one and the Qumran document 4Q521, Bird believes it "highly probable" that "Jesus regarded his ministry as demonstrating that the messianic signs of deliverance were present. . . ." Further, Jesus "saw himself in some sense as the king of God's kingdom. . . ." Jesus's "repeated reference to royal figures" that he compared himself to certainly was "provocative." Jesus's uses of "I have come" sayings "possess messianic connotations." Jesus, according to Bird, "identified the role of Messiah with a different constellation of categories" that possibly "led him to place the messianic vocation within a matrix of restoration eschatology, vicarious suffering, and the onset of the final tribulation." The incidents of Jesus's anointing in Bethany, his triumphal entry into Jerusalem, and his episode in the temple were all "deliberately provocative" in confirming his messianic position; together they justify the claim that Jesus sought to exercise a "messianic praxis." In fact, so Bird claims, "Jesus saw himself as the messianic shepherd. . . ." When Jesus answers the question standing before the high priest, he makes "a tacit messianic claim" and places himself "in the sphere of divine sovereignty." These are some significant and tantalizing conclusions reached by Bird in the course of his study.

The verbs that Bird uses are themselves provocative: Jesus "uses," "refers," "exercises," "regarded," "saw himself," makes "constant reference," "identifies," "placed," "exercised," and "sought," among others. All of these verbs may well indicate more than we might first expect in this treatment of Jesus's messianism. If Bird is right in his depiction of Jesus—and I think that he essentially is—then the Gospels contain much more than simply a depiction of Jesus. These words that Bird uses attribute intentions and motives to Jesus, and more than that, a specific type of knowledge, a messianic knowledge. The language attributes a particular kind of self-knowledge and internal cognizance to Jesus that result in the outward manifestation of a self-aware inner reality. Bird rightly indicates that Jesus actually did more than simply perform some actions or use some words that were seen to be messianic. He did and said certain things because he intended to do and say them. He intended to say and do them because he knew that he was the Messiah.

I raised the question above of whether we have enough information to provide an analysis of Jesus's self-consciousness or self-awareness. The current opinion is that we do not. However, unless actions or words are random or wholly unconsidered, there must be some previous thought and knowledge that motivates and drives them. Jesus's actions and behavior, as Bird has clearly shown, are not the result of inadvertent or haphazard behavior. We may wish to shy away from overpsychologizing our knowledge of Jesus, or any other person, ancient or modern, for that matter. That should not necessarily inhibit us from realizing the intentions that legitimately lie behind particular words and actions. I believe that Bird has provided strong evidence and support for going even further than we at first imagined, to a penetration of the knowledge and intentions of Jesus the Messiah. A book that helps us to do this is a book to be enthusiastically welcomed.

Stanley E. Porter
President and Dean
Professor of New Testament
McMaster Divinity College
Hamilton, Ontario, Canada

Preface

This volume argues that the historical Jesus understood his mission, ministry, or vocation (or whatever we want to call it) in messianic categories. Jesus understood himself to be designated by God as the Messiah of Israel. There are many bricks used to construct this argument, and I recognize that while the foundations for the conclusion seem strong, some of the walls are stronger than others. As for which ones are the strongest or which less persuasive—that will be for others to decide. My overall objective is to demonstrate that the early Christian confession that "Jesus is the Christ" has pre-Easter roots in Jesus's own mission and purpose. This is a contention that stands in direct opposition to a number of recent studies including Joseph A. Fitzmyer's volume *The One Who Is to Come*,[1] which in many ways has inspired this project and is one of my primary dialogue partners.

Toward that task I have enjoyed a great deal of assistance. First of all, the Highland Theological College librarian, Martin Cameron, secured for me many secondary sources, including several obscure journal articles from Germany. Second, Craig A. Evans of Acadia Divinity School discussed the matter with me a couple of times, and I was grateful for his interaction on the subject. Third, I have to thank Danny Zacharias, a colleague of Professor Evans at Acadia and also a PhD student with me at the Highland Theological College, who made his article on 4Q521 available to me in advance of its publication. Fourth, I am grateful to Professor Stanley E. Porter, President and Dean of McMaster Divinity College, for reading the manuscript and writing the foreword. Professor Porter has been a role model for me in terms of both the productivity of his writing schedule and the breadth of his learning in New Testament studies. Fifth, my dear wife, Naomi, and my daughters, Alexis and Alyssa, also deserve a mention because of their support of me, and they now

---

1. Grand Rapids: Eerdmans, 2007.

know what I was doing between 9:00 p.m. and 1:00 a.m. most evenings. Sixth, Dr. Bob Webb, editor for the *Journal for the Study of the Historical Jesus*, was largely responsible for the development of this book. What started out as a single article destined for *Journal for the Study of the Historical Jesus* then became two articles, then three, then it morphed into a book. My thanks for Bob's patience in allowing me to defer that article project while this book was being completed. Seventh, Chris and Anja Tilling studiously checked my German translations and corrected several infelicities. Eighth, a number of persons read all or part of the initial manuscript, and I have benefited from their comments and criticisms; these include Brant Pitre, Jason Hood, James Crossley, Doug Chaplin, and Ben Reynolds. Ninth, I am most grateful to the good folks at Baker Academic (esp. James Ernest) for the support that they gave me in bringing this manuscript to fruition. Tenth, I want to thank Dr. Rick Strelan of the University of Queensland, who has to live with the infamy of being known as my *Doktorvater*. For three and a half years, Rick shared with me the most intimate aspects of my intellectual existence as well as the frustration of being my tennis partner. Because of Rick, my tennis is better and so is the standard of my research, writing, and teaching. Rick taught me to fight the arguments that I know I can win and to follow the line of the text and nothing else. To him I dedicate this book, in gratitude for his patience, time, and efforts on my behalf.

All biblical quotations not otherwise attributed are my own.

Abbreviations

Bibliographic and General

AB	Anchor Bible
ABD	*Anchor Bible Dictionary*
ABRL	Anchor Bible Reference Library
ANE	ancient Near East(ern)
ANYAS	Annals of the New York Academy of Sciences
b.	*ben* (= son of)
BAR	*Biblical Archaeology Review*
BBR	*Bulletin for Biblical Research*
BCE	before the Common Era
BETL	Bibliotheca ephemeridum theologicarum lovaniensium
Bib	*Biblica*
BJRL	*Bulletin of the John Rylands Library*
BSL	Biblical Studies Library
BTS	Biblisch-theologische Studien
BZ	*Biblische Zeitschrift*
BZAW	Beihefte zur Zeitschrift für die alttestamentliche Wissenschaft
ca.	circa, around
CBQ	*Catholic Biblical Quarterly*
CE	Common Era
CIL	*Corpus inscriptionum latinarum*

CIS	Copenhagen International Seminar
COQG	Christian Origins and the Question of God
DBAT	*Dielheimer Blätter zum Alten Testament und seiner Rezeption in der Alten Kirche*
DNTB	*Dictionary of New Testament Background*
DSD	*Dead Sea Discoveries*
DSS	Dead Sea Scrolls
ed.	editor/edited by; edition
EDNT	*Exegetical Dictionary of the New Testament*
EHJ	*Encyclopedia of the Historical Jesus*
EQ	*Evangelical Quarterly*
ExpT	*Expository Times*
FRLANT	Forschungen zur Religion und Literatur des Alten und Neuen Testaments
FS	Festschrift
Heb.	Hebrew
HTKNT	Herders theologischer Kommentar zum Neuen Testament
HTR	*Harvard Theological Review*
HTS	*Hervormde teologiese studies*
ICC	International Critical Commentary
JAAR	*Journal of the American Academy of Religion*
JBL	*Journal of Biblical Literature*
JBT	*Jahrbuch für biblische Theologie*
JETS	*Journal of the Evangelical Theological Society*
JGRChJ	*Journal of Greco-Roman Christianity and Judaism*
JSHJ	*Journal for the Study of the Historical Jesus*
JR	*Journal of Religion*
JSJ	*Journal for the Study of Judaism in the Persian, Hellenistic, and Roman Period*
JSNT	*Journal for the Study of the New Testament*
JSNTSup	Journal for the Study of the New Testament: Supplement Series
JSOTSup	Journal for the Study of the Old Testament: Supplement Series
JSPSup	Journal for the Study of the Pseudepigrapha: Supplement Series
JTS	*Journal of Theological Studies*

L	Luke's special material
LCL	Loeb Classical Library
lit.	literally
LNTS	Library of New Testament Studies
LXX	Septuagint
M	Matthew's special material
MS(S)	manuscript(s)
NICNT	New International Commentary on the New Testament
NIDNTT	*New International Dictionary of New Testament Theology*
NIGTC	New International Greek Testament Commentary
NovT	*Novum Testamentum*
NRSV	New Revised Standard Version
NTS	*New Testament Studies*
OTP	*The Old Testament Pseudepigrapha*
P.Oxy.	*The Oxyrhynchus Papyri*, London, 1898–
Q	*Quelle*, source (written?): Material common to Matthew and Luke that does not depend on Mark. When preceded by a number, Q = Qumran; 1Q = Cave 1, and so forth; DSS
R.	Rabbi
RB	*Revue biblique*
rev.	revised
RHPR	*Revue d'histoire et de philosophie religieuses*
RTR	*Reformed Theological Review*
SBET	*Scottish Bulletin of Evangelical Theology*
SBLMS	Society of Biblical Literature Monograph Series
SBT	Studies in Biblical Theology
SJT	*Scottish Journal of Theology*
SNTSMS	Society for New Testament Studies Monograph Series
ST	*Studia theologica*
SUNT	Studien zur Umwelt des Neuen Testaments
TDNT	*Theological Dictionary of the New Testament*
trans.	translated by; translation
TrinJ	*Trinity Journal*
TSAJ	Texte und Studium zum antiken Judentum
TynBul	*Tyndale Bulletin*

UBS	United Bible Society
UBS⁴	United Bible Societies Greek New Testament, 4th edition
UBW	Understanding the Bible and Its World
vol(s).	volume(s)
WBC	Word Biblical Commentary
WTJ	*Westminster Theological Journal*
WUNT	Wissenschaftliche Untersuchungen zum Neuen Testament
ZAW	*Zeitschrift für die alttestamentliche Wissenschaft*
ZNW	*Zeitschrift für die neutestamentliche Wissenschaft*
ZTK	*Zeitschrift für Theologie und Kirche*

Old Testament

Gen.	Genesis
Exod.	Exodus
Lev.	Leviticus
Num.	Numbers
Deut.	Deuteronomy
Josh.	Joshua
Judg.	Judges
Ruth	Ruth
1–2 Sam.	1–2 Samuel
1–2 Kings	1–2 Kings
1–2 Chron.	1–2 Chronicles
Ezra	Ezra
Neh.	Nehemiah
Esther	Esther
Job	Job
Ps(s).	Psalms
Prov.	Proverbs
Eccles.	Ecclesiastes
Song	Song of Songs
Isa.	Isaiah
Jer.	Jeremiah
Lam.	Lamentations

Ezek.	Ezekiel
Dan.	Daniel
Hosea	Hosea
Joel	Joel
Amos	Amos
Obad.	Obadiah
Jon.	Jonah
Mic.	Micah
Nah.	Nahum
Hab.	Habakkuk
Zeph.	Zephaniah
Hag.	Haggai
Zech.	Zechariah
Mal.	Malachi

New Testament

Matt.	Matthew
Mark	Mark
Luke	Luke
John	John
Acts	Acts
Rom.	Romans
1–2 Cor.	1–2 Corinthians
Gal.	Galatians
Eph.	Ephesians
Phil.	Philippians
Col.	Colossians
1–2 Thess.	1–2 Thessalonians
1–2 Tim.	1–2 Timothy
Titus	Titus
Philem.	Philemon
Heb.	Hebrews
James	James
1–2 Pet.	1–2 Peter

1–3 John	1–3 John
Jude	Jude
Rev.	Revelation

Other Jewish and Christian Writings

Add. Esth.	Additions to Esther
Adv. Marc.	Tertullian, *Against Marcion*
Apoc. Abr.	Apocalypse of Abraham
Apoc. Pet.	Apocalypse of Peter
1 Apol.	Justin Martyr, *First Apology*
Bar.	Baruch
2 Bar.	2 Baruch
1 Clem.	1 Clement
Comm. Matt.	Origen, *Commentary on the Gospel of Matthew*
Dial.	Justin Martyr, *Dialogue with Trypho*
Did.	Didache
1–3 En.	1–3 Enoch
Exag.	Ezekiel the Tragedian, *Exagōgē*
Gos. Phil.	Gospel of Philip
Gos. Thom.	Gospel of Thomas
Haer.	Hippolytus, *Refutation of All Heresies* or Irenaeus, *Against Heresies*
Herm. *Vis.*	Shepherd of Hermas, *Vision*
Hist. eccl.	Eusebius, *Ecclesiastical History*
Ign. *Eph.*	Ignatius, *To the Ephesians*
Ign. *Magn.*	Ignatius, *To the Magnesians*
Ign. *Pol.*	Ignatius, *To Polycarp*
Ign. *Rom.*	Ignatius, *To the Romans*
Ign. *Smyrn.*	Ignatius, *To the Smyrnaeans*
Ign. *Trall.*	Ignatius, *To the Trallians*
Jdt.	Judith
Jub.	Jubilees
L.A.B.	Liber antiquitatum biblicarum (Pseudo-Philo)
Lam. Rab.	Lamentations Rabbah

Lev. Rab.	Leviticus Rabbah
1–4 Macc.	1–4 Maccabees
Mart. Pol.	Martyrdom of Polycarp
Midr. Cant.	Midrash on Canticles/Song of Songs
Midr. Pss.	Midrash on Psalms
Num. Rab.	Numbers Rabbah
Odes Sol.	Odes of Solomon
Paed.	Clement of Alexandria, *Christ the Educator*
Pesiq. Rab.	Pesiqta Rabbati
Pss. Sol.	Psalms of Solomon
Recog.	Pseudo-Clement, *Recognitions*
Sib. Or.	Sibylline Oracles
Sir.	Sirach
T. Benj.	Testament of Benjamin
T. Jud.	Testament of Judah
T. Levi	Testament of Levi
T. Mos.	Testament of Moses
T. Reub.	Testament of Reuben
T. Sol.	Testament of Solomon
T. Zeb.	Testament of Zebulun
Tob.	Tobit
Wis.	Wisdom of Solomon

Josephus and Philo

Ant.	Josephus, *Jewish Antiquities*
Moses	Philo, *On the Life of Moses*
Rewards	Philo, *On Rewards and Punishments*
Spec. Laws	Philo, *On the Special Laws*
War	Josephus, *Jewish War*

Rabbinic Tractates

The abbreviations below are used for the names of the tractates in the Mishnah (indicated by a prefixed *m.*), Tosefta (*t.*), Babylonian Talmud (*b.*), and Jerusalem/Palestinian Talmud (*y.*).

Ber.	*Berakot*
Ḥag.	*Ḥagigah*
Ned.	*Nedarim*
Pesaḥ.	*Pesaḥim*
Šabb.	*Šabbat*
Sanh.	*Sanhedrin*
Sukkah	*Sukkah*
Taʿan.	*Taʿanit*

Targumim

Tg. Hos.	Targum of Hosea
Tg. Isa.	Targum of Isaiah
Tg. Lam.	Targum of Lamentations
Tg. Mic.	Targum of Micah
Tg. Neof.	Targum Neofiti
Tg. Onq.	Targum Onqelos
Tg. Ps.-J.	Targum Pseudo-Jonathan
Tg. Pss.	Targum of Psalms
Tg. Ruth	Targum of Ruth
Tg. Zech.	Targum of Zechariah

Qumran/Dead Sea Scrolls

1QapGen	Genesis Apocryphon
1QH	Thanksgiving Hymns
1QM	War Scroll
1QPs^j	Psalms, copy *j*
1QS	Rule of the Community
1QS^a	Rule of the Congregation (appendix *a* to 1QS)
1QS^b	Rule of the Blessings (appendix *b* to 1QS)

4Q161	Pesher on Isaiah, copy *a*
4Q174	Florilegium
4Q175	Testimonia
4Q246	Aramaic Apocalypse
4Q252	Pesher on Genesis, copy *a*
4Q254	Pesher on Genesis, copy *c*
4Q285	War Scroll, copy *g*
4Q369	Prayer of Enosh
4Q376	Liturgy of the Three Tongues of Fire
4Q381	Non-canonical Psalms, copy *b*
4Q382	Paraphrase of Kings
4Q458	Narrative, copy *a*
4Q521	Messianic Apocalypse
4QMMT	Halakic Letter
4QpIsa[a]	Pesher on Isaiah, copy *a*
11QMelch	Melchizedek
11QPs[a]	Psalms Scroll, copy *a*
CD	Cairo Damascus Document, MSS CD-A and CD-B from the Cairo Genizah; copies also in DSS

Classical Writers

Claud.	Suetonius, *Claudius*
Hist.	Dio Cassius, *Roman History* or Tacitus, *Histories*
Mor.	Plutarch, *Moralia*
Orat.	Dio Chrysostom, *Orations*
Peregr.	Lucian, *The Passing of Peregrinus*
Vesp.	Suetonius, *Vespasian*

1

"Jesus Who Is Called the Christ"

Matthew and Josephus both refer to "Jesus who is called 'Messiah.'" Matthew places the remark on the lips of Pilate at Jesus's trial, while Josephus mentions "Jesus who is called Messiah" almost as a side remark in his narration of the death of James the brother of Jesus, who was put to death at the instigation of the high priest Ananus in the early 60s CE.[1] Both of these authors are writing in the last quarter of the first century of the Common Era and refer to Jesus who is called "Messiah." But by whom was Jesus called "Messiah"? The obvious answer surely is, by Christians, and Josephus himself traces the name of the Christians back to the founder of their movement, to Jesus, which implies that he was known as "Christ" (*Ant.* 18.64).[2] Matthew, in

---

1. Matt. 27:17, 22: Ἰησοῦν τὸν λεγόμενον Χριστόν; and Josephus, Ant. 20.200: Ἰησοῦ τοῦ λεγομένου Χριστοῦ. See also Justin Martyr (*Dial.* 32) where Trypho refers to "this so-called Christ of yours [οὗτος δὲ ὁ ὑμέτερος λεγόμενος Χριστός]."

2. On the authenticity of elements of the *testimonium Flavianum*, see John P. Meier, *A Marginal Jew: Rethinking the Historical Jesus*, 3 vols. (ABRL; New York: Doubleday, 1991–2001), 1:56–69. Meier concludes that the phrase "He was the Messiah" in *Ant.* 18.63 is an interpolation by a Christian scribe but that the references to "the tribe of Christians named after him has not died out" (*Ant.* 18.64) and "Jesus who is called Messiah" (*Ant.* 20.200) are probably original and authentic to Josephus. In favor of the authenticity of a messianic reference to Jesus in the *testimonium Flavianum*, Alice Whealey ("The Testimonium Flavianum in Syriac and Arabic," *NTS* 54 [2008]: 573–90) draws attention to the testimonia preserved by Michael the Syrian (twelfth century) and Jerome (fourth century), which independently attest to a reading of "he was thought to be the Messiah," and this corresponds to Origen's claim (*Comm. Matt.* 1.15) that Josephus did not believe in Jesus as the Messiah. A variant is also found in the Arabic chronicles of Agapius of Hierapolis (tenth century): "he was perhaps the Messiah." In light of this, there probably was a reference to Jesus as Messiah in the testimonium, but probably in a

contrast, would have us believe that Jesus was known as "Messiah" during the course of his final ministry in Jerusalem and in particular at his trial. While no one disputes that Jesus was proclaimed and heralded as Messiah in the early church, the question as to whether or not he was recognized as such during his own lifetime is a much more complex and disputed topic. Moreover, it is equally debated as to whether Jesus claimed to be the Messiah and whether we can legitimately talk of a "messianic self-consciousness" on the part of the historical Jesus.[3]

Scholarship on the Messianic Question

This "messianic question" as to whether or not Jesus believed himself to be the Messiah is a recurring riddle of historical Jesus scholarship. Julius Wellhausen wrote that of all the problems facing scholarship on the life of Jesus, "among the most important questions is whether and in what sense he [Jesus] believed and claimed himself to be the Messiah."[4] Similarly, H. J. Holtzmann said that the messianic consciousness of Jesus was "the main problem of New Testament theology."[5] The nature of the dilemma, as Albert Schweitzer recognized long ago, is that researchers have had to wrestle with the problem of the purportedly nonmessianic character of Jesus's public ministry in contradistinction to his messianic vocation and identity as affirmed by early Christian sources.[6]

---

way that held that the messianic status of Jesus was dubious. Christian scribes who transmitted the text of Josephus removed this dubiety from the testimonium and inserted instead, "He was the Messiah."

3. Paul W. Meyer ("The Problem of the Messianic Self-Consciousness of Jesus," *NovT* 4 [1960]: 122–38) posits the question of Jesus's messianic self-consciousness as one of the many dividing lines between the heirs of Wrede and the heirs of Schweitzer.

4. Julius Wellhausen, *Einleitung in die drei ersten Evangelien* (Berlin: Georg Reimer, 1905), 89: "Darunter ist das wichtigste, ob und in welchem Sinne er selber sich für den Messias gehalten und gegeben habe." Oscar Cullmann (*The Christology of the New Testament* [trans. S. C. Guthrie and C. A. M. Hall; 2nd ed.; London: SCM, 1963], 117) wrote something similar: "The question whether Jesus had a 'messianic self-consciousness' is one of the major problems for understanding both his life and teachings." James H. Charlesworth ("From Messianology to Christology: Problems and Prospects," in *The Messiah* [ed. James H. Charlesworth; Minneapolis: Fortress, 1992], 35) said: "We have been left with numerous questions, most notably this one: Why did Jesus' followers claim above all that he was the Messiah?" More recently Christopher Tuckett (*Christology and the New Testament: Jesus and His Earliest Followers* [Louisville: Westminster John Knox, 2001], 210) has commented: "One of the most vexed questions in current New Testament research is whether Jesus regarded himself as in any sense a 'Messiah' figure."

5. H. J. Holtzmann, *Lehrbuch der neutestamentlichen Theologie* (ed. D. A. Jülicher and W. Bauer; 2nd ed.; 2 vols.; Tübingen: Mohr, 1911), 295: "das Hauptproblem der neutest. Theologie."

6. Albert Schweitzer, *The Quest of the Historical Jesus* (ed. John Bowden; 6th ed.; London: SCM, 2000), 299–302; N. A. Dahl, "The Crucified Messiah," in *Jesus Is the Christ: The Historical Origins of Christological Doctrine* (ed. Donald H. Juel; Minneapolis: Fortress, 1991), 35, 44.

Primitive Christianity was a messianic movement that venerated a figure with the appellation Χριστός (Christ/Messiah/Anointed One), and followers of Jesus were even given the name Χριστιανοί (Christians/Messianists) to distinguish them from other Jewish sects. Did a self-professedly messianic claimant lie at the root of this messianic movement, or was the messianic identity of Jesus a subsequent development in the christological reflection of the early Christian communities that attributed the title to him in the course of their post-Easter theologizing? In the last one hundred years of historical Jesus research, mainly under the influence of William Wrede and Rudolf Bultmann, the consensus has largely rejected the position that the historical Jesus regarded himself as the Messiah. In fact, Martin Hengel goes so far as to state: "Today the unmessianic Jesus has almost become a dogma among many New Testament scholars. One is tempted to describe this phenomenon as 'non-messianic dogmatics.'"[7] Just in case one thinks that Hengel is exaggerating the state of scholarship, consider the following collection of comments:

> For this is the truly amazing thing, that there is in fact not one single certain proof of Jesus' claiming for himself one of the Messianic titles which tradition has ascribed to him. . . . Not a single one of his words speaks of the *Messias designatus*.[8]

> Jesus is never once recalled as using the title "Messiah" of himself or as unequivocally welcoming its application to him by others.[9]

> To claim Jesus is the Messiah is absurd.[10]

> There is not a single genuine saying of Jesus in which he refers to himself as the Messiah.[11]

> It seems that before the passion Jesus did not openly claim to be the Messiah.[12]

> Scenes in the Gospels in which Jesus is addressed or acknowledged as the Messiah are very few and acceptance of that title by Jesus is marred by complications.[13]

7. Martin Hengel, "Jesus, the Messiah of Israel," in *Studies in Early Christology* (Edinburgh: T&T Clark, 1995), 16.

8. Günther Bornkamm, *Jesus of Nazareth* (trans. Irene McLuskey et al.; London: Hodder & Stoughton, 1973), 172, 178.

9. James D. G. Dunn, *Jesus Remembered*, vol. 1, *Christianity in the Making* (Grand Rapids: Eerdmans, 2003), 653.

10. Donald H. Juel, "The Origin of Mark's Christology," in Charlesworth, *The Messiah*, 453.

11. Eduard Schweizer, *Jesus* (trans. D. E. Green; London: SCM, 1971), 14.

12. Dahl, "Crucified Messiah," 40.

13. Raymond E. Brown, *The Death of the Messiah* (2 vols.; ABRL; New York: Doubleday, 1994), 1:475.

There is thus no certainty that Jesus thought of himself as bearer of the title "Messiah." On the contrary, it is unlikely that he did so: all the gospel writers so regarded him, but they could cite little direct evidence.[14]

Jesus never chose to call himself "Messiah" or "Son of God" and even when others questioned him about his Messiahship, he usually declines to give a straight answer.[15]

As a possible role model he was more hostile than welcoming to the idea of the royal messiah.[16]

The historical-critical work on the Gospels regarding the question of the work and the self-understanding of the "earthly" Jesus leads to the following result: Jesus did not designate himself as "Messiah."[17]

Such skepticism is unsurprising given that Jesus in the Gospels never explicitly refers to himself as the Messiah, but he is called the Messiah, King, or Son of David by others, such as Peter (Mark 8:29/Matt. 16:16/Luke 9:20), Bartimaeus (Mark 10:47–48), the high priest (Mark 14:61), Nathanael (John 1:49), the Galilean crowds (John 6:15; Matt. 12:23), Passover pilgrims (Mark 11:9–10), and Martha (John 11:27). By itself such data might suggest that Jesus inspired messianic hopes but did not embrace the title himself.

In Quest of Jesus's Self-Understanding

One may wish to look elsewhere in the hope of finding more explicit evidence that Jesus claimed to be a messianic figure. There are several places where Jesus accepts the title of "Messiah," according to the evangelists. In John 4, during Jesus's encounter with the Samaritan woman at the well, she claims, "I know that Messiah[18] is coming [Μεσσίας ἔρχεται]. . . . When he comes, he will proclaim all things to us," to which the Johannine Jesus replies, "I am he, the one who is speaking to you" (John 4:25–26). In the Markan trial scene the high priest asks Jesus: "Are you the Messiah, the Son of the Blessed One?" and Jesus replies, "I am" (Mark 14:61b–62; but see the different responses

14. E. P. Sanders, *The Historical Figure of Jesus* (London: SCM, 1993), 242.

15. Geza Vermes, *The Authentic Gospel of Jesus* (London: Penguin, 2004), 402.

16. James D. G. Dunn, "Messianic Ideas and Their Influence on the Jesus of History," in Charlesworth, *The Messiah*, 374.

17. Otfried Hofius, "Ist Jesus der Messias?" *JBT* 8 (1993): 119: "Die historisch-kritische Arbeit an den Evangelien führt hinsichtlich der Frage nach dem Wirken und dem Selbstverständnis des 'irdischen' Jesus m. E. zu den folgenden Ergebnissen: Jesus hat sich nicht selbst als 'Messias' bezeichnet."

18. The word μεσσίας for "Messiah" (John 1:41; 4:25) is a grecized version of the Aramaic משיחא (*mĕšîḥā'*) and the Hebrew המשיח (*hammāšîaḥ*).

in Matt. 26:64; Luke 22:67–68; John 18:33–34). Elsewhere Jesus does refer to the Messiah, but never with first-person personal pronouns. In Mark we read: "For I tell you the truth, whoever gives you a cup of water to drink because you are of Messiah [Χριστοῦ ἐστε] will by no means lose the reward" (Mark 9:41). A titular occurrence appears also in Matthew: "Nor are you to be called instructors, for you have one instructor, the Messiah [ὁ Χριστός]" (Matt. 23:10). Jesus warns of false messiahs (ψευδόχριστοι) in the Olivet Discourse of the synoptic tradition (Mark 13:21–22/Matt. 24:24) and poses a riddle about the Messiah as the Son of David (Mark 12:35–37). Since most of these texts comport with the Christology and kerygma of the primitive church, scholars have been reluctant to regard them as historically authentic and usually suppose that they are accretions to the Jesus tradition by the early church, which invested the tradition with its own christological convictions concerning Jesus's identity.

The notion that Jesus of Nazareth never claimed to be the Messiah has thus remained a well-worn position in modern research, although it is probably not as strongly held as it once was. There has been a reevaluation of the messianic question in some quarters of research inspired partly by more nuanced studies on the diversity of Jewish beliefs in the Second Temple period, as well as further studies on the various messianisms of ancient writings, and aided by the discovery of the Dead Sea Scrolls. All of these have led to renewed interest in Jewish and Christian notions of the Messiah. Scholars operating in the "Third Quest"[19] for the historical Jesus exercise a range of views on the matter, as a mere comparison of Geza Vermes, N. T. Wright, and E. P. Sanders demonstrates. As such, any bifurcation between a "messianic" or "nonmessianic" consciousness on the part of Jesus can obscure the complexity of the subject as it has been handled in contemporary discussion. There are four main ways in which the messianic question has been handled:

1. Jesus never claimed to be the Messiah, and the early church proclaimed Jesus as Messiah as an inference based on belief in his resurrection or more generally out of their post-Easter faith.[20]

---

19. While a taxonomy of modern research along the lines of Old Quest–No Quest–New Quest–Third Quest has come under attack as a naive and inadequate description of currents in research on the historical Jesus in the twentieth century, see my defense of a modified form of the taxonomy in Michael F. Bird, "Is There Really a 'Third Quest' for the Historical Jesus?" *SBET* 4 (2006): 195–219.

20. William Wrede, *The Messianic Secret* (trans. J. C. G. Greig; Cambridge: James Clark, 1971); Reginald H. Fuller, *The Mission and Achievement of Jesus* (SBT 12; London: SCM, 1954), 108, 116; Cullmann, *Christology*, 133–36; Schweizer, *Jesus*, 13–15, 70–71, 91; B. L. Mack, "The Christ and Jewish Wisdom," in Charlesworth, *The Messiah*, 217; E. P. Sanders, *Jesus and Judaism* (London: SCM, 1985), 307–8; idem, *Historical Figure of Jesus*, 242–43; H. J. de Jonge, "The Historical Jesus' View of Himself and of His Mission," in *From Jesus to John: Essays on Jesus and New Testament Christology in Honour of Marinus de Jonge* (ed. Martin C. de Boer;

2. The disciples or crowds proclaimed Jesus as Messiah during his lifetime, but Jesus himself rejected the title.[21]

3. Jesus did not claim the title "Messiah" for himself in his ministry, but neither did he actually reject it at a key moment at his trial, which resulted in the erection of the *titulus* on the cross.[22]

4. Jesus claimed to be the Messiah of Israel even if he revised the meaning of the role.[23]

Sheffield: JSOT Press, 1993), 21–37; Jürgen Becker, *Jesus of Nazareth* (trans. J. E. Crouch; New York: de Gruyter, 1998), 197; Marcus Borg, *Conflict, Holiness, and Politics in the Teachings of Jesus* (Harrisburg, PA: Trinity, 1998), 17–18; G. S. Oegema, "Messiah/Christ," in *EHJ* (ed. C. A. Evans; New York: Routledge, 2008), 399.

21. Günther Bornkamm, *Jesus of Nazareth* (trans. Irene McLuskey et al.; London: Hodder & Stoughton, 1973), 172; Geza Vermes, *The Religion of Jesus the Jew* (London: SCM, 1973), 154; Dahl, "Crucified Messiah," 42–43; Brown, *Death of the Messiah*, 1:478–79; Paul Fredriksen, *Jesus of Nazareth, King of the Jews* (New York: Vintage, 1999), 234, 244–59; Dunn, *Jesus Remembered*, 1:653–54.

22. Dahl, "Crucified Messiah," 43–44; C. K. Barrett, *Jesus and the Gospel Tradition* (London: SPCK, 1967), 19–24; E. Dinkler, "Peter's Confession and the Satan Saying: The Problem of Jesus' Messiahship," in *The Future of Our Religious Past: Essays in Honour of Rudolf Bultmann* (ed. James M. Robinson; New York: Harper & Row, 1971), 169–72; Brown, *Death of the Messiah*, 1:479–80; C. H. Dodd, *The Founder of Christianity* (London: Collins, 1971), 103; Joseph A. Fitzmyer, *The One Who Is to Come* (Grand Rapids: Eerdmans, 2007), 140–41; Tuckett, *Christology and the New Testament*, 212–13; cf. Hengel, "Messiah of Israel," 58, 69.

23. W. Waldensperger, *Das Selbstbewusstsein Jesu im Lichte der messianischen Hoffnungen seiner Zeit* (2nd ed.; Strassburg: Heitz, 1892); W. Mundle, "Die Geschichtlichkeit des messianischen Bewusstseins Jesu," *ZNW* 21 (1922): 299–311; Johannes Weiss, *Jesus' Proclamation of the Kingdom of God* (ed. R. H. Hiers and D. Larrimore Holland; 1971; repr., Chico, CA: Scholars Press, 1985), 127–28; Schweitzer, *Quest of the Historical Jesus*, 316–19; Adolf Schlatter, *The History of the Christ: The Foundation of New Testament Theology* (trans. A. Köstenberger; Grand Rapids: Baker Academic, 1997), 109, 124–26, 280, 283–85; C. J. Cadoux, *The Historic Mission of Jesus: A Constructive Re-examination of the Eschatological Teaching in the Synoptic Gospels* (London: Lutterworth, 1941), 51–60; William Manson, *Jesus the Messiah* (London: Hodder & Stoughton, 1943); Otto Betz, "Die Frage nach dem messianischen Bewusstsein Jesu," *NovT* 6 (1963): 24–37; T. W. Manson, *The Servant Messiah* (Cambridge: Cambridge University Press, 1961); Joachim Jeremias, *New Testament Theology* (trans. J. Bowden; London: SCM, 1971), 254–55; C. F. D. Moule, *The Origin of Christology* (Cambridge: Cambridge University Press, 1977), 31–35; Hengel, "Messiah of Israel," 1–72; Ben F. Meyer, *The Aims of Jesus* (London: SCM, 1979), 174–202; Christopher Rowland, *Christian Origins* (London: SCM, 1985), 182; Peter Stuhlmacher, *Jesus of Nazareth, Christ of Faith* (trans. S. Schatzmann; Peabody, MA: Hendrickson, 1988), 22–29, 47–49; H. C. Kee, *What Can We Know about Jesus?* (New York: Cambridge University Press, 1990), 111; Markus Bockmuehl, *This Jesus: Martyr, Lord, Messiah* (Edinburgh: T&T Clark, 1994), 51–58; G. B. Caird, *New Testament Theology* (ed. L. D. Hurst; Oxford: Clarendon, 1994), 306–10; Ben Witherington, *The Christology of Jesus* (Minneapolis: Fortress, 1990), 115–16, 118, esp. 143, 215, 263–77; W. D. Davies and Dale C. Allison, *The Gospel according to Saint Matthew* (3 vols.; ICC; Edinburgh; T&T Clark, 1991), 2:595–601; Craig A. Evans, *Jesus and His Contemporaries* (Leiden: Brill, 1995), 437–56; N. T. Wright, *Jesus and the Victory of God* (vol. 2 of *Christian Origins and the Question of God*; London: SPCK, 1996), 477–539, esp. 538; Robert Stein, *Jesus the Messiah* (Downers Grove, IL: InterVarsity, 1996), 147–49, 248; Marinus de Jonge, *Jesus, the Servant-Messiah* (New Haven: Yale University Press,

The subject is quite complex. To make matters worse, it is further complicated by debates concerning messianic expectations in Jewish and Christian
sources, by issues relating to the development of primitive Christology, and
by questions about the authenticity of messianic texts in the Gospels. Be that
as it may, the goal of this work is to argue for the fourth position: that Jesus
of Nazareth did claim, in action and speech, to be the Messiah of Israel. In
brief, I want to reopen the messianic question and place it at the forefront of
studies in Christian origins and the historical Jesus.

That said, I do not like the term "messianic self-consciousness," since the
mental states and psychological profiles of individuals from antiquity are
beyond the bounds of historical inquiry. I prefer the phrase "messianic self-
understanding," by which I mean Jesus's identifying himself in a messianic
role and couching his activities as messianic in character and purpose. I am
not going to set out to demonstrate that Jesus used the title "Messiah" of
himself, because I am fairly confident that he did not.[24] What I am going to do,
rather, is argue that Jesus saw himself in messianic categories, as enacting a
messianic role or a messianic vocation as part of his aim to renew and restore
Israel through his various activities. I am interested in *intentions* and *identity*
as they pertain to Jesus and messiahship. I think this can be properly derived
from our sources through critical analysis of the authentic traditions in the
Gospels. I will contend that it is the messianic nature of Jesus's ministry that
explains the reason for Jesus's death and accounts for the messianism of the
early church, including its Christology. Anyone familiar with the contours of
the debate will realize that I stand on the shoulders of others such as Albert
Schweitzer, Martin Hengel, Craig A. Evans, and N. T. Wright in order to make
my case. I hope in greater detail to pursue what these scholars have already
paved the way for in their respective works.

This book proceeds in several stages. In chapter 2, I offer some brief
notes about the origins of messianism as it relates to the Second Temple
period. In chapter 3, I deal with the objections against the historical Jesus
as a messianic claimant. I will try to show that such reasons are actually

---

1991), 68–72; idem, *God's Final Envoy: Early Christology and Jesus' Own View of His Mis-
sion* (Grand Rapids: Eerdmans, 1998), 98–109; Dale C. Allison, *Jesus of Nazareth: Millenarian
Prophet* (Minneapolis: Fortress, 1998), 67–68n251; Scot McKnight, *A New Vision for Israel:
The Teachings of Jesus in National Context* (Grand Rapids: Eerdmans, 1999), 6; Jonathan
Knight, *Jesus: An Historical and Theological Introduction* (UBW; London: T&T Clark, 2004),
145; Gerd Theissen and Annette Merz, *The Historical Jesus: A Comprehensive Guide* (trans.
J. Bowden; Minneapolis: Fortress, 1998), 538; Giorgio Jossa, *Jews or Christians?* (trans. Molly
Rogers; WUNT 202; Tübingen: Mohr Siebeck, 2006), 54–63; David Flusser with R. Stephen
Nutley, *The Sage from Galilee: Rediscovering Jesus' Genius* (Grand Rapids: Eerdmans, 2007),
115; Andrew Chester, *Messiah and Exaltation: Jewish Messianic and Visionary Traditions and
New Testament Christology* (WUNT 207; Tübingen: Mohr Siebeck, 2007), 307–24.

24. Cf. similarly James H. Charlesworth, *Jesus within Judaism: New Light from Exciting
Archaeological Discoveries* (London: SPCK, 1989), 131–32.

lacking in substance. In chapters 4 and 5, I then set out and evaluate all the arguments both for and against regarding the historical Jesus as a messianic claimant. Finally, in chapter 6, I dare to ask what is at stake in this debate for modern theology and what significance can be attached to the confession "Jesus is the Christ."

2

Messianic Expectations
in Second Temple Judaism

Before undertaking a study on the historical Jesus and the messianic question, it is necessary to say something about messianic expectations, messianic hopes, and messianic figures/failures in antiquity because they form the backdrop for the discussion that follows. However, studies in the messianism of the Old Testament, the intertestamental period, Second Temple Judaism, Christianity, and rabbinic Judaism are ubiquitous, and I have no desire to embark on an exhaustive survey of the many pertinent texts in any great depth, since this would no doubt require treading upon all of their scholarly paraphernalia.[1] I want briefly to outline some of the essential factors

1. W. O. E. Oesterley, *The Evolution of the Messianic Idea: A Study in Comparative Religion* (London: Pitman, 1908); Emil Schürer, *The History of the Jewish People in the Age of Jesus Christ* (rev. and ed. G. Vermes, F. Millar, and M. Black; 3 vols; Edinburgh: T&T Clark, 1973–87), 2:488–554; Sigmund Mowinckel, *He That Cometh* (Nashville: Abingdon, 1954); Joseph Klausner, *The Messianic Idea in Israel from Its Beginning to the Completion of the Mishnah* (New York: Macmillan, 1955); H. Ringgren, *The Messiah in the Old Testament* (SBT 18; London: SCM, 1956); Abba Hillel Silver, *A History of Messianic Speculation in Israel from the First through the Seventeenth Centuries* (1927; repr., Boston: Beacon, 1959); Richard A. Horsley and John S. Hanson, *Bandits, Prophets, and Messiahs: Popular Movements in the Time of Jesus* (Minneapolis: Winston, 1985); Jacob Neusner, William S. Green, and Ernest Frerichs, eds., *Judaisms and Their Messiahs at the Turn of the Christian Era* (Cambridge: Cambridge University Press, 1987); Charlesworth, *The Messiah*; E. P. Sanders, *Judaism: Practice and Belief 63 BCE–66 CE* (London: SCM, 1992), 295–98; N. T. Wright, *The New Testament and the People of God* (vol. 1 of *Christian Origins and the Question of God*; Minneapolis: Fortress, 1992), 307–20; John J. Collins, *The Scepter and the Star: The Messiahs of the Dead Sea Scrolls*

and general characteristics of messianic expectations as they relate to Second
Temple Judaism.

The Paucity and Diversity of Messianic Expectations

It has to be said straightaway that hopes for a Messiah were not unanimous in
the Second Temple period, and what expectations did exist are to be characterized as highly diverse in form and content.[2] The prophetic hope for a renewed
Davidic dynasty that would carry the nation forward into an age of deliverance
and prosperity did not eventuate; therefore, expectations in the early fifth to late
second century BCE were largely lacking messianic content. It was the rise and
demise of the Hasmonean dynasty, in the context of the sociopolitical milieu of
Palestine in the mid-second century and onward, that provided the catalyst for a
radical reinterpretation of certain scriptural traditions that eventually developed
into Jewish messianism. The exhibition of hopes for national redemption and
spasmodic resistance to foreign rule were inspired by renewed interpretation of
Israel's sacred traditions. These texts provided a number of potential messianic
paradigms that were subsequently taken up by others.

However, messianism remained only one way of telling the story of Israel's
hope for the future. For many Jews, collaboration with Rome was a sensible

and Other Ancient Literature (ABRL; New York: Doubleday, 1995); Kenneth Pomykala, *The
Davidic Dynasty Tradition in Early Judaism: Its History and Significance for Messianism* (At-
lanta: Scholars Press, 1995); Antti Laato, *A Star Is Rising: The Historical Development of the
Old Testament Royal Ideology and the Rise of the Jewish Messianic Expectations* (Atlanta:
Scholars Press, 1997); Dan Cohn-Sherbok, *The Jewish Messiah* (Edinburgh: T&T Clark, 1997);
Gerbern S. Oegema, *The Anointed and His People: Messianic Expectations from the Maccabees
to Bar Kochba* (JSPSup 27; Sheffield: Sheffield Academic Press, 1998); William Horbury, *Jewish
Messianism and the Cult of Christ* (London: SCM, 1998); idem, *Messianism among Jews and
Christians: Twelve Biblical and Historical Studies* (London: Continuum/T&T Clark, 2003);
J. H. Charlesworth, H. Lichtenberger, and G. Oegema, eds., *Qumran-Messianism: Studies
on the Messianic Expectation in the Dead Sea Scrolls* (Tübingen: Mohr Siebeck, 1998); John
Day, ed., *King and Messiah in Israel and the Ancient Near East* (JSOTSup 270; Sheffield: Shef-
field Academic Press, 1998); Richard S. Hess and M. Daniel Carroll R., eds., *Israel's Messiah
in the Bible and the Dead Sea Scrolls* (Grand Rapids: Baker Academic, 2003); Fitzmyer, *The
One Who Is to Come*; Markus Bockmuehl and James Carleton Paget, eds., *Redemption and
Resistance: The Messianic Hopes of Jews and Christians in Antiquity* (London: T&T Clark,
2007); Magnus Zetterholm, ed., *The Messiah: In Early Judaism and Christianity* (Minneapolis:
Fortress, 2007).

2. Cf. similar warnings by Marinus de Jonge, "The Use of the Word 'Anointed' in the Time
of Jesus," *NovT* 8 (1966): 147–48; Sanders, *Judaism: Practice and Belief*, 295; Charlesworth,
"Messianology to Christology," 6, 35; N. T. Wright, *People of God*, 307–8; J. Collins, *Scepter
and the Star*, 3–4, 11; Theissen and Merz, *Historical Jesus*, 537–38; Dunn, *Jesus Remembered*,
618; L. T. Stuckenbruck, "Messianic Ideas in the Apocalyptic and Related Literature of Early
Judaism," in *The Messiah in the Old and New Testaments* (ed. S. E. Porter; Grand Rapids:
Eerdmans, 2007), 112–13.

way forward for the nation, with manifold advantages such as imperial pa-
tronage and external security especially in light of the Parthian threat from
the east (Josephus, *War* 1.142–43; *Ant.* 14.332, 363–64; *War* 1.268–69). For
some peasants a limited good or putting up with poor circumstances was to
be preferred to the war and bloodshed of revolution. Some could even prefer
the Romanized Herodians to the corrupt and volatile Hasmoneans (*Ant.* 15.3).
While messianism could figure prominently in eschatological hopes for the
future, not all eschatology necessarily required a Messiah (e.g., 2 Macc. 2:18;
14:15; Tob. 13:11–17; 14:4–7; Bar. 2:27–35; 4:36–37; 5:5–9; Sir. 36:11–17; Jub.
23.27–31).

I would also shy away from the opinion, once commonly held, that there
was a uniform hope for the coming Davidic king in common Judaism. What
messianic aspirations did exist displayed a variety of beliefs about a coming
deliverer. One obvious distinction is that some conceived of the Messiah
as an earthly warrior (1QM; Pss. Sol. 17–18), while there were others who
conceived of him as a preexisting and transcendent figure (1 Enoch; 4 Ezra).
Or there again, some, like those at Qumran, could conceive of two Messiahs, one of Aaron and one of Israel (1QS 9.11; CD 12.22–23; 13.20–22;
14.18–19; 19.34–20.1; CD-B 1.10–11; 2.1; 1QSa 2.17–22). This pattern might
be predicated on a tradition of the duumvirates of Aaron-Moses and Joshua-
Zerubbabel and even replicated later with Eleazar-Kosiba in the 132–135
CE revolt.[3] These figures could be variously related to one or more of the
offices of prophet, priest, and king. Such idealized figures could fit a number
of patterns or different types of savior/deliverer models from Israel's sacred
traditions. Various expectations were projected onto them in order to line
up with known and celebrated concepts of liberation. The "Messiah" of the
Psalms of Solomon has priestly functions ascribed to him (17.30, 36, 48–49),
and the Servant of the Lord in Isaiah exhibits royal, priestly, and prophetic
traits.[4]

This caveat must not obscure the fact that, even without a uniform and
monochrome notion of "Messiah" waiting in the wings to be applied to some
charismatic and ambitious individual, there could be elements of messianism
that were shared, repeatable, and constant even if they were never completely
identical. A messiah is ordinarily someone raised up, sent, or anointed for a

3. The notion of two Messiahs may be indebted to Zech. 6:11 and Jer. 33:14–18 (as well
as T. Reub. 6.8; T. Jud. 21.2–5; T. Mos. 9.1). On the two Messiahs of Qumran, see Schürer,
History of the Jewish People, 2:550–54; Shemaryahu Talmon, "Waiting for the Messiah: The
Spiritual Universe of the Qumran Covenanters," in Neusner, Green, and Frerichs, *Judaisms
and Their Messiahs at the Turn of the Christian Era*, 111–137; J. Collins, *Scepter and the Star*,
74–95; Mark Adam Elliott, *The Survivors of Israel: A Reconsideration of the Theology of
Pre-Christian Judaism* (Grand Rapids: Eerdmans, 2000), 479–83; and the skepticism of L. D.
Hurst, "Did Qumran Expect Two Messiahs?" *BBR* 9 (1999): 157–80.

4. G. W. E. Nickelsburg, *Ancient Judaism and Christian Origins: Diversity, Continuity, and
Transformation* (Minneapolis: Fortress, 2003), 92–93, 105.

particular task as it relates to the liberation of Israel from its perceived travail and suffering.[5]

The Extent of Messianic Ideas in the Old Testament

Another subject for discussion is the extent to which messianic ideas have their roots in the Old Testament or Hebrew Bible. Anointing was associated with three primary offices or ministries in ancient Israel: king,[6] priest,[7] and prophet,[8] but mostly with the first of these. More to the point, the word מָשִׁיחַ, "anointed one," was not used of eschatological figures in the Old Testament. The exception is perhaps Dan. 9:24–27, although the sense there is ambiguous.[9] Marinus de Jonge comments: "One should realize that in the OT the term 'anointed' is never used of a future savior/redeemer, and that in later Jewish writings of the period between 200 BC and AD 100 the term is used only infrequently in connection with agents of divine deliverance expected in the future."[10] Thus, to what extent can we speak of a "Christology" or messiah in the Old Testament?[11]

A Christology of the Old Testament is something that can be spoken of, quite legitimately, as a feature of canonical interpretation undertaken retrospectively by Christian interpreters in light of their Scriptures and traditions. As for messianism in the Old Testament, it depends on what criteria one develops for determining a messianic text. The mistake of an older generation was to erroneously posit a correlation between eschatological expectations and messianic expectations. As such, Joseph Fitzmyer (following Sigmund Mowinckel) opts for a definition of a messianic text as one that contains a reference to "an awaited or future anointed agent of God."[12] Thus, Fitzmyer sees messianic texts in the Old Testament as

5. For an attempt to situate messianism as part of a broader eschatological narrative, see Schürer, *History of the Jewish People*, 2:514–47. On shared elements of messianism, see J. Collins, *Scepter and the Star*, 12; N. T. Wright, *People of God*, 320. On the "coherence" of Jewish messianism, see Horbury, *Jewish Messianism*, 64–108.

6. 1 Sam. 10:1; 12:3; 16:1, 13; 24:6, 10; 2 Sam. 2:4, 7; 5:3, 17; 19:21; 1 Kings 1:39; 19:15–16; Pss. 2:2; 89:20, 38, 51; 132:10. Note especially Ps. 18:50 (Ps. 17:51 LXX), which sets מֶלֶךְ/βασιλεύς and מָשִׁיחַ/χριστός in parallel.

7. Exod. 28:41; 30:30; Lev. 4:3, 5, 16; 6:22; Dan. 9:25–26; cf. 2 Macc. 1:10; T. Levi 17.2–3.

8. 1 Kings 19:16; 1 Chron. 16:22; Ps. 105:15; Isa. 61:1–3.

9. Cf. John E. Goldingay, *Daniel* (WBC; Dallas: Word, 1989), 257–63; J. Collins, *Scepter and the Star*, 34–35; Fitzmyer, *The One Who Is to Come*, 56–64.

10. Marinus de Jonge, "Messiah," *ABD* 4:777.

11. Cf. J. Gordon McConville, "Messianic Interpretation of the Old Testament in Modern Context," in *The Lord's Anointed: Interpretation of Old Testament Messianic Texts* (ed. P. E. Satterthwaite, R. S. Hess, and G. J. Wenham; Carlisle, UK: Paternoster, 1995), 1–17. On various definitions of "Messiah," see Oegema, *The Anointed*, 23–26.

12. Fitzmyer, *The One Who Is to Come*, 5; Mowinckel, *He That Cometh*, 155–56; cf. also M. de Jonge, "Anointed," 133. Cf. Charlesworth ("Messianology to Christology," 4), who defines "messiah" as "God's eschatological Anointed one, the Messiah"; he takes "messianic" as des-

tied quite strictly to the use of the word מָשִׁיחַ (anointed one) in connection with teaching about a continuing Davidic dynasty in the subsequent history of Israel.[13] The consequence is that messianism is seen as a postexilic phenomenon. But that is a rather narrow lexical approach to the matter, and one wonders if Fitzmyer has exchanged the elastic rubber-band definition of messianism for one that is caught up in a linguistic straitjacket.[14] When we come to messianic hopes, biblical and postbiblical, we see that functions and roles are often more important than a single title.[15] Before 70 CE we can hardly find any occurrence of the absolute term "the Messiah"; instead the word in Greek or Hebrew occurs with a genitive or possessive pronoun like "Messiah of Israel," "Messiah of Aaron," "Messiah of the LORD," or "his Messiah": the designation is always qualified rather than absolutized, and no single meaning is ever assumed.[16] What is more, messianic figures could go by a variety of names other than "Messiah," including Son of David, Son of God, Son of Man, the Prophet, Elect One, Prince, Branch, Root, Scepter, Star, Chosen One, Coming One, and so forth.[17] Consequently I prefer the

ignating "images, symbols or concepts, either explicitly or implicitly linked to ideas about the Messiah," and "messianology" as signifying "Jewish ideas or beliefs in the Messiah."

13. Fitzmyer, *The One Who Is to Come*, 7, 11–13.

14. In *The Messiah*, a volume edited by James Charlesworth, several contributors see messianism as much wider than a lexical link to "anointed one" (מָשִׁיחַ); see J. J. M. Roberts ("The Old Testament's Contribution to Messianic Expectations," 39): "A discussion of the Old Testament's contribution to the development of later messianic expectations can hardly be focused on the Hebrew word for Messiah, מָשִׁיחַ"; S. Talmon ("The Concepts of *Māšîaḥ* and Messianism in Early Judaism," 80): "I differentiate between the epithet מָשִׁיחַ, which is preponderantly used in the Hebrew Bible in reference to an actual ruling king or his immediate successor, and the concept of messianism, which derives from that noun but becomes increasingly invested as Jewish thought develops with a credal and visionary dimension that transcends the original and terrestrial signification of the term *māšîaḥ*." P. D. Hanson ("Messiahs and Messianic Figures in Proto-apocalyptic Judaism," 67–68) sees a category of material that does not mention the word מָשִׁיחַ but that remains "relevant to our subject due to the presence of other terms undergoing transformation in the direction of eschatological connotations in a manner parallel to *māšîaḥ*." According to Chester (*Messiah and Exaltation*, 201, 204): "A messiah is a figure who acts as the agent of the final divine deliverance, whether or not he is specifically designated as 'messiah' or 'anointed.' . . . I wish to emphasize again that the use (or lack) of the term מָשִׁיחַ (and equivalent) should not be allowed to be determinative for the definition of messianism." See also Stefan Schreiber, *Gesalbter und König: Titel und Konzeptionen der königlichen Gesalbtenerwartung in frühjudischen und urchristlichen Schriften* (BZAW 105; Berlin: de Gruyter, 2000), 29–32. The biggest problem that I have with Fitzmyer's approach is his failure to engage messianism on a social, cultural, and theological level.

15. According to M. de Jonge ("Anointed," 147), "Not the person as such, but his calling and his function are of importance." Earlier H. H. Rowley ("The Suffering Servant and the Davidic Messiah," in *The Servant of the Lord and Other Essays on the Old Testament* [ed. H. H. Rowley; Oxford: Blackwell, 1963], 63) wrote: "While the term Messiah, or Christ, does not appear to be actually used of the Davidic descendent in the Old Testament, the concept of the Davidic Messiah is familiar enough." Charlesworth ("Messianology to Christology," 13) observes: "There was considerable fluidity among the various titles that could be or become messianic titles."

16. M. de Jonge, "Anointed," 133–34.

17. Cf. similarly Chester, *Messiah and Exaltation*, 204.

definition of messianism given by John Collins, who proposes that a messianic figure is one who is "an agent of God in the end-time who is said somewhere in the literature to be anointed, but who is not necessarily called 'messiah' in every passage."[18] There are two crucial elements in messianism: (1) The sociological status of the messianic functionary is that of royalty; or more specifically, he is regal and sometimes priestly. By virtue of this status as a royal arbiter between the people and God, he can reign over Israel, defeat Israel's enemies, and represent Israel before God. (2) The temporal orientation of messianism is always toward the future, even though the sequence of events or the leadership paradigm may be drawn from Israel's sacred traditions about the past.[19]

What can be said about the Old Testament is that very early on there emerged an idealization of the Davidic dynasty or something that we might call "proto-messianism."[20] The future of Israel is tied to the fortunes and affairs of the Davidic line, and this notion has preexilic roots. In 2 Sam. 7:12–16 is an oracle by Nathan concerning God's promises to David:

> When your days are fulfilled and you lie down with your ancestors, I will raise up your offspring after you, who shall come forth from your body, and I will establish his kingdom. He shall build a house for my name, and I will establish the throne of his kingdom forever. I will be a father to him, and he shall be a son to me. When he commits iniquity, I will punish him with a rod such as mortals use, with blows inflicted by human beings. But I will not take my steadfast love from him, as I took it from Saul, whom I put away from before you. Your house and your kingdom shall be made sure forever before me; your throne shall be established forever.

This oracle promises that after David's passing (1) God will continue his dynasty through a physical descendant; (2) that descendant will build a house for God's name, and God in turn will establish his throne eternally; and (3) the king will have a unique filial relationship with Israel's God. The final declaration in verse 16, "Your throne shall be established forever," turns the oracle into a covenantal promise that is said to endure for all eternity.

This theme is taken up in several places. It is prominent in the royal psalms, especially in Pss. 2; 72; 89; and 132. In Ps. 2, an enthronement psalm, we read in verse 6: "I have set my king on Zion, my holy hill," which links the divine election of the king to the election of Zion in the divine design. Consequently it is an exercise in futility for the nations to "conspire" or "plot" against "the LORD's anointed" (v. 2), since he is installed by divine fiat. The scope of the

---

18. John J. Collins, " 'He Shall Not Judge by What His Eyes See': Messianic Authority in the Dead Sea Scrolls," *DSD* 2 (1995): 146; cf. idem, *Scepter and the Star*, 11–12.

19. Mark J. Boda, "Figuring the Future: The Prophets and Messiah," in Porter, *The Messiah in the Old and New*, 36–43.

20. Craig A. Evans, "Messianic Hopes and Messianic Figures in Late Antiquity," *JGRChJ* 3 (2006): 10; Chester, *Messiah and Exaltation*, 229.

king's reign is even said to include "the ends of the earth." The nations, instead of plotting the demise of the Israelite king, should freely subjugate themselves to him in humble reverence or risk destruction (vv. 9–12).[21]

Psalm 89 explicitly reiterates 2 Sam. 7:11–16 and describes the promise as a "covenant" (ברית) in verses 3, 28, 34. From Yahweh's perspective, David is recalled as "my servant David," whom "with my holy oil I have anointed [משחתיו]" (v. 20). The following verses describe the inviolability and security of the divine promises to sustain David's line, including honors such as being able to say to Yahweh: "You are my Father, my God" (v. 26); he will be the "firstborn" and "highest of the kings of the earth" (v. 27); and "his line shall continue forever, and his throne endure before me like the sun" (v. 36). This promise remains certain even if Israel fails to keep the law and walk according to the ordinances. In the face of judgment and destruction, the psalmist urges Yahweh to remain faithful to those promises; hence, the Davidic covenant becomes the basis of the hope for national restoration in the face of threat or national destruction.

In Ps. 132 the promises made to David are again invoked in order to plead for Yahweh to meet them in their worship in the temple. The psalmist pleads: "For your servant David's sake do not turn away the face of your anointed one" (v. 10). The psalmist also recalls God's oath: "One of the sons of your body I will set on your throne" (v. 11). Importantly, the election of David is related to the election of Zion (v. 13). Because Zion is God's resting place, he is bound to bless it, and he says furthermore, "There I will cause a horn to sprout up for David; I have prepared a lamp for my anointed one. His enemies I will clothe with disgrace, but on him, his crown will gleam" (vv. 17–18). While it is perhaps misguided and even anachronistic to find in the Psalms messianism in a highly developed sense, we find here already the convergence of kingship, future hopes, and national restoration. If this is not messianism, it contains at least the key ingredients for it.[22]

In prophetic literature the Davidic covenant and Davidic dynasty are explicated in several places. The development of the Davidic tradition in the prophetic oracles meant that the royal ideology associated with the Davidic line began to be infused with eschatological expectations. This mix of royal ideology and eschatological hopes provided the fertile soil in which subsequent

---

21. Fitzmyer (*The One Who Is to Come*, 19–20) detects in Ps. 2 not messianism but adoptionism. Though the liturgy behind Ps. 2 may reflect a sacralization of secular kingship, it also sets up the expectations and paradigm of what Israel's king should look like and how the king relates to God; it quite easily casts the model into a future horizon, given the promise of vv. 8–9. If (or when) the monarchy crumbled, the royal Psalms as a whole depict what the monarchic restoration would look like. In fact, Ps. 89's allusion to 2 Sam. 7:13–14 and possibly Ps. 2 reflects exactly that: the idealization of kingship has been transported to a matrix of eschatological expectations focused on the king. See further Tremper Longman, "The Messiah: Explorations in the Law and Writings," in Porter, *The Messiah in the Old and New*, 17–20.

22. Contra Fitzmyer, *The One Who Is to Come*, 25.

messianism developed.[23] In the book of Hosea one finds the hope that in "the latter" days the exiled northern tribes will repent and seek out "David their king" (3:4–5). In the book of Micah is a prophetic promise for a Davidic king to rise again from Bethlehem: "From you [Bethlehem] shall come forth for me one who is to rule in Israel, whose origin is from of old, from ancient days" (5:2). The prophet sees God as bringing in a new beginning with a new David. The dark and somber judgment oracles of Amos stand in juxtaposition with the promise at the end of the book that God will "raise up the booth of David that is fallen" (Amos 9:11).

In Isa. 9 is a prediction of a child to be born during a period of national threat (probably Hezekiah's reign), and it is said of him: "There shall be endless peace for the throne of David and his kingdom," and "He will establish and uphold it with justice and with righteousness" (9:7). The child is also to be called "Mighty God" and "Everlasting Father" (9:6; cf. 7:14). While this might reflect nothing more than throne names of the ancient Near East for monarchs, such honors clearly transgress language used in divine worship of Yahweh. Another prophetic oracle reflecting a similar royal ideology is found in the opening of Isa. 11.

> A shoot shall come out from the stump of Jesse, and a branch shall grow out of his roots. The Spirit of the LORD shall rest on him, the spirit of wisdom and understanding, the spirit of counsel and might, the spirit of knowledge and the fear of the LORD. His delight shall be in the fear of the LORD. He shall not judge by what his eyes see, or decide by what his ears hear; but with righteousness he shall judge the poor, and decide with equity for the meek of the earth; he shall strike the earth with the rod of his mouth, and with the breath of his lips he shall kill the wicked. (Isa. 11:1–4)

The figure envisaged clearly stands in the Davidic line and is endowed with the "Spirit of the LORD" in a particular way (cf. Isa. 61:1). He has a special relationship with Yahweh, executes judgments justly and effectively, and is able to dominate all that lies in his path.

Similar Davidic traditions are reinterpreted, expanded, intensified, and re-applied in the exilic prophets Jeremiah and Ezekiel. In Jeremiah we read: "For if you will indeed obey this word, then through the gates of this house shall enter kings who sit on the throne of David, riding in chariots and on horses, they, and their servants, and their people" (Jer. 22:4). The oracle implies that a Davidic deliverer will come when and only when the survivors of Israel have taken to obeying God's word; this is highly reminiscent of the later talmudic doctrine teaching that "if Israel repents for one day, the son of David shall come

---

23. Evans, "Messianic Hopes and Messianic Figures," 12; and on the royal dynasty of David in the Old Testament, see especially Laato, *A Star Is Rising*, 33–47.

immediately."[24] Another oracle highly significant for messianic interpretation is found in Jer. 23:5–6.

> The days are surely coming, says the LORD, when I will raise up for David a righteous scion, and he shall reign as king and deal wisely, and shall execute justice and righteousness in the land. In his days, Judah will be saved and Israel will live in safety. And this is the name by which he will be called: "The LORD is our righteousness."

In context it reflects the failure of the leadership of Zedekiah, who has not lived up to his name ("Righteousness of Yahweh"), and the prophet envisages God sending a new king to rule in his stead.[25] God raises up a righteous "scion" (צמח), reminiscent of the shoot (חטר) and branch (נצר) in Isa. 11:1. Elsewhere it is stated that God's act of releasing the exiles from slavery will coincide with his exalting "David their king, whom I will raise up for them" (Jer. 30:9). The hope is rehearsed again in relation to the inviolability of God's promise to David. What is more, one begins to see the interlocking relation of the Davidic dynasty to the continuing services of the Levitical priesthood:

> For thus says the LORD: David shall never lack a man to sit on the throne of the house of Israel, and the levitical priests shall never lack a man in my presence to offer burnt offerings. . . . If any of you could break my covenant with the day and my covenant with the night, so that day and night would not come at their appointed time, only then could my covenant with my servant David be broken, so that he would not have a son to reign on his throne, and my covenant with my ministers the Levites. (Jer. 33:17–22)

In Ezekiel one finds the coming of a new Davidic king, who has the vocation of shepherding his people and will do so in contrast to the neglect and suffering of the flock under the false shepherds (Ezek. 34:23–24; 37:24–25). Moreover, it is narrated that God himself comes to shepherd his people in and through the pastoral and royal reign of a Davidic king.

> I will save my flock, and they shall no longer be ravaged; and I will judge between sheep and sheep. I will set up over them one shepherd, my servant David, and he shall feed them: he shall feed them and be their shepherd. And I, the LORD, will be their God, and my servant David shall be prince among them; I, the LORD, have spoken. (Ezek. 34:22–24)

Though the future Davidic king prophesied in Jeremiah and Ezekiel is never called the "Messiah," I fail to see how either portrayal is "without any remote

24. See *y. Ta'an.* 1.1; cf. *b. Sanh.* 97a; *b. Šabb.* 118b.
25. J. Collins, *Scepter and the Star*, 25.

connection to a 'Messiah' ":[26] surely kingship, future deliverance, and restoration are being obviously mixed together. It is true that monarchic restoration is not strictly equivalent to messianism.[27] Nonetheless, the concepts overlap significantly in their future orientation and by placing the center of gravity on kingship.

The postexilic period continued this hope for a coming Davidic king who would pastor Israel, obey the Torah, establish authentic worship, and inaugurate an era of prosperity and peace. The community would then be morally purified and cleansed of all contamination and would flourish despite the fact that it lived under Gentile hegemony. One also finds concomitant idealizations of another anointed figure, the priest, resulting in what Evans calls "diarchic restoration." He finds this schema implicit in Haggai (1:12–14; 2:2–4, 20–23) and Zechariah (3:6–10; 4:2–5, 11–14). During this era Zerubbabel, the Persian-appointed governor, was of Davidic descent, and the high priest, Joshua, was of Zadokite descent. Together they began to rebuild Judean society amid idealized conceptions of priesthood and kingship.[28] In Zechariah these two figures are the "sons of oil" (4:12–14); it is likely that these two anointed offices are even collapsed together (6:11–12).[29]

A significant writing for the development of messianism is the book of Daniel. This writing seems to have taken its final form during a period of social disempowerment and amid perceptions of accommodation to a foreign culture. The whole book is arguably more kingdom centered than any other writing from the Old Testament, and it marks the beginning of a shift from a prophetic to an apocalyptic orientation by certain Judeans. In the interpretation of Nebuchadnezzar's dream, the stone cut out of the mountain and not made by human hands strikes the idolatrous statue and smashes its feet (Dan. 2:34–35, 41–43). The collapse of the pagan kingdom is contrasted with the kingdom that follows it:

> And in the days of those kings the God of heaven will set up a kingdom that shall never be destroyed, nor shall this kingdom be left to another people. It shall crush all these kingdoms and bring them to an end, and it shall stand forever; just as you saw that a stone was cut from the mountain not by hands, and that it crushed the iron, the bronze, the clay, the silver, and the gold. (Dan. 2:44–45)

The mountain is probably identifiable with Mount Zion, and the "stone" could signify a range of possibilities, including a revitalized Jewish kingdom,

26. Fitzmyer, *The One Who Is to Come*, 50.

27. So Joachim Becker, *Messianic Expectation in the Old Testament* (trans. David A. Green; Philadelphia: Fortress, 1980), 50.

28. Evans, "Messianic Hopes and Messianic Figures," 15–18.

29. J. Collins, *Scepter and the Star*, 31.

a Jewish monarchy, or even a king (there is a possible wordplay between אבן [*eben*, stone] and בּן [*ben*, son]).[30] References to God's kingdom, which is set over and against human kingdoms, are found throughout the book in subsequent sections (esp. Dan. 4:3, 17; 6:26; 7:18, 27). The theological center of gravity is arguably the sovereignty of God's kingdom over human kingdoms and the participation of God's people in God's coming reign.

The coming of "one like a son of man" in Dan. 7:13 (RSV) is a much-disputed piece of text, though I find it persuasive that "son of man" here is a metaphor with a variety of referents (Israel, God's kingdom, a future Judean king, and perhaps an angelic figure). The enthronement of the mysterious human figure and the everlasting dominion bestowed upon him in verses 13–14 correspond to the way the "saints of the Most High" in verses 15–18, 27 receive a kingdom that also lasts forever and ever (as stated in the explanation of the vision). That said, there is no absolute bifurcation between an individual and a corporate entity since representation of the nation before God was presupposed in the roles of prophet, priest, and king and also for angelic intermediaries. The royal and ruling function of the son of man and the saints of the Most High and their association with the dominion of God are easily worked into a messianic matrix.

In Dan. 9:24–27 is a reinterpretation of Jeremiah's "seventy years" (Jer. 25:11–12; 29:10) as seventy weeks of years. This section provides a chronological scheme for the coming of an anointed leader and the advent of one who is to desecrate the holy place. Overall this section serves to demonstrate the lordship of Yahweh over secular history and human kingdoms. After transgression is finished, when sin is ended and iniquity is atoned for, then the people are to "anoint a most holy place," which is probably tantamount to a cleansing and rededication of the temple. This is followed by the coming of an "anointed one" (משיח) and "prince" (נגיד) that is arguably a reference to "Messiah King" (Dan. 9:25). The text does not specify who this is: it could signify a non-Israelite ruler or either Zerubbabel and Joshua, the "sons of oil" of Zech. 4:12–14. Then in Dan. 9:26–27 there is an interval of sixty-two weeks; then another anointed one (perhaps different from the first in v. 25) is "cut off," and another prince comes to destroy the city and the sanctuary, and he ends sacrifices in the temple. The problem here is that "in both cases in which Daniel uses the word ['anointed one'], there

---

30. Josephus (*Ant.* 10.205) changes Dan. 2:29 from "To you . . . came thoughts of what would be hereafter" to "You were worried concerning those who would be reigning over the whole world after you." N. T. Wright (*People of God*, 313) suggests that while this refers to all kingdoms that follow Nebuchadnezzar, it is focusing predominantly on the reign associated with the coming of the "stone." See references to this passage from Daniel in Justin Martyr, *Dial.* 70; 100; 126; 4 Ezra 13.6–7, 36; Didascalia (Eth.) 30.v.20; and Num. Rab. 13.14, which interpret the stone/mountain messianically.

are two persons designated. Both are hard to define, but are certainly not 'messianic.'"[31]

The aspirations of Daniel are not incompatible with the expectation of a messianic figure, but neither do they require it.[32] Yet, in summarizing Daniel's contribution, it seems that "the kernel of Daniel's messianic hope is therefore the universal dominion of the devout" (2:44; 7:14, 27).[33] The terms "stone," "son of man," and "anointed one" are not strictly messianic in the sense of referring to a future eschatological redeemer who is anointed by God to deliver Israel, but they contain linguistic and ideological perspectives that enclose many of the ingredients for later messianism.

In the intertestamental period, one observes the idealization of the Davidic line evolving into a full-blown messianism, with prophetic hopes for restoration. The sociopolitical circumstances of Judea provide the primary catalyst for this shift. This reexpression was often, though not always, articulated in the categories of apocalyptic eschatology. In that development the Jewish Scriptures were of vital importance. The Scriptures were of extensive significance in fermenting and defining the nature of messianic hopes and messianic movements as they arose. According to Josephus, this is exactly what occurred during the Jewish war against Rome:

> But what more than all else incited them to the war was an ambiguous oracle, likewise found in their sacred scriptures, to the effect that at that time one from their country would become ruler of the world. This they understood to mean someone of their own race, and many of their wise men went astray in their interpretation of it. (*War* 6.312–13)

It is tragic and frustrating for historians of Judaism and early Christianity that Josephus does not tell us which oracle he means, and it is impossible to identify the oracle with any certainty. A text like Num. 24:17 is a good candidate, but he may have had another in mind or perhaps no single text at all.[34]

Several scholars have tried to establish a criterion in order to determine messianic texts of the Old Testament and so bridge the gap between text and appropriation of a text in the subsequent history of interpretation. Gerd

31. Florentino García Martínez, "Messianische Erwartungen in den Qumranschriften," *JBT* 8 (1993): 173: "In beiden Fällen, wo Daniel das Wort verwendet, sind es zwei Personen, die schwer genau zu bestimmen, jedoch sicher keine 'messianischen' Gestalten sind." Cf. similarly Fitzmyer, *The One Who Is to Come*, 64.

32. J. Collins, "Messianism in the Maccabean Period," in *Judaism and Their Messiahs at the Turn of the Christian Era* (ed. J. Neusner, W. S. Green, and E. S. Frerichs; Cambridge: Cambridge University Press, 1987), 100.

33. Schürer, *History of the Jewish People*, 2:498.

34. Cf. N. T. Wright, *People of God*, 312–13, and arguments for an association with the book of Daniel.

Theissen and Annette Merz offer a three-point criterion to identify messianic figures in the Old Testament:[35]

- They usher in an eschatological turning point.
- They have a soteriological function.
- They have a charismatic status beyond that of other human beings.

The problem I have with this criterion is that it could apply equally to Moses, Saul, Elijah, and even John the Baptist. Yet we cannot regard any of them as messianic figures as far as they were remembered and revered in Jewish and Christian writings. There is also a certain feel of circularity in any definition of a messianic text that is derived from the Old Testament texts and then applied back to those texts. If one begins by looking at the biblical texts for certain patterns and paradigms about national saviors and eschatological deliverers and then develops from that a definition of a "messianic figure" based on those texts, then when that definition is taken back to the texts, it will obviously cohere with the proposed definition and will be regarded as a messianic text. In other words, if you use Isa. 11:1–2 as the basis for creating a definition of "messianic," of course you will regard Isa. 11:1–2 as a messianic text.

An alternative approach would be to define a messianic text through a comparative religious approach (e.g., comparison with ANE literature) or through a sociological model (e.g., "hero" or "savior" figures in other cultures and religions). The danger in this latter approach is that it risks importing foreign ideas into the texts and presses them into the service of a definition that presupposes things (historical, cultural, theological, or cosmological) that are either irrelevant or alien to the world of the texts and the world behind the texts.

I suggest that a better criterion for establishing what constitutes a messianic text in the Old Testament is to take into account the texts that were read messianically by Jews and Christians. Some will no doubt object that this disregards the authorial intent of the Old Testament authors; they may ask, Who is to say that Jewish and Christian authors were right in the first place when they attributed messianic significance to certain texts? Not everyone agrees with the Peter of Acts that Ps. 16 speaks of the resurrection of the Messiah (Acts 2:25–28), or with Josephus that Vespasian was the prophesied ruler of the world (*War* 3.400–404; 6.313–15),[36] and not all will concur with

---

35. Theissen and Merz, *Historical Jesus*, 532. On the problem of developing a set of criteria for messianism, see Chester, *Messiah and Exaltation*, 191–205.

36. Linking messianic hopes to a non-Jewish king was hardly unprecedented; see Isa. 45:1 and Sib. Or. 3.652–56.

Rabbi Akiba that Num. 24:17 referred to Simon ben Kosiba (*y. Ta'an.* 4.5; Lam. Rab. 2.4).

There are several reasons why messianic readings of Old Testament texts can be considered legitimate even if a messianic sense is not explicit in the original context. First, we should consider some texts as deliberately "open" and susceptible to further interpretation (by which I do not mean completely indeterminate!). Fitzmyer considers Ps. 72 and its echoing of the phraseology of 2 Sam. 7:11–16 as rendering it "open" to further interpretation in the Jewish tradition along messianic lines, as was the case in Pss. Sol. 17, which is largely an imitation of Ps. 72.[37] I do not know precisely what Fitzmyer means by "open," but I have in mind Umberto Eco's distinction between "closed texts" and "open texts."[38] Although some texts are relatively "closed" in that they evoke a prescripted response, some texts are open in the sense that they invite reinterpretation in a new context which, while in some respects innovative, is not completely out of step or at variance with the original intent. I suggest that this is indeed the case with Gen. 49:10 and Num. 24:17. Both texts look toward a future moment; though that moment may be historical, it could also be typological.

Second, reinterpretation of sacred traditions is already taking place within the development of the Old Testament corpus. This is what Michael Fishbane calls "inner-biblical exegesis."[39] Such reinterpretations already place the original texts on a messianic trajectory. A good example of this would be the intensification of 2 Sam. 7:12–16 in Ps. 89:3–4, 19. Another instance is the combination of the "scion" or "branch" of Jer. 23:5; 33:15 (cf. Isa. 11.1) with the "servant" of Isa.

37. Fitzmyer, *The One Who Is to Come*, 43. Cf. Roberts ("The Old Testament's Contribution," 51), who thinks that most messianic texts in the Old Testament refer to a continuing Davidic dynasty, but he acknowledges that some of these texts are "open" to the interpretation that they refer to visions of a final Davidic ruler who will rule for all time to come.

38. Umberto Eco, *The Limits of Interpretation* (Bloomington: Indiana University Press, 1990), cited in Kevin J. Vanhoozer, *Is There a Meaning in This Text? The Bible, the Reader, and the Morality of Literary Knowledge* (Grand Rapids: Zondervan, 1998), 151–52.

39. Michael A. Fishbane, *Biblical Interpretation in Ancient Israel* (Oxford: Clarendon, 1985). Fishbane (ibid., 542–43) writes: "The whole phenomenon of inner-biblical exegesis requires the latter-day historian to appreciate the fact that the texts and traditions, the received traditum of ancient Israel, were not simply copied, studied, transmitted, or recited. They were also, and by these means, subject to redaction, elucidation, reformation, and outright transformation. Accordingly, our received traditions are complex blends of traditum [what is transmitted] and traditio [the act of transmitting] in dynamic interaction, dynamic interpretation, and dynamic interdependence. They are, in sum, the exegetical voices of many teachers and tradents [those who transmit tradition], from different circles and times, responding to real and theoretical considerations as perceived and as anticipated. To retrace this substantial achievement is, then, correspondingly to encounter traces of ancient Israelite exegetical thinking in its attentive relations to textual contexts and historical memories, in its complex correlations of traditions and situations, and literary form."

41–53, with the result that Zech. 3:8 refers to "my servant the Branch."[40] What is more, the editing, collecting, and translation of the Hebrew texts also led to the formation of messianism within the interpretive development of the Old Testament itself. When the Prophets or Psalms are read after the Pentateuch, the pentateuchal prophecies are taken up and continued by another series that expresses the particularity of the Davidic covenant and hope. When heard in the context of the Pentateuch and Prophets, the royal Psalms can readily be understood as oracles of the future related to Davidic kingship and national restoration (esp. Pss. 89 and 132).[41]

Translations into Greek and Aramaic also created messianism.[42] In Num. 24:7 LXX the translators combine the prophetic oracle "There shall come forth a man" with the reference to "Gog" from Ezek. 38–39, with the result that "there shall come a man out of his seed, and he shall rule over many nations; and his kingdom shall be made higher than Gog, and his kingdom shall be increased" (ἐξελεύσεται ἄνθρωπος ἐκ τοῦ σπέρματος αὐτοῦ καὶ κυριεύσει ἐθνῶν πολλῶν, καὶ ὑψωθήσεται ἢ Γωγ βασιλεία αὐτοῦ, καὶ αὐξηθήσεται ἡ βασιλεία αὐτοῦ). This is a clear instance of combining the original oracle with exilic hopes for national deliverance from Israel's arch-enemy of the last days. And also in Hab. 2:3 LXX we find: "For *he* will surely come, and will not tarry" (ὅτι ἐρχόμενος ἥξει καὶ οὐ μὴ χρονίσῃ), which changes the "it" (i.e., the vision) to a person "he will come" (i.e., a divine agent) in the future. Thus, the messianic interpretation of certain texts in the Second Temple era is merely an extension of what was already happening within the Old Testament itself. The process of the reinterpretation and reapplication of certain texts along royal, messianic, and eschatological lines had long since begun.

Third, while literary context is a crucial arbiter for the creation and limitation of meaning, it is not the only context of the authors and audiences. It might be better to speak of contexts in the plural as they relate to wider factors as diverse as canon and community or Scripture and society and how the process of creating meaning is deeply affected by these factors. We must take into account the canonical and sociological contexts of readers as they received the books of the Old Testament. Isaiah may show signs of different levels of redaction between chapters 1–39 and chapters 40–55, and commentators may accordingly write commentaries on Deutero-Isaiah. Nonetheless, the ancients did not compartmentalize their sacred traditions nor study them in an atomized form. It was perfectly normal to read Isa. 11 in tandem with Isa. 53. Ancient readers did not think about source criticism

---

40. For a similar link to the new David as a "servant," see Ezek. 34:23.

41. Horbury, *Jewish Messianism*, 25–29.

42. Samson H. Levey, *The Messiah: An Aramaic Interpretation; The Messianic Exegesis of the Targum* (New York: Ktav, 1974); M. A. Knibb, ed., *The Septuagint and Messianism* (BETL 195; Louvain: Leuven University Press, 2006).

or eisegesis. There was nothing to stop interpreters from reading Dan. 7:9, 13–14 in the light of Ps. 110:1–2 and the like. Sociological factors such as deprivation and disempowerment may also provide another impetus toward readings that promote hopes for deliverance. Such readings might remain indebted to sentiments imbibed by several texts that, although dealing with similar issues of repression, were not obviously related to the particular situation of the readers.[43] Thus, as far as ancient readers go, the meaning of Isa. 61:1 is not the exclusive property of Trito-Isaiah, and it belongs to the manifold contexts in which it was read. Meaning, though not necessarily open-ended, was created through the dynamic interplay of a text with other texts and between the fusion of the worlds of the audience, the author, and the text.

Fourth and finally, we must consider the viability of *Wirkungsgeschichte* (effective history) as an indicator of the meaning of texts. The gap between implied readers and real readers in antiquity may not be as broad as is often thought. Accordingly, it is surely of paramount significance that a text like Num. 24:17 was consistently given a messianic spin by Philo, by rabbinic authors, and in the Qumran scrolls. This may seem to give way to a rampant exegetical subjectivity whereby all messianic texts of the Old Testament are authenticated by the often-eccentric readings of later interpreters. However, a safeguard may be provided by insisting on some semantic correlation that seems at least capable of sustaining a messianic sense and in regarding Old Testament texts as at least potentially messianic (i.e., "open") where there is multiple attestation for a messianic reading of them in antiquity.

In light of that, what I propose then is that we identify an Old Testament text as "messianic" when the plain sense of the text (i.e., its semantic and linguistic operation)[44] designates a figure with royal qualities who is sent by God, and also that either the text itself was treated as messianic in postbiblical interpretation, or else the pattern of activity that the figure embodies corresponds to a pattern of activity often expected of messianic figures in antiquity.[45]

---

43. On the relationship between sociology and ideology in fermenting messianism, J. Collins (*Scepter and the Star*, 41) writes: "No would-be messiah was motivated only, or primarily, by the desire to act out a textual paradigm. Political and especially social factors provided the obvious occasions of most of the messianic movements of the Roman era. But actions are also shaped by ideologies, and in Judaism at the turn of the era the available ideologies were predominantly shaped by scriptural traditions."

44. Cf. John Barton, *The Nature of Biblical Criticism* (Louisville: Westminster John Knox, 2007), 101–16.

45. Roberts ("The Old Testament's Contribution," 41n2) is surely right to note that there is a basic consistency in the choice of texts that are considered messianic by interpreters of antiquity. If every messianic document had a completely different selection of proof texts, one could grant the capricious nature of their messianic exegesis, but the fact that certain texts kept being recalled for their messianic content is a highly significant feature of Jewish and Christian interpretation.

Table 1. Old Testament Texts and Messianic Interpretations

OT/Hebrew Bible	Messianic interpretation
Gen. 49:10	4QpIsaᵃ frgs. 7–10.iii.25; 4Q252 5.1–7; T. Jud. 22.1–3; 24.1; LXX; Sib. Or. 5.415; Tg. Onq.; Tg. Neof.; Justin Martyr, *1 Apol.* 32, 54; *Dial.* 52, 120; Clement of Alexandria, *Paed.* 1.5–6; Irenaeus, *Haer.* 4.10.2
Num. 24:17	1QSb 5.20–29; CD 7.18–20; 1QM 11.6–7; 4Q175 1.9–13; 1QPsʲ 9–13; Philo, *Moses* 1.290; *Rewards* 95; T. Jud 24.5; T. Levi 18.3; *y. Ta'an.* 4.5; Tg. Onq.; Justin Martyr, *Dial.* 106; Irenaeus, *Haer.* 3.9.2
2 Sam. 7:12–16	Pss. 89; 132; Sir. 47:11; 4Q174 2.19–3.11; 4Q246 1.8–9; 2.1; 4Q254 4.2–3; 4Q369 frg. 1 2.6; Pss. Sol. 17.4; 4 Ezra 13.32, 37
Ps. 2	4Q174 3.10–13; 3.18–19; Pss. Sol. 17.23; 1 En. 48.10; 4 Ezra 13.32, 37, 52
Isa. 11:1–6	1QSb 5.22, 25, 26; 4Q161 8, 9, 10, 15–29; 4Q285 5.1–6; 1 En. 62.2; Pss. Sol. 17.24, 29, 36–37; T. Jud. 24.6; T. Levi 18.7; Tg. Isa.; Matt. 2:23; Acts 13:23; Heb. 7:14; Rev. 5:5; 22:16; Justin Martyr, *1 Apol.* 32; *Dial.* 87; Clement of Alexandria, *Paed.* 1.7
Isa. 53	1 En. 37–70; Tg. Isa.
Jer. 23:5; 33:15; Zech. 6:12	4Q161 8+9+10 15–16, 22; T. Jud. 24.4–6
Dan. 7:9, 13–14	Mark 14:61–62; 1 En. 37–70; 4 Ezra 13; *b. Ḥag.* 14a; *b. Sanh.* 38b; Justin Martyr, *Dial.* 31–32
Amos 9:11	4Q174 3.10–13

Messianic Claimants in the First Century

On messianism in the first century, Raymond Brown stated: "There seems to be no identifiable Jew hailed as the kingly Messiah other than Jesus of Nazareth."[46] While strictly speaking this is true, we need to distinguish between a messianic claimant and a messianic leader. The former designation of an explicit "messianic claimant" would apply only to Simon ben Kosiba and (as I will argue) Jesus of Nazareth, but the latter category of "messianic leader" applies to those who deliberately invoked messianic themes or inspired messianic hopes by their actions. Not everyone grasping for the throne of Judea was a messianic pretender claiming to restore the Davidic line, thinking of himself as ushering in an eschatological age of salvation, and counting on bringing biblical prophecies to fulfillment. Nonetheless, several royal pretenders did echo messianic themes in their actions and intentions.

It is historically naive to depict first-century Palestine as ravaged with continual uprisings and to posit some Roman occupying forces as having to put

46. Brown, *Death of the Messiah*, 1:475; cf. J. Collins, *Scepter and the Star*, 208–9; Jossa, *Jews or Christians?* 59.

down one messianic pretender after another. Alternatively, it is equally reductionistic to suppose that many of the tumultuous events of the first century were untouched by messianism. The death of Herod the Great led to several uprisings; although things cooled for a while, in the period 4 BCE to 66 CE, there were many socioreligious movements at the time of the procurators that show expectation and hope for God's miraculous interventions and gradually a spirit of zealotry beginning to emerge. I doubt that we have to wait as long as Simon ben Kosiba in 135 CE to find another messianic leader after the death of Jesus. The following lists indicate messianic expectations that are explicitly titular or implicitly messianic.[47]

Expectations using the title "Messiah":

"Messiah of Aaron and Israel" (CD 12.23–13.1; 14.19; 19.10–11; 20.1; 1QS 9.11)

"Messiah of Israel" (1QSa 2.12, 14, 20)

"Messiah of righteousness" (4Q252 frg. 1 5.3–4)

"Heaven and earth will obey his Messiah" (4Q521 2.1)

"Their king shall be the Lord's Messiah" (Pss. Sol. 17.32; cf. 18.7)

"May God cleanse Israel for the day of mercy and blessing for the appointed day when his Messiah will reign" (Pss. Sol. 18.5)

"Lord of the Spirits and his Messiah" (1 En. 48.10)

"authority of the Messiah" (1 En. 52.4)

"For my son the Messiah shall be revealed with those who are with him" (4 Ezra 7.28)

"This is the Messiah whom the Most High has kept until the end of days, who will arise from the offspring of David" (4 Ezra 12.32)

"The Messiah will begin to be revealed" (2 Bar. 29.3)

"when the time of the appearance of the Messiah has been fulfilled" (2 Bar. 30.1)

"the kingship of the house of David, thy righteous Messiah" (Shemoneh 'Esreh 14)

Expectations not using the title "Messiah":

Son of Man (Dan. 7:13–14; 1 En. 46.1–5; 48.2; 62.1–15; 63.11; 69.27–29; 71.14–17; 4 Ezra 13.1–13, 25–26; Justin Martyr, *Dial.* 31–32)

Man/Ruler (Philo, *Rewards* 95; Num. 24:7, 17 LXX)

Rod (CD 7.19–20; Justin Martyr, *Dial.* 100, 126)

---

47. Adapted from Theissen and Merz, *Historical Jesus*, 537; and Craig A. Evans, "Messianism," in *DNTB* (ed. C. A. Evans and S. E. Porter; Downers Grove, IL: InterVarsity, 2000), 701–2.

Prince (Ezek. 34:24; 37:25; Dan. 9:25–26; CD 7.20; 1QSb 5.20; 1QM 3.16; 5.1; 4Q285 frgs. 4–6; Jub. 31.18; Sib. Or. 3.49–50)

Branch of David (4Q161 frgs. 8–10.15, 22; 4Q252 5.3; 4Q285 frg. 5.3–4; T. Jud 24.4–6)

Scepter (1QSb 5.27–28; 4Q161 frgs. 2–4 2.9–13; frgs. 5–6 3.17; frgs. 8–10, 22–26; 4Q252 5.2)

Son of God (4Q246 1.9; 2.1; Mark 15:39)

Elect/Chosen One (1 En. 39.6; 40.5; 45.3; 48.6; 49.2, 4; 51.3, 5; 52.6, 9; 53.6; 55.4; 61.5, 8, 10; 62.1; Apoc. Abr. 31.1)

King (Mark 15.32 and par.; Sib. Or. 3.286–87, 652)

Snow-white cow/horned ram (1 En. 90.9–12, 37–38)

Star (T. Levi 18.3; T. Jud. 24.1; Sib. Or. 5.158–60)

Righteous One (Acts 3:14; 22:14; 1 John 2:1; 1 En. 38.2; 53.6)

Historical figures referred to as "Messiah":

Jesus of Nazareth
Simon ben Kosiba

Implicitly messianic historical figures not referred to as "Messiah":

Judas the Galilean
Simon the servant of Herod
Athronges
Menahem
Simon bar Giora

Let us not forget that Josephus attributes the outbreak of the Jewish war to the interpretation of an "ambiguous oracle found in their sacred scriptures" about one who would become "ruler of the world" (*War* 6.312). If there is some degree of continuity between the Jewish War (66–70 CE) and the uprisings of an earlier period, then the uprisings staged from 4 BCE onward may well have had a messianic impetus in some form or other that surfaces in the character and conduct of different would-be rulers.

The death of Herod the Great and the deposition of Archelaus were occasioned by several revolts and disturbances that required military action.[48] We are told that the "Fourth Philosophy," mentioned by Josephus, was derived from Judas the Galilean, who led a violent uprising against the Romans during a census imposed in 6 CE for the purpose of taxation. This "movement" (note

48. Cf. Josephus, *Ant.* 17.269; *War* 2.55.

the quotation marks!) claimed that "God is their only Governor [ἡγεμών] and Master [δεσπότης]" and was related to notions of "liberty" (ἐλεύθερος) or national redemption (*Ant.* 18.23; cf. 18.4–6; Acts 5:37). Two of Judas's sons were executed by Tiberius Alexander some years later (ca. 46–48 CE; *Ant.* 20.102), and another of his descendants (son or grandson) was Menaham, who was a short-term leader of the revolt of 66–70 CE and even made royal gestures in his actions (*War* 2.433–34). Ten years earlier, after the death of Herod the Great in 4 BCE, Judas the son of Hezekiah (whose father was one of the bandits of Syria that Herod the Great had captured and killed; *Ant.* 14.159–60; 17.271; *War* 2.56) himself led an insurrection in Sepphoris of the Galilee, and Josephus says that this bloodshed was motivated by "zeal for royal honor [ζηλώσει βασιλείου τιμῆς]" (*Ant.* 17.272).

At the same time, a certain Athronges, a shepherd in Judea, led a revolt in Judea with his brothers and "set himself up in kingship [βασιλεία]." He was also "called a king [βασιλεύς]," and he put a "diadem [διάδημα] on his head" (*Ant.* 17.278, 280–81; *War* 2.60–62). The fact that Athronges was a shepherd may have counted in his favor and invoked imagery of David as the shepherd-become-king of Israel as in 2 Sam. 5:2 or of the prophesied Davidic shepherd king of Ezek. 34:23–24. However, we should also note that placing a diadem was a typically Hellenistic act of conferring royal status in contrast to the Jewish tradition of anointing kings with oil. In Perea, Simon a servant of Herod also put a diadem on his head (*Ant.* 17.273; *War* 2.57) and was "declared to be king [βασιλεὺς ἀναγγελθείς]" by a number of people (*Ant.* 17.274). Josephus says that both Athronges and Simon were noted for their physical attributes, which was a Davidic quality (*Ant.* 17.273, 278; *War* 2.60).[49]

Josephus tells us that a certain Menahem—a descendant of Judas the Galilean, a leader of the Sicarii—led a small contingent of men, who seized the fortress at Masada and looted the armory. Menahem then "returned to Jerusalem like a king [βασιλεύς]" (*War* 2.434) and appointed himself leader of the siege against the Roman troops barricaded in the Antonian fortress. Menahem also had the high priest Ananias killed; this deed, Josephus tells us, made Menahem think of himself as the unrivaled leader to the degree that he went to worship in the temple "adorned in royal [βασιλικῇ] apparel" (*War* 2.444). A faction of the insurgents loyal to Eleazar, the son of Ananias the high priest murdered by Menahem, despised Menahem's tyranny and did not enjoy the prospect of having someone from a social station lower than themselves (ἑαυτῶν ταπεινότερον) ruling over them. The insurgents launched an attack on Menahem, who initially fled and hid, but was eventually captured, tortured, and executed (*War* 2.441–48).

Another figure, Simon bar Giora (in Aramaic בר גיורא means "son of the proselyte," which may tell us something of Simon's origins), led thousands in

---

49. Cf. Martin Hengel, *The Zealots* (Edinburgh: T&T Clark, 1989), 292.

the insurrection with some degree of success early on, especially in subjugating Idumea (*War* 4.521–34), which has parallels to David's military career in conquering neighboring tribes. We are told by Josephus that his army was "subservient to his command as to a king [βασιλέα]" (*War* 4.510). Josephus also describes his message as being along the lines of "proclaiming liberty for slaves and rewards for the free" (*War* 4.508). Such a statement seems to echo Lev. 25:13 and Isa. 61:1 and is perhaps close to what Jesus said in Luke 4:18–21 and what is found in 11QMelch 2. What is more, the quest for liberty[50] and a belief that Israel was still in slavery[51] were well-known motifs in Jewish restoration eschatology. Like Simon ben Kosiba in the second century, Simon bar Giora also minted coins celebrating the redemption of Zion. Simon bar Giora took control of Jerusalem from John of Gischala, leader of the Zealots, around 69 CE (*War* 4.577). When the Romans stormed the city and razed the temple, Simon initially hid and then emerged dressed in white tunics and a purple cloak and appeared before the Roman soldiers on the place where the temple had stood (*War* 7.29). His apparel was designed to "astonish" and "elude" the Romans, but instead he was seized, chained, sent to Rome, and eventually executed (*War* 7.154–55). Richard Horsley states: "By far the most important 'messianic' movement of the first century was that focused on Simon bar Giora, who eventually became the principal political-military commander in Jerusalem during the Jewish Revolt and whom the Romans ceremonially executed as, in effect, the king of the Jews."[52]

Moving to the second century,[53] in the Jewish revolt of 132–135 CE led by Simon ben Kosiba, we encounter diverse evidence for a messianic claim on his part.[54] To begin with, Kosiba is never designated as "Messiah" in extant letters, inscriptions, and coinage. He is called נשיא (prince), which had a long history as a messianic title. In any case, the later literary evidence clearly associates Kosiba with a messianic claim.[55] One of the leading Tannaitic rabbis, Akiba, regarded Kosiba as the Messiah (*y. Ta'an.* 4.5; *Lam. Rab.* 2.4). While

50. Isa. 45:13; 61:1; Jer. 34:8, 15; 1 Macc. 10:33; 2 Macc. 1:27; 4 Ezra 12.34; Luke 4:18; Josephus, *War* 2.259; 5.396; T. Jud. 23.5; T. Zeb. 9.8.

51. Ezra 9:8–10; Neh. 9:36; Jdt. 8:22–23; Add. Esth. 14:8; 2 Macc. 1:27; Josephus, *War* 5.395–96; *Ant.* 18.4.

52. Richard A. Horsley, " 'Messianic' Figures and Movements in First-Century Palestine," in Charlesworth, *The Messiah*, 277.

53. The Jewish revolt of 117–118 CE in Cyrene and Egypt may have been directed by either Lucuas or Andreas, whom Eusebius calls a "king." Unfortunately, it is exceedingly difficult to say anything concrete about these figures and their aspirations because of our scant sources, which do not always agree on the details. The most that can be said is that there was a Jewish uprising and that it had leaders (Eusebius, *Hist. eccl.* 4.2.1–5; Dio Cassius, *Hist.* 68.32; 69.12–13). However, several scholars (listed in J. Collins, *Scepter and the Star*, 211n24) argue that the revolt was inspired by messianism.

54. Cf. Evans, *Jesus and His Contemporaries*, 183–211; J. Collins, *Scepter and the Star*, 202–3.

55. Cf. Eusebius, *Hist. eccl.* 4.6; Dio Cassius, *Hist.* 69.12–14; *b. Sanh.* 93b.

rabbinic traditions about Akiba may contain legendary accretions, there is no need to doubt his claim that Kosiba was the Messiah.[56] Justin Martyr records: "Barchochebas [= bar Kokhba], the leader of the revolt of the Jews, gave orders that Christians alone should be led to cruel punishments unless they would deny Jesus Christ and utter blasphemy" (Justin Martyr, 1 Apol. 31.5–6). The Apocalypse of Peter identifies the coming of false Christs and martyrdom for believers with the persecution of Christians under Kosiba, and this may provide an indication of Jewish Christians being persecuted for failing to deny that Jesus is the Messiah (Apoc. Pet. 2). At the height of this revolt, there was a persecution of Jewish Christians, and this was perhaps undertaken because their own brand of messianism did not square with the ideology of the revolt led by Kosiba. The denunciation of Kosiba as a false Messiah in both Christian and Jewish literature constitutes good evidence that he was regarded as such during his lifetime, since such a view would not likely have arisen after his death if he was never associated with messianic hopes.[57]

The primary pattern we find here is that sociopolitical and economic factors led to revolts, insurrections, and banditry. Hopes for deliverance in this context were often associated with themes of national deliverance for the Jewish nation: restoration eschatology is anchored in hopes from Israel's sacred traditions. The leaders of these revolts were frequently heralded as king; quite often they made deliberate royal gestures and were even known to have royal aspirations. When this fact is coupled with Josephus's remarks that the 66–70 CE revolt was linked to the interpretation of an oracle from the Jewish Scriptures, then we are certainly in the messianic ballpark. Thus, though it is true that we know of no other figure who is named as or claimed to be the Messiah in the first century besides Jesus, we still have a number of spasmodic revolts that seem to echo messianic ideas in the portraits that they presented of their leaders, most likely as a feature of political propaganda designed to win adherents. Horsley concludes: "The messianic and prophetic movements of late Second Temple times constituted widespread, organized popular resistance to Roman imperial rule and its client regimes in Palestine."[58]

56. Cf. Brook W. R. Pearson, "The Book of the Twelve, Aqiba's Messianic Interpretations, and the Refuge of Caves of the Second Jewish War," in The Scrolls and the Scriptures: Qumran Fifty Years After (ed. S. E. Porter and C. A. Evans; Sheffield: Sheffield Academic Press, 1997), 221–39.

57. Cf. Adele Reinhartz, "Rabbinic Perceptions of Simeon Bar Kosiba," JSJ 20 (1989): 177.

58. Horsley, "Messianic Figures and Movements," 294; cf. N. A. Dahl, "Messianic Ideas and the Crucifixion of Jesus," in Charlesworth, The Messiah, 385, who states: "It is more likely than not that messianic ideas in a wider sense of the term played a role for the freedom fighters."

Sources and a Sketch

The role of the Messiah(s) in the literature is multifarious.[59] There was no single and uniform description of the messianic task. Likewise the means through which a Messiah accomplished his mission, including the degree of divine assistance, were diverse in the minds of interpreters. Nonetheless, some scholars have posited a core and common set of expectations that a Messiah could fulfill. According to N. T. Wright:

> The main task of the Messiah, over and over again, is the liberation of Israel, and her reinstatement as the true people of the creator god [sic]. This will often involve military action, which can be seen in terms of judgment as in a lawcourt. It will also involve action in relation to the Jerusalem Temple, which must be cleansed and/or restored and/or rebuilt.[60]

Generally speaking, this is correct, but we can be slightly more specific in looking over several key texts and what they have to say about messianic figures.

1. The Psalms of Solomon constitute a primary source for unearthing messianic expectations, especially in chapters 17 and 18. The document was probably written some time after the death of Pompey since there is a reference to a Gentile conqueror who came from the west (17.12), who laid siege to the temple (2.1), entered it and thereby desecrated its precincts (2.2), and was eventually assassinated in Egypt (2.25–29). If Pompey was killed around 48 BCE, then Psalms of Solomon was probably composed sometime afterward and was perhaps written just before or during the reign of Herod the Great (37–4 BCE).[61]

The characteristics of the Messiah include the following:

- He is of the Davidic line and establishes the throne of David over and against those who have usurped his authority by their arrogance (17.4–6, 21).
- He appears on the appointed day (18.5).
- He purges Jerusalem of Gentiles, destroys the unrighteous rulers, shatters the unlawful nations, and condemns sinners, meaning Jews who live as Gentiles (17.21–25).
- He gathers up the scattered people of the Diaspora, distributes land among the tribes, and judges the tribes of the people; Gentiles are his

59. I have not included a survey of the Testament of the Twelve Patriarchs because it is impossible to determine if it is a Jewish composition with Christian editing or a Christian composition that makes use of traditional Jewish material. In either case, in its current form it contributes more to Christian views of eschatology and messianism than to Second Temple perspectives.

60. N. T. Wright, *People of God*, 320.

61. Cf. Michael Lattke, "Psalms of Solomon," in *DNTB*, 885.

servants as they come from the ends of the earth to worship God and
to return the exiles to Jerusalem (17.26–32).

• He inaugurates a period of holiness and covenant righteousness and
  also purifies/cleanses the people (17.29–32, 43–44; 18.4–9).

• He is compassionate, sinless, blessed, full of the Holy Spirit, wise, and
  divinely strengthened to reign and shepherd over "the house of Israel"
  (17.34–42).

The coming of the "king of Israel" (17.32, 42) is an act of God. God raises
up the king for Israel's benefit, and the text never for a moment forfeits the
view that God alone is the true king (17.1, 34, 46); and it is his kingdom that
brings salvation (17.3). While the Messiah/king figures prominently, this never
eclipses the strong theocentric element of God as the ultimate hope and deliverer of the Israelites.

Psalms of Solomon (17.32; 18.7) even refers to the "Lord Messiah" (χριστὸς
κύριον and χριστοῦ κυρίου). Though this text could be a gloss by a later Christian scribe or a mistranslation from a Semitic original concerning the "Messiah of the Lord" (e.g., Tg. Pss. 89:52 [משיחך יהוה]),[62] several things are worth
pointing out: (1) in context "Lord Messiah" makes better sense than "Messiah
of the Lord"; (2) the reading is attested by the Greek and Syriac manuscripts;
(3) Lam. 4:20 LXX and Luke 2:11 include similar phrasing of the Greek; (4) it
is probable that in Pss. Sol. 17.32 and 18.7 κύριος does not render יהוה and that
it merely signifies a royal title like "lord" or "king" and is more equivalent to
"King Messiah" (see משיחא מלכא in, e.g., Tg. Ps.-J. Gen. 3:15; 35:21; 49:1; Tg.
Ruth 1:1; Tg. Lam. 2:22 and similar expressions in y. Ber. 2.3; y. Ta'an. 4.5;
b. Sanh. 99a; cf. Mark 15:32; Luke 23:2). In context then "Lord Messiah" attests
the lordship of the anointed one over Israel on God's behalf.[63]

2. The messianism of the Dead Sea Scrolls[64] continues to fascinate and
perplex commentators. While much of what is known of messianism from
this period comes from the scrolls, the Qumran sect did not make messianism
a central part of their communal beliefs. Messianism is lacking, for instance,

62. So, e.g., Klausner, Messianic Idea, 321.
63. See further Craig A. Evans, "The Aramaic Psalter and the New Testament: Praising the
Lord in History and Prophecy," in From Prophecy to Testament: The Function of the Old Testament in the New (Peabody, MA: Hendrickson, 2004), 67; Lattke, "Psalms of Solomon," 856;
and R. B. Wright, "Psalms of Solomon," in OTP (ed. James H. Charlesworth; 2 vols.; ABRL;
New York: Doubleday, 1983–85), 2:667–78 n. z. Fitzmyer (The One Who Is to Come, 116–17)
still prefers the genitive expression "the Lord's Messiah."
64. For an overview, cf. Martin G. Abegg and Craig A. Evans, "Messianic Passages in the
Dead Sea Scrolls," in Charlesworth, Lichtenberger, and Oegema, Qumran-Messianism, 191–203;
García Martínez, "Messianische Erwartungen in den Qumranschriften," 171–208; and in more
depth, J. Zimmerman, Messianische Texte aus Qumran: Königliche, priesterliche und prophetische Messiasvorstellungen in den Schriftfunden von Qumran (WUNT 104; Tübingen: Mohr
Siebeck, 1998).

from the Halakic Letter (4QMMT), which denominates the sect's distinctive beliefs and practices in comparison to other Jewish groups (although if messianism was not a point of contention, this could conceivably explain its omission). In the extant text of the 867 scrolls from Qumran, only six to eight explicitly mention an "anointed" person who is understood as the eschatological Messiah. These include the following:

CD	The Damascus Document
1QS	The Rule of the Community
1QSa	The Rule of the Congregation
4Q252	Pesher on Genesis[a]
4Q381	Non-canonical Psalms[b] (possibly)
4Q382	Paraphrase of Kings (possibly)
4Q458	Narrative[a]
4Q521	The Messianic Apocalypse

To this we can add the messianic exegesis of certain biblical texts such as Num. 24:17; Gen. 49:10; and 2 Sam. 7:12–16 (see table 1 above). Taken together, the primary messianic texts are CD, 1QS, 1QSa, 1QSb, 1QM, 4Q161, 4Q174, 4Q175, 4Q252, 4Q376, 4Q458, and 4Q521.[65] We have already mentioned the diarchic messianism of Qumran, with a Messiah of Aaron and a Messiah of Israel, and we can state that Qumran messianism had the following characteristics for the expected leader or leaders:

- He executes judgment against oppressors of God's people at the time of punishment and subdues the *Kittim* (= Romans) and nations (CD 19.10–11; 1QSb 5.20–29; 1QM 11.6–13).
- He leads a new exodus (1QM 11.9–12).
- He is from the Davidic line (4Q161, 4Q174, 4Q252, 4Q285).
- He/they shall preside over an eschatological banquet for the congregation of the renewed covenant (1QSa 2.11–22).
- The restoration of the Davidic dynasty is related to the deliverance of Israel (1Q174 3.6–12).
- He reigns over Israel, gives dominion to Israel, and establishes the covenant and kingdom (4Q252 5.1–5).
- He is the firstborn, prince, and ruler of the inhabited world (4Q369 2.1–11).
- He keeps the law with the congregation (4Q252 5.5).

65. Craig A. Evans, "Qumran's Messiah: How Important Is He?" in *Religion in the Dead Sea Scrolls* (ed. J. J. Collins and R. A. Kugler; Grand Rapids: Eerdmans, 2000), 135–37.

- He is endowed with special insight in order to achieve God's deliverance (4Q381 15.1–10).
- His coming will be indicated with signs from God relating to healing, preaching good news, leading the poor, and raising the dead (4Q521 2.1–14).

While the scrolls are not exactly saturated in messianism, it does figure prominently in hopes for the future of the sect, especially if the Messiahs of Aaron and Israel are said to rise up from within their own ranks.

3. Since eschatological categories and hopes do not dominate Philo's writings, it is all the more significant when he employs themes known to relate to national deliverance and to a coming Jewish ruler of the world. In Philo there is a dynamic interface between particularism and universalism. For instance, while the law given to Israel is their unique possession, it is also the supreme principle of the universe. Philo hopes that the nations will put aside their own customs and take on the laws of Israel's God (e.g., *Moses* 2.43–44). Peder Borgen comments: "Thus the central role of the Jewish nation as the head (and ruler) of all nations is a fundamental element of Philo's eschatological hope."[66]

In regard to messianism, there are two basic starting points. Philo depicts Moses as the one whom God has made king over Israel and the vocation of Israel as a kingdom of priests that offers up prayers to God for every human tribe.[67] God rewards Moses for his virtue by giving him the whole world to be his portion, including all its wealth and riches (Philo, *Moses* 1.149, 155–57; *Spec. Laws* 1.97). At several points Philo echoes Num. 24:17 and the expectation of a coming Jewish ruler to defeat Israel's enemies (Philo, *Moses* 1.289–90; *Rewards* 91–97, 163–72). Important for Philo, Moses's words are set within the context of expectations for the future since Moses himself was "possessed by the spirit, no longer uttering general truths to the whole nation but prophesying to each tribe in particular the things which were to be and hereafter must come to pass. Some of these have already taken place, others are still looked for, since confidence in the future is assured by fulfillment in the past" (*Moses* 2.288). I list the constituent elements of Philo's messianism:

- The triumph of the Hebrew nation through its messianic leader is derivative of the kingship that God holds over the universe (*Moses* 1.217).
- The triumph of the Hebrew nation is contingent upon their obedience to the Mosaic law and confession of their sins (*Rewards* 79, 163–64).

66. Peder Borgen, " 'There Shall Come Forth a Man': Reflections on Messianic Ideas in Philo," in Charlesworth, *The Messiah*, 346.

67. On Moses as a king, see also *Exag.* 67–89; Exod. 4:20 LXX; and possibly Deut. 33:5, which could refer to Moses or to the LORD where it states, "He was king at Jeshurun."

- The messianic leader will rule over the nations and extend the kingdom of the Hebrew people (*Moses* 1.290–91; *Rewards* 95–97).
- The day of deliverance, where a messianic leader is not explicitly mentioned, includes the reversal of the Deuteronomic curses, the end of the exile of the Jewish people from among the nations, and liberty for the Hebrew nation (*Rewards* 163–72).

In many ways, this is similar to the Qumran scrolls and the Psalms of Solomon in the expectation of a coming Jewish ruler to defeat Israel's enemies, the return of the exiles to Palestine, and the use of Num. 24:17 as prophesying an appointed ruler.

4. Several apocalypses that reached their final form in the post–70 CE period (although their sources and ideas are very probably earlier) are also useful for our discussion. The documents 1 Enoch, 4 Ezra, and 2 Baruch are significant because they press the messianic idea into service of an apocalyptic eschatological narrative. By focusing on a heavenly figure rather than on an earthly one, they may witness to dissatisfaction and disillusionment with messianic figures of purely human origin.[68]

The messianic passages of 1 Enoch are found predominantly in the Similitudes of chapters 37–71 (but see also chaps. 83–90). Dating the Similitudes is notoriously difficult, and I have nothing further to add to the debate other than affirming that it was probably written sometime after the composition of Daniel and before the second century CE. If one wanted to be more specific, then Martin Hengel's suggestion of a period between the Parthian invasion of 40 BCE and the Jewish war of 66 CE sounds eminently plausible (cf. 1 En. 56.5–57.3).[69] Titles designating the eschatological deliverer include Righteous One, Messiah, Elect/Chosen One, and Son of Man. This transcendent figure is clearly preexistent. He is the judge of humanity who will reign on the earth and who is to be enthroned with God. The various functions of the Enochic figure emulate those of the Servant from Isa. 42, 49, 53 and the Son of Man from Dan. 7. Both of these backgrounds imply that this eschatological figure is also the representative of Israel. The tradition behind 1 Enoch then represents a synthetic compilation of Danielic and Isaianic themes centered on a particularized conception of the Messiah as a superhuman and transcendent being.

The document known as 4 Ezra (= 2 Esdras in the Old Testament Apocrypha) is a Jewish apocalyptic writing concerned mainly with matters of theodicy

---

68. J. Collins, *Scepter and the Star*, 189. Even so, the Christology of Revelation, with its dual focus on the human existence and heavenly exaltation of Jesus, indicates that although the two contrasting forms of messianism (transcendent and earthly) are different in origin and function, they are not mutually exclusive (see J. Collins, "Messianism," 103).

69. Martin Hengel, "The Effective History of Isaiah 53 in the Pre-Christian Period," in *The Suffering Servant: Isaiah 53 in Jewish and Christian Sources* (ed. B. Janowski and P. Stuhlmacher; Grand Rapids: Eerdmans, 2004), 99.

in the post–70 CE era. In the third vision, after narrating God's act of creation, Ezra is informed about the coming new creation, where the future deliverance transpires because "my son the Messiah shall be revealed with those who are with him, and those who remain shall rejoice four hundred years. After those years my son the Messiah shall die, and all who draw human breath" (4 Ezra 7.28–29). That in turn sends the world back into a state of primeval silence before awakening with the dawn of the resurrection.[70] In the fifth vision of the book, the Roman Empire, symbolized by an eagle, meets its defeat by the Messiah, symbolized by a lion. The Messiah is the one "whom the Most High has kept until the end of days, who will arise from the offspring of David, and will come and speak with them. He will denounce them for their ungodliness and for their wickedness, and will display before them their contemptuous dealings. For first he will bring them alive before his judgment seat, and when he has reproved them, then he will destroy them" (4 Ezra 12.32–33). The sixth vision combines elements of Dan. 2 and Dan. 7. The author describes a "figure of a man" who comes out of the sea. This figure flies on the clouds of heaven (= Dan. 7:13), and he carved out for himself a great mountain (4 Ezra 13.3–7). The human figure makes war on all who have gathered against him, but he fights unarmed and for weapons uses the fire, flaming breath, and sparks from his mouth (4 Ezra 13.8–12). Then it is reported that "many people came to him, some of whom were joyful and some sorrowful; some of them were bound, and some were bringing others as offerings," which probably hints at the nations coming before the human figure and bringing Jewish exiles with them (4 Ezra 13.13). In the interpretation of the dream, the figure is identified as "he whom the Most High has been keeping for many ages, who will himself deliver his creation" (4 Ezra 13.26) and is also called "Son" echoing Ps. 2:2, 7 (4 Ezra 13.32, 37, 52; as in 7.28).

The Syriac Apocalypse of Baruch known as 2 Baruch was originally a Hebrew composition and probably stems from the same period as 4 Ezra, sometime after 70 CE. Here the Messiah is revealed by God (2 Bar. 29.3), defeats the kingdoms opposed to God's people (2 Bar. 39.7; 40.1–2; 72.1–6; 82.2–9), inaugurates the resurrection of the dead (2 Bar. 30.1), and delivers people from various catastrophes (2 Bar. 70.9).[71]

Although the characteristics vary considerably in these documents, four main features largely stand out about the Messiah in these apocalypses:

- He is a preexistent and transcendent figure endowed with supernatural power.
- He establishes a messianic kingdom.

---

70. The Latin text is obviously Christianized with its reference to "my son Jesus [*filius meus Iesus*]" as opposed to the Syriac, which reads "my son, the Messiah."

71. Cf. Klausner, *Messianic Idea*, 330–48; Fitzmyer, *The One Who Is to Come*, 123.

- He comes to deliver God's people at a time of judgment.
- He defends and restores the nation over and against their adversaries.

5. Second-century literature written by both Jews and Christians also contributes to our picture of first-century conceptions of a Messiah. As a sample of what can be gleaned, here I cite evidence from Justin Martyr, Hippolytus, and selections from rabbinic writings.

Justin Martyr was exposed to forms of Judaism in both Palestine and the Diaspora, and he makes several comments pertaining to messianic hopes in *Dialogue with Trypho the Jew*. Here we find a window into messianic expectations largely through what Trypho does not believe to be true of the Messiah.[72] Justin's Trypho rejects the notion of a preexistent Messiah incarnated in human form (*Dial.* 48), and Trypho says, "We all expect the Messiah to be a man born of men" (*Dial.* 49), which stands in contrast to Christian claims of the deity of Jesus and his virgin conception. Trypho also contrasts the Son of Man, who receives an everlasting kingdom from the Ancient of Days, with the so-called Christ, who was inglorious and cursed through the cross (*Dial.* 32). This implies that it certainly was possible for Jews and Christians to read Dan. 7:13–14 messianically. Trypho is also open to the possibility that the Messiah had to suffer (*Dial.* 39, 89).

Hippolytus, a presbyter in Rome (d. ca. 235 CE), wrote of Jewish messianic beliefs in *Against All Heresies* 9.25:

Still all parties alike expect Messiah, inasmuch as the Law certainly, and the prophets, preached beforehand that He was about to be present on earth. Inasmuch, however, as the Jews were not cognizant of the period of His advent, there remains the supposition that the declarations (of Scripture) concerning His coming have not been fulfilled. And so it is, that up to this day they continue in anticipation of the future coming of the Christ,—from the fact of their not discerning Him when He was present in the world. And (yet there can be little doubt but) that, on beholding the signs of the times of His having been already amongst us, the Jews are troubled; and that they are ashamed to confess that He has come, since they have with their own hands put Him to death, because they were stung with indignation in being convicted by Himself of not having obeyed the laws. And they affirm that He who was thus sent forth by God is not this Christ (whom they are looking for); but they confess that another Messiah will come, who as yet has no existence; and that he will usher in some of the signs which the law and the prophets have shown beforehand, whereas, regarding the rest (of these indications), they suppose that they have fallen into error. For they say that his generation will be of the stock of David, but not from a virgin and the holy spirit, but from a woman and a man according as it is natural for all to be procreated from seed. And they allege that he will

72. Cf. Stefan Heid, "Frühjüdische Messianologie in Justins 'Dialog,'" *JBT* 8 (1993): 219–38.

be king over them, a warlike and powerful man, who, when he has gathered together the entire people of the Jews, and when he had done battle with all the nations, will restore for them Jerusalem the royal city. Into this city he will bring together the entire race, and will once again reinstate them in the ancient circumstances as a nation exercising royal and priestly functions, and dwelling in security for a long time. Then, when they are gathered together, war will be waged against them, and in this war Christ will fall by the sword. Then, after a short time, the end and conflagration of the universe will follow. In this way, their opinions concerning the resurrection will be fulfilled, and a recompense be rendered to each man according to his works.[73]

In this work, Hippolytus is trying to narrate "the diversities among the Jews," including the Pharisees, Sadducees, Essenes, and even the Jewish Christian Elkasites. Here (1) Hippolytus regards messianic hopes as widespread among Jews of different parties; (2) there is perhaps a denial of the preexistence of the Messiah, "who as yet has no existence," or it could comprise a Jewish denial of the Christian claim of Jesus Christ as divine and preexistent; (3) the Messiah is expected to "usher in some of the signs which the law and the prophets have shown beforehand," which may correspond to the type of signs narrated in Isa. 61:1; 4Q521; and Luke 7:22–23/Matt. 11:4–5; and (4) the Messiah will "fall by the sword" during a time of war. This resonates with one strand of messianic hopes that appears to have envisaged a dying Messiah and connected messianism to wider narrative of eschatological woes and a final tribulation that falls upon the elect.

Although rabbinic literature has a great deal to say about "the age to come," comparatively little of it is associated specifically with a Messiah. There also seems to have been some doubt among the sages as to when or even whether a Messiah would actually come. In response to Rabbi Akiba's identification of Simon ben Kosiba as the promised Messiah of Num. 24:17, Rabbi Yohanan ben Toreta is reported to have said: "Akiba! Grass will grow on your cheeks before the Messiah will come!" (*y. Ta'an.* 4.5). The same tractate states that Israel had to choose between the war fought by Kosiba and the war fought for Torah: "Why had they [Israel] been punished? It was because of the weight of the war, for they had not wanted to engage in the struggles over the meaning of the Torah" (*y. Ta'an.* 3.9; cf. *y. Šabb.* 16.8; 15d). According to Jacob Neusner, many of the sages saw Torah and Messiah as two mutually exclusive options and thought that victory would be achieved through arguments about ritual matters.[74]

At any rate, there are enough references to a Messiah in rabbinic literature to show that hope for a Messiah persisted or at least remained a topic of discussion

73. Hippolytus, *Haer.* 9.25 (adapted from *The Ante-Nicene Fathers* [ed. A. Roberts and J. Donaldson; repr., Peabody, MA: Hendrickson, 1994], 5:138).

74. Jacob Neusner, *Rabbinic Judaism: Structure and System* (Minneapolis: Fortress, 1995), 153–54.

in the post–135 CE era. Even if we cannot firmly date rabbinic traditions back to the first century, several good examples do illustrate rabbinic conceptions of the Messiah. In the Mishnah tractate *Soṭah* we read: "With the footprints of the Messiah presumption shall increase and dearth reach its height; . . . the wisdom of the Scribes shall become insipid and they that shun sin shall be deemed contemptible, and truth shall nowhere be found. Children shall shame the elders, and the elders shall rise up before the children" (*m. Soṭah* 9.15 = Mic. 7:6). The "footprints of the Messiah" is probably a reference to signs of social disintegration that precede the Messiah's coming and is equivalent to the "birth pangs of the Messiah" (see *b. Sanh.* 98b; Mark 13:3–8). In another Mishnah tractate, the biblical command to "remember the day that you came out of the land of Egypt all the days of your life" (Exod. 13:3) makes "days of your life" inclusive of the "Days of the Messiah" (*m. Ber.* 1.5; cf. *t. Ber.* 1.10). In the Jerusalem Talmud the coming of the Messiah is preceded by Israel repenting and obeying the law. Thus Rabbi Tanhum ben R. Hiyya said, "If Israel repents for one day, forthwith the son of David will come." And Rabbi Levi declared, "If Israel would keep a single Sabbath in the proper way, forthwith the son of David will come" (*y. Ta'an.* 1.1). The ideas that the future age will be preceded by a time of tribulation and that Israel needs to prepare itself by way of covenant righteousness to inaugurate the reign of the Messiah are part of a view that may be safely traced to the first century and may have been characteristic of Pharisaism.

The Shemoneh 'Esreh, or Eighteen Benedictions, probably took shape around 100 CE, thus showing how hopes for national restoration continued in the post-70 environment even with a tacit messianic element. In a well-rehearsed theme, the tenth benediction prays for the regathering of the Diaspora, the eleventh for the reinstatement of a national government, the fourteenth for the rebuilding of Jerusalem, the fifteenth for the arrival of the Son of David and the establishment of the kingdom, and the seventeenth for the reinstitution of the sacrifices. In the Palestinian recension, the fifteenth berakah is missing, and the prayer for the coming of the Son of David is an addendum to the fourteenth berakah.[75]

Taken collectively, the shared features of messianic hopes in these sources include the following:

- The Messiah will be Israel's king.
- He will be a Son of David.
- He will defeat the Gentiles and Israel's enemies.
- He will restore Jerusalem and the cultus.
- He will inaugurate a period of proper law observance.

75. Schürer, *History of the Jewish People*, 2:455–63, 512.

- He will come during a time of trial or tribulation.
- His coming will mark a return from the Diaspora, a regathering of the Jewish tribes.

Though this material is later than the first century, the fact that it comports with materials from an earlier period is sound proof that we have here evidence of first-century messianic hopes from second-century sources.

Conclusion

The preceding analysis is little more than an overview of the materials related to messianic expectations and the interpretive issues that emerge out of handling this material. This is my attempt to provide a backdrop to further discussion on Jesus and the early church in relation to messianism as opposed to a concerted study of messianism in antiquity, which would require a more detailed review and analysis.

In this chapter I hope to have established several things: (1) It is anachronistic to speak of a Christology of the Jewish Scriptures (apart from a Christian canonical perspective). Yet one observes a developing process from the idealization of kingship in the preexilic era, to expectation of a renewed kingship placed in the context of wider eschatological hopes, to the emergence of prophetic descriptions of the age of deliverance through intermediary figures and divine agents that have regal characteristics in the postexilic period, to the emergence of militant messianism amid the political turmoil and social upheaval of the Hasmonean and Herodian periods, and to the transformation of messianism into a transcendent form in the post–70 CE era. Rather than call this protomessianism, I prefer to see the Hebrew writings as being set within a messianic trajectory. (2) When it comes to messianism, functions are more important than titles. (3) An eschatological savior does not necessarily equate to a messianic figure, even though messianic figures can perform a variety of eschatological roles absorbed from Israel's sacred traditions. (4) In Second Temple Judaism, messianic beliefs were diversified and perhaps even in the minority, but they were nonetheless recognizable and arose from a common pool of tradition. (5) Finally, key texts from Israel's sacred writings played a determinative role in the development of Jewish and Christian messianism.

3

Messiah Jesus—a Role Declined?

At some point most books on the historical Jesus have to ask how Jesus understood his own role, mission, or identity given his social, cultural, and religious milieu. Many commentators—while acknowledging that Jesus saw himself as an important figure who, deliberately or not, imbued his followers and the crowds with eschatological hopes—think that he fell short of declaring himself to be the Messiah and even rejected the title when it was applied to him.[1] For example, Rudolf Bultmann (following the tradition of Adolf von Harnack) regarded Jesus's message as primarily about God and God's kingdom rather than about himself, which provides no room for Jesus to speak of himself with titles analogous to "Messiah." For John Dominic Crossan, Jesus was a Palestinian Cynic philosopher and did not entertain other worldly hopes for salvation as much as he sought the transformation of this world along the lines of a brokerless kingdom of equals. According to Geza Vermes, Jesus was a Galilean holy man and "spirit person," not a revolutionary or a Messiah. Even E. P. Sanders, who made eschatology fashionable again in historical Jesus scholarship, shrinks from having Jesus claim to be a Messiah: he settles for a Jesus who sees himself as having a regal role in a future kingdom.

The denial of a messianic shape to Jesus's ministry often leads to several reasons being given to account for the origin of the title "Messiah" and its application to him. The messianic question then becomes a prime example

1. The phrase "a role declined" in the chapter title is indebted to Dunn, *Jesus Remembered*, 647.

of discontinuity between Jesus and the early church. In light of that, the purpose of this chapter is to examine several reasons for denying that Jesus had a messianic intention and to demonstrate the weakness inherent in each one. The arguments examined include these: (1) messiahship inferred from the resurrection; (2) the "messianic secret" as proposed by William Wrede; (3) the disciples' enthusiasm for Jesus as Messiah and the authorities' perception of Jesus as Messiah; (4) an inference from the *titulus* on the cross; and (5) the scripturizing of the tradition. In sum, this chapter seeks to demonstrate that the case against a messianic Jesus is far weaker than it appears to be.

Messiahship Inferred from the Resurrection

It is quite evident that a number of texts representing traditional material (Rom. 1:4; 2 Tim. 2:8) and kerygmatic summaries of the early church (Acts 2:36; 13:33) clearly link the resurrection of Jesus to his status as Messiah. Based on this, Wrede argued the following:

> The view that Jesus only becomes messiah after his death is assuredly not merely an old one, but the oldest of which we have any knowledge. Had the earthly life of Jesus been looked upon from the start as the actual life of the messiah, it would have been only with difficulty that, by way of supplement to this, the idea could have been hit upon of regarding the resurrection as the formal beginning of the messiahship and the appearance in glory as the *single* coming of the messiah.[2]

Nevertheless, there are several problems with this line of argument. First, the most significant problem is logical: there is nothing about a resurrection that itself would connect or conjure up the issue of messianic identity in the absence of a prior messianic claim by Jesus and/or a messianic hope among his disciples.[3] The messiahship of Jesus does not figure prominently in the resurrection narratives where one might expect to find a clear announcement of messiahship on the lips of Jesus or confession by one of the disciples if

2. Wrede, *Messianic Secret*, 218.
3. Cf., e.g., Schweitzer, *Quest*, 309–10; Johannes Weiss, *Das Urchristentum* (Göttingen: Vandenhoeck & Ruprecht, 1917), 22; W. Manson, *Jesus the Messiah*, 6–7, 11; Vincent Taylor, *The Gospel according to St. Mark* (London: Macmillan, 1952), 122–23; Jeremias, *New Testament Theology*, 255; Ulrich Wilckens, *Resurrection* (Atlanta: John Knox, 1977), 102; B. F. Meyer, *Aims of Jesus*, 177–78; Meier, *A Marginal Jew*, 1:219; Larry W. Hurtado, "Christ," in *Dictionary of Jesus and the Gospels* (ed. J. B. Green, S. McKnight, and I. H. Marshall; Downers Grove, IL: InterVarsity, 1992), 113; Dahl, "Messianic Ideas," 390–91; Stein, *Messiah*, 147; Theissen and Merz, *Historical Jesus*, 540–41; Allison, *Jesus of Nazareth*, 67; Dunn, *Jesus Remembered*, 626–27; N. T. Wright, *Jesus and the Victory of God*, 487–88; idem, *The Resurrection of the Son of God* (vol. 3 of *Christian Origins and the Question of God*; Minneapolis: Fortress, 2003), 24, 575–76; Chester, *Messiah and Exaltation*, 308–9.

Jesus's messianic status was derived from Easter faith.[4] I concur with Martin Hengel: "The mere revivification of a person or, as the case may be, his translation into the heavenly realm, establishes neither messianic majesty nor eschatological mission, nor could it, of itself, supply the content of a message of salvation."[5]

Second, there is a *Religionsgeschichte* problem in that we have no analogy for a suffering righteous one who is resurrected, ascended, exalted, and designated as Messiah.[6] John the Baptist had an eschatological message, was killed, and some hoped or thought he had been raised (Mark 6:14–16), but at no point in the tradition did he become the Messiah.[7] If one of the two bandits crucified with Jesus had been seen alive three days later, it would have amazed the crowds and delighted their family, but no one would have necessarily thought that he was the Messiah redivivus.[8]

Third, we can and should admit that belief in the resurrection did shape the messianic beliefs about Jesus in the early church. The resurrection, as an article of belief in the primitive Jerusalem church, transformed the debris of messianic failure into a messianic triumph; it vindicated a prior claim that was seemingly doubted, overturned the mockery of the *titulus*, but did not create the title or the web of expectations that went with it.[9] Without the resurrection, the disciples probably would have remained in a state of melancholic disappointment and lamented how they "had hoped that he was the one who would redeem Israel" (Luke 24:21). Their hopes might have been dashed in the same way they were for the followers of Judas the Galilean, Simon the servant of King Herod, Athronges, Simon bar Giora, and Simon bar Kosiba (see chap. 2 above). Thus, in the traditional formula of Rom. 1:3–4, we do not have here an adoptionist Christology, nor an inference from resurrection to messiahship. Rather, what we find is that Jesus's Davidic heritage is already presupposed for his resurrection, and divine sonship is transposed rather than triggered by the event of resurrection. Jesus's resurrection marks a transition into a higher rank of sonship, and his sonship exercises a new eschatological function that he did not previously discharge before Easter.[10] In the words of Johannes Weiss: "Only because

4. Dahl, "Crucified Messiah," 38.

5. Hengel, "Messiah of Israel," 10.

6. Ibid., 12.

7. On Mark 6:14–16 and "resurrection," see Klaus Berger, *Die Auferstehung des Propheten und die Erhöhung des Menschensohnes: Traditionsgeschichtliche Untersuchung zur Deutung des Geschickes Jesu in frühchristlichen Texten* (SUNT 13; Göttingen: Vandenhoeck & Ruprecht, 1976).

8. N. T. Wright, *Resurrection of the Son of God*, 24, 574–76.

9. Cf., e.g., Bockmuehl, *This Jesus*, 56–57; N. T. Wright, *Jesus and the Victory of God*, 488.

10. James D. G. Dunn, *Romans 1–8* (WBC; Dallas: Word, 1988), 14; Douglas J. Moo, *The Epistle to the Romans* (NICNT; Grand Rapids: Eerdmans, 1996), 48; Hengel, "Messiah of Israel," 11.

his death seemed to be a proof against messiahship could his resurrection be perceived as a proof in favor of it."[11]

The "Messianic Secret"

A theme central in the Gospel of Mark is the progressive revelation of Jesus's messiahship to the disciples. Throughout its narrative the Markan Gospel gradually unfolds the significance and meaning of the incipit of 1:1, "The gospel of Jesus Christ."[12] The nature of Jesus's identity remains a mysterious question in the first half of the Gospel (1:27; 2:7; 4:41; 8:27–29a). When Jesus's identity does surface in the story, it is often accompanied by commands to secrecy (8:29–30; 9:9–10). Earlier in the narrative the insight of the demons is explicitly silenced (1:23–25, 34; 3:11–12; 5:6–7); after several miracles, silence is likewise enjoined (1:44; 5:43; 7:36; 8:26). Wrede argued that this secrecy motif was not historical: it was a theological motif[13] already extant in Mark's tradition but amplified by the evangelist. The purpose of this "secret" was to account for the fact that Christians believed Jesus to be the Messiah since his resurrection (see above), though there was no extant memory of Jesus ever claiming to be so. The messianic secret is, "so to speak, a transitional idea and *it can be characterised as the after-effect of the view that the resurrection is the beginning of the messiahship at a time when the life of Jesus was already being filled materially with messianic content.*"[14] In the end the messianic secret becomes *"positive historical testimony for the idea that Jesus actually did not give himself out as messiah."*[15] Wrede's proposal has significantly affected the course of Markan scholarship,[16] and he has been followed by many who

11. Johannes Weiss, "Das Problem der Entstehung des Christentums," *Archiv für Religionswissenschaft* 16 (1913): 470: "Nur weil der Tod ein Gegenbeweis gegen die Messianität zu sein schien, konnte die Erhöhung als der Beweis dafür empfunden werden."

12. On the secondary nature of "Son of God," see Peter M. Head, "A Text-Critical Study of Mark 1:1: 'The Beginning of the Gospel of Jesus Christ,'" *NTS* 37 (1991): 621–29.

13. Wrede, *Messianic Secret*, 67. On the unhistorical nature of Mark and the commands to secrecy, see ibid., 9–10, 33, 49, 69.

14. Ibid., 229, with original emphasis.

15. Ibid., 230, with original emphasis.

16. Cf., e.g., H. J. Ebeling, *Das Messiasgeheimnis und die Botschaft des Markusevangelium* (Berlin: A. Töpelmann, 1939), 1–113; Georg Strecker, "Zur Messiasgeheimnistheorie im Markusevangelium," *ST* 3 (1964): 87–104; Norman Perrin, "The Wredestrasse Becomes the Hauptstrasse," *JR* 46 (1966): 296–300; Lewis S. Hay, "Mark's Use of the Messianic Secret," *JAAR* 35 (1967): 16–27; G. Minette de Tillesse, *Le secret messianique dans l'Évangile de Marc* (Paris: Cerf, 1968); James L. Blevins, *The Messianic Secret in Marcan Research, 1901–1976* (Washington, DC: University of America Press, 1981); Christopher Tuckett, ed., *The Messianic Secret* (London: SPCK, 1983); H. Räisänen, *The "Messianic Secret" in Mark's Gospel* (Edinburgh: T&T Clark, 1990); John M. Perry, *Exploring the Messianic Secret in Mark's Gospel* (Kansas City: Sheed & Ward, 1997).

similarly regard the secrecy motif as a theological construct and garner it as further proof that Jesus did not claim to be the Messiah.[17]

However, Wrede's thesis has received its own fair share of criticism as well,[18] including a devastating review early on from Schweitzer.[19] To begin with, Wrede regarded all of the christological titles in Mark as designating a Christian conception of messiahship that is then negated by the injunctions to silence.[20] However, the title "Holy One of God" (Mark 1:24) seems to be a general acclamation of charismatic authority and is not necessarily synonymous with messianic identity. The silences also relate to more than a messianic status and include Jesus's sonship (3:11), miracles (5:43), and the kingdom (4:10–12). Mark has just as much a kingdom secret and a miracle secret as he has a messianic secret.[21] When Wrede says, "For nothing is more obvious than that Mark understood the miracles as manifestations of the Messiah,"[22] this is far from obvious to most scholars now.[23] Wrede's attempt to compress all miracle and kingdom traditions under the aegis of messiahship must be regarded as a failure.[24] On top of that, the only supplicant of healing who hails Jesus in explicitly messianic terms (i.e., "Son of David") in Mark 10:46–52 is not silenced at all. Thus, messiahship is not silenced, and what is silenced is not necessarily messianic. There are also indications that the injunctions to secrecy are ineffective at certain points as the reports of Jesus's activities, whereabouts, and identity spread further and are speculated upon (Mark 1:28,

17. Rudolf Bultmann, *Theology of the New Testament* (trans. Kendrick Grobel; 2 vols.; London: SCM, 1952), 1:32; Ernst Käsemann, "The Problem of the Historical Jesus," in *Essays on New Testament Themes* (trans. W. J. Montague; London: SCM, 1964), 43; Bornkamm, *Jesus*, 171–72, 206–10.

18. Cf., e.g., David Aune, "The Problem of the Messianic Secret," *NovT* 11 (1969): 1–31; R. N. Longenecker, "The Messianic Secret in the Light of Recent Discoveries," *EQ* 41 (1969): 207–15; James D. G. Dunn, "The Messianic Secret in Mark," *TynBul* 21 (1970): 92–117; Christopher L. Mearns, "Parables, Secrecy and Eschatology in Mark's Gospel," *SJT* 44 (1991): 423–42; Charlesworth, "Messianology to Christology," 34; David F. Watson, "The 'Messianic Secret': Demythologizing a Non-existent Markan Theme," *Journal of Theology* 110 (2006): 33–44. A letter possessed by Gerd Lüdemann (to date unpublished) is believed to contain evidence that Wrede himself changed his mind about the messianic secret in Mark; see reference to it in Hengel, "Messiah of Israel," 17n16. Further discussion of Wrede's change of mind is given in Chester, *Messiah and Exaltation*, 309n370.

19. Schweitzer, *Quest*, 303–14.

20. N. T. Wright, *Jesus and the Victory of God*, 478.

21. Cf. Ulrich Luz, "Das Geheimnismotiv und die markinische Christologie," *ZNW* 56 (1965): 9–30.

22. Wrede, *Messianic Secret*, 17.

23. An exception is perhaps Francis Watson ("The Social Function of Mark's Secrecy Theme," *JSNT* 24 [1985]: 51–52), who sees miracles and messiahship as inextricably linked together in Mark's narrative. Although miracles can be incorporated into some kind of messianism, not all miracles are necessarily messianic. I am also not so sure that Peter's confession at Caesarea Philippi was inspired *exclusively* by Jesus's miraculous acts in the Markan narrative.

24. Schweitzer, *Quest*, 311–12.

45; 3:20; 5:19–20; 6:2–3, 14–16, 31; 7:24, 36–37; 8:28). Indeed, people widely publicize Jesus's actions and mighty deeds. It thus is better to think of a messianic *misunderstanding* as opposed to a messianic *secret*.[25]

That leads to my second point: Mark's Gospel, with its apocalyptic orientation, exhibits a dual conceal-reveal pattern indicative of apocalypticism (Mark 4:22; 9:9). Apocalyptic groups often regard themselves as possessing insider knowledge that cannot be revealed until an appointed time (Dan. 12:4; Rev. 22:10). One such secret was the identity of Jesus as Messiah. Knight comments: "The secrecy of which Mark speaks is not the secrecy of someone who is replacing one concept of Messiahship with another. It is the secrecy of someone who believes that he possesses heavenly secrets, revealed to him at baptism and . . . conceivably at other points of his ministry."[26] This secrecy motif is not a Markan invention but probably derives from the historical Jesus.[27] If Jesus is situated in the context of apocalypticism and hopes buoyed by apocalyptic eschatology, then the messianic secret is indebted not to the historicizing tendency of the tradition, but is a historical theme in the career of one who shared the apocalyptic worldview and understood himself as possessing a decisive role in the fulfillment of eschatological hopes. Jesus may have spoken of his identity and mission in deliberately opaque and enigmatic terms so as to avoid messianic connotations among the crowds, believing that it was not time for God to reveal the true extent of his identity and mission. Additionally, Jesus probably kept his answer to the Messiah question concealed from others besides his disciples (John 10:24–26)[28] until an appropriate time (Mark 8:31–33; 9:9). This coheres with many sources stating that God has concealed the Messiah (1 En. 48.6; 62.7; cf. Isa. 49:2) and will reveal him on the appointed day (Pss. Sol. 18.5; 4 Ezra 7.28–29; 12.31–34; 13.26; 2 Bar. 30.1–2; Odes Sol. 41.15). The messianic secret might also exude from a sense of predestination concerning knowledge being given to insiders over against outsiders in understanding the secret of Jesus's identity. This could be true for both the historical Jesus and in apocalyptic circles of the Jesus movement.[29]

Third, there is another reason for the essential historicity of a "messianic secret" originating in Jesus's ministry. The political reality of Palestine, with diverse messianic expectations, many of them militaristic, would have made it necessary for Jesus to keep the messianic question under wraps. A transparent

25. Dunn, "Messianic Secret," 100.
26. Knight, *Jesus*, 143 (esp. 138–45); cf. Hengel, "Messiah of Israel," 59.
27. All proposals as to how the secret functioned in Jesus's own mind should be prefaced with the warning from Schweitzer (*Quest*, 319): "The question why Jesus made a secret of his expectation that he would be revealed as the Messiah cannot be answered with any accuracy. All we can determine from his behaviour is that he seriously intended to preserve this secret; we cannot make out motives for this."
28. Theissen and Merz, *Historical Jesus*, 540.
29. On this point, see F. Watson, "Mark's Secrecy Theme," 54–65.

and clear messianic claim by Jesus would have triggered revolutionary fervor and a severe response from either Jewish or Roman authorities, who saw it in their interests to put down prophetic and messianic movements long before they led to uprisings. If Jesus wished to avoid the militaristic associations of "Messiah" or to refrain from exciting crowds with nationalistic zeal, then his intention to keep a messianic theme either undisclosed or at least ambiguous is perfectly understandable. In the Johannine tradition, we have an episode narrated where Jesus explicitly rejects the attempt to make him king by force, where his reputation as a miracle worker has kindled hopes of national deliverance (John 6:14–15).[30] We cannot assume that if Jesus thought himself to be the Messiah, he was bound to make it explicit or to publicize it from the outset.[31]

Fourth, if certain events in Jesus's life have a historical character—such as Peter's confession at Caesarea Philippi, the triumphal entry, the temple-judging episode, and the high priest's charge that he is a messianic pretender—then we have an account of Jesus's messiahship that cannot be dumped at the feet of the evangelists and their communities.[32] This is in counterpoint to Wrede, who accepts the messianic connotations of the triumphal entry and must regard it as "a completely isolated story in Mark."[33] Here it looks as though Wrede is sweeping away data that does not fit his theory.

The secrecy motif operates quite differently at the literary, theological, and historical levels. We should add that John's Gospel has its own messianic secret, and the narrator leads his audience on a quest to discover the Messiah through the various signs and witnesses that he provides. While Wrede's thesis captured the attention of a previous generation of scholarship, it is (quite rightly) fading from the scene as a serious explanation of Mark's theology and narrative. It is even less useful for determining the origin of the messianic idea in relation to Jesus. As Joseph Klausner put it sometime ago:

> A theory has been put forward [i.e., Wrede] that Jesus never regarded himself as the Messiah and only after his death was he acclaimed as Messiah by his disciples. But had this been true it would never have occurred to his disciples (simple-minded Jews) that one who had suffered crucifixion ("a curse of God is he that is hanged") could be the messiah; and the messianic idea meant nothing whatsoever to the Gentile converts. *Ex nihilo nihil fit* [out of nothing comes noth-

30. On the historicity on this passage, see C. H. Dodd, *Historical Tradition in the Fourth Gospel* (Cambridge: Cambridge University Press, 1963), 213–16; Raymond E. Brown, *The Gospel according to John 1–12* (AB; New York: Doubleday, 1966); 249–50; Witherington, *Christology of Jesus*, 99; Craig L. Blomberg, *The Historical Reliability of John's Gospel* (Downers Grove, IL: InterVarsity, 2002), 120–21.

31. Charlesworth, "Messianology to Christology," 13.

32. Schweitzer, *Quest*, 334–54. Note the remark of Davies and Allison (*Saint Matthew*, 2:599): "More importantly, the motifs of sonship, temple building, and kingship do not simply converge in one Markan paragraph: they also converge in the historical ministry of Jesus."

33. Wrede, *Messianic Secret*, 16, 46.

ing]: when we see that Jesus' messianic claims became a fundamental principle of Christianity soon after his crucifixion, this is a standing proof that even in his lifetime Jesus regarded himself as the Messiah.[34]

It surely is correct to see the early church attributing theological significance to the title "Christ." After all, for the early church, Jesus was, is, and will be the Messiah and Savior of the people.[35] Yet it is singularly inappropriate to conclude from this that all the messianic passages in the Gospels are indebted to the faith of the early church.[36] Wrede's messianic secret tried to lend some credence to this perspective, but the theory is no longer acceptable.

Disciples' Enthusiasm and Authorities' Perception

As we have observed, several scholars argue that Jesus was believed to be the Messiah either by his followers or by the crowds during his lifetime, but that Jesus himself rejected this category for describing his mission and ministry. In contrast to Wrede, this approach recognizes the pre-Easter nature of the disciples' messianic faith and the authenticity of the *titulus* "King of the Jews," while maintaining that Jesus never claimed to be the Messiah, except perhaps at the very end of his life.[37] This explains why the Roman and Judean coalition charged him with claiming to be the Messiah, but it does not *adequately* account for (1) why the charge was successful and (2) why the disciples believed Jesus to be the Messiah in the first place.

34. Joseph Klausner, *Jesus of Nazareth: His Life, Times, and Teaching* (trans. Herbert Danby; London: Allen & Unwin, 1929), 255–56; see also Hengel, "Messiah of Israel," 14:

> If Jesus never possessed a messianic claim of divine mission, rather sternly rejected every third-hand question in this regard, if he neither spoke of the coming, or present, "Son of Man," nor was executed as a messianic pretender and alleged king of the Jews—as is maintained with astonishing certainty by radical criticism unencumbered by historical arguments—then the emergence of Christology, indeed, the entire history of primitive Christianity, is completely baffling, nay, incomprehensible. But this is not all—all four gospels, and above all the Passion narrative as their most ancient component, would be a curious product of the imagination very difficult to explain, for the Messiah question is at the centre of them all. If Mark 1–10 stands under the rubric of the "messianic secret," the remainder of the gospel, following the Entry into Jerusalem (Mark 11:1–11), dissolves this step by step. Is this no more than a construct of the novelistic art and christological imagination of the evangelist? With regard to Christology, are not the gospels also a part of the *Religionsgeschichte* derived from the Jewish heritage?

Cf. N. T. Wright, *Resurrection of the Son of God*, 555; Dunn, *Jesus Remembered*, 653.

35. Bockmuehl, *This Jesus*, 59.

36. Cf., e.g., Bornkamm, *Jesus of Nazareth*, 172–73.

37. See esp. W. Grundmann, "Χριστός," *TDNT*, 9:538; Brown, *Death of the Messiah*, 1:478–80.

Regarding point 1, due to the nature of the evidence, we cannot have certainty about what happened at the trial. What is more, the charge of being a messianic pretender was probably one issue among others—such as blasphemy, speaking against the temple, and leading the nation astray—that required an official response and some form of public reprisal. But the messianic charge was what secured the death penalty and was the decisive outcome of the trial, as evidenced by the crucifixion (a punishment for bandits and brigands) and the *titulus* (a mocking of Jewish messianic hopes). However, all things being equal, the enthusiasm of the disciples and crowds would be insufficient to substantiate the charge that Jesus was a would-be Messiah. Jesus looked nothing like Judas the Galilean, and his followers were not exactly poised for a coup d'état.[38] Jesus was captured on the Mount of Olives, not in Masada. As far as we know, he did not go to the cross while screaming, "I am not the Messiah, I am not the Messiah, I am but a prophet of God!" If it was known that Jesus did not claim to be the Messiah, then early Jewish polemics against Christianity missed out on what was perhaps their best opportunity to pose a counterassertion to early Christian proclamation. More likely, the charge must have stuck due to something Jesus himself said or did not say at the proceedings. It thus seems probable that Jesus either outed himself as a messianic claimant, or else he did not deny the title at his trial when the question was put to him. In either case we can explain why the messianic charge was successful on the grounds that the trial settled the messianic issue in the affirmative and led to the crucifixion and the *titulus*, not because of the messianic hopes of the crowds and his followers, but due to Jesus's own testimony.

We must also consider point 2, the problem of how pre-Easter messianic hopes originated if Jesus made no such claim. Brown himself acknowledges that "one cannot argue that if Jesus' followers thought he was sent by God, they would have had to say he was the Messiah."[39] Claiming to be an eschatological "somebody" (e.g., Acts 5:36) did not amount to a messianic claim. Preaching

---

38. Cf. Michael F. Bird, "Jesus and the Revolutionaries: Did Jesus Call Israel to Repent of Nationalistic Ambitions?" *Colloquium: Australian and New Zealand Theological Review* 38, no. 2 (2006): 127–39; and see discussion in Markus Bockmuehl, "Resistance and Redemption in the Jesus Tradition," in Bockmuehl and J. C. Paget, *Redemption and Resistance*, 65–77.

39. Brown, *Death of the Messiah*, 1:475. See Fitzmyer (*The One Who Is to Come*, 2–3) and Mowinckel (*He That Cometh*, 3–4), who point out that an eschatological redeemer figure is not coterminous with a Messiah. Cf. Nickelsburg (*Ancient Judaism and Christian Origins*, 116), who points out that given the spectrum of divine agents in Second Temple Judaism, "the historical Jesus could have had a high understanding of his place in God's scheme of things without having claimed to be the 'Anointed one.' Certainly the prophets did." Jürgen Becker (*Jesus of Nazareth*, 188) writes similarly that just because messianic hopes were in the air, "it was not the case, therefore, that Jesus and his Galilean followers were under some sort of historical compulsion to think of his activity in messianic terms." One of the weaknesses of Hengel's otherwise exemplary argument ("Messiah of Israel," 63–71, esp. 66) is that in some cases he seems to assume a logic of "eschatological" and therefore "Messiah."

the kingdom does not automatically make Jesus the king or Messiah or the coming one.[40] Why then did they think him to be the Messiah? I believe it was because he did and said things that gave them that obvious impression. The question of whether John the Baptist was a messianic deliverer arose, and we have multiple attestation that the Baptist regarded himself as a forerunner of the Messiah (Mark 1:7–8; Luke 3:15–18/Matt. 3:11–12; John 1:19–28; Acts 13:25). Likewise, there is multiple attestation that the question of Jesus as the Messiah came up before his trial in Jerusalem, and in most cases we are given a positive albeit mysterious answer (Mark 8:27–30; 10:46–48; 11:1–10; 12:35–37; Luke 7:18–22/Matt. 11:1–6; John 4:25–26; 7:25–44; 12:30–34).[41] Jesus did not have to make an overt and clear messianic claim to get this across. Given the climate of Galilee and Jerusalem, such a statement would have been rash or foolish. But as he made an oblique comment here, performed a symbolic action there, threw in a few quotes about the anointed one from Isa. 61, used "Son of Man" as a self-reference, talked of kingdom and great reversals—it did not take a colloquium of rabbis to read between the lines as to what Jesus was saying. Jesus himself injected messianic enthusiasm into his disciples even if he was not responsible for the direction in which they took it. It was in Jerusalem that this cryptic messianism was found out by the Judean leadership, who could no longer tolerate his incendiary actions, prophetic outbursts, and subversive teaching. In Jerusalem at Passover, when hopes for liberation from pagan rule were at their highest, they moved against him swiftly and violently.

Here we must also draw attention to Paula Fredriksen's view that Jesus was crucified as a political insurrectionist, but his followers were not sought out and executed as leading an insurrection.[42] This is a good observation, and we have two options as to why the followers were not rounded up and executed after Jesus's death. (1) Jesus's disciples proclaimed him as Messiah, Jesus rejected the title, the Judean authorities knew Jesus rejected it, Pilate knew it, but they crucified him anyway as a nuisance on a trumped-up charge as "King of the Jews." And because the whole messianic charge was a sham anyway, there was no need to round up the followers since there was no real military threat looming. Or (2) at his trial Jesus lived up to the messianic rumors, albeit with a unique spin about a coming "Son of Man," but the authorities knew that a dead messiah was a failed messiah: by destroying him they had dashed the hopes of his followers—regardless of whether those hopes were political, spiritual, or cultic; their leader was gone, and the movement was effectively quashed unless a descendant or blood relative from Galilee rose in his place.

40. Contra Fredriksen, *Jesus of Nazareth*, 245–46, 251–52.

41. Several scholars, while acknowledging that the question did arise during Jesus's prepassion period (e.g., Dahl, "Crucified Messiah," 43; Bornkamm, *Jesus of Nazareth*, 172–73), deny that Jesus answered affirmatively or even hinted at an affirmative answer; yet these scholars can do this only by discounting a large part of the tradition as inauthentic.

42. Fredriksen, *Jesus of Nazareth*, 9; cf. Sanders, *Jesus and Judaism*, 317–18.

They equally knew that Jesus's followers were not staging a revolution since there had been no banditry associated with Jesus, no skirmishes had broken out along the frontiers at his instigation, and the crowds of followers were not drawn from hideouts in caves of Judea or from mountain fortresses east of the Jordan. In terms of a discernible threat, the followers of Jesus lacked any known intent or capability to stage a serious military action. Thus, it is quite possible to explain why his disciples were not rounded up despite the fact that Jesus did make a messianic claim.

An Inference from the *Titulus* on the Cross

Nils A. Dahl's influential article "The Crucified Messiah" set about plotting the origins of the title of "Messiah" and its application to Jesus. The genius of Dahl's article is that he rejected Wrede's view that Jesus's messiahship was inferred from his resurrection, and he also took seriously the problem of finding sufficient grounds for postulating Jesus as a messianic claimant in the prepassion period.[43] Dahl finds the impetus toward Jesus's messiahship in the *titulus* or inscription against him placarded on the cross: "The King of the Jews." Dahl acknowledges that Jesus's activities may have given cause for a messianic question to be raised at his trial, and Jesus may have even refused to deny the charge, but it remains "uncertain" to deduce from this a messianic consciousness on the part of Jesus. Instead, Dahl avers:

> But we may take it as a historical fact that Jesus did nothing to avoid his condemnation and crucifixion as "King of the Jews." Only in the form of this "good confession" before Pontius Pilate does a "messianic claim" of Jesus become historically accessible. But this is precisely the one thing that is a necessary presupposition for the New Testament gospel of the crucified Messiah. . . . The formulation of the confession "Jesus is the Messiah" presupposes the formulation of the charge and was occasioned by it. It is quite probable that the title "Messiah" was first brought forth as an expression of false expectation, as an accusation and as a mockery of Jesus. Only later, after the appearance of the risen Lord, was it taken up as a unifying expression of confession and preaching.[44]

There is much to be said here. For a start, I think that the *titulus* is certainly part of the fabric of evidence for Jesus's messianism. As I will argue in chapter 5, the *titulus* implies a charge, the charge implies a question, and the question implies a range of activities by Jesus that brought the messianic question to the surface. That being said, the *titulus* alone could not have created the messianic

---

43. Dahl ("Crucified Messiah," 38, 40) wrote: "But his resurrection would not necessarily mean that he is the Messiah. . . . It seems certain that before the passion Jesus did not openly claim to be the Messiah."

44. Ibid., 43–44.

faith of the early church. While Dahl disagrees with Bultmann's rejection of the authenticity of the *titulus* on the cross and rejects Wrede's theory of "resurrection = Messiah" in primitive Christology, he nonetheless is not too distant from Wrede in all actuality. For Dahl, it is the *titulus* plus resurrection faith that allowed the placard to be transformed into a messianic title and become an article of faith. That in turn provides an instance of historical continuity between Jesus and the church's faith regarding the issue of messiahship. But that leads to a further problem: why did the disciples, who knew that Jesus rejected political messianism, embrace the verdict of the Romans? The resurrection thereby becomes not so much the vindication of Jesus but rather the validation of the mocking jibe of his executioners.[45]

Moreover, the *titulus* by itself can have hardly have fostered belief in Jesus as the Messiah. For a start, the title is framed in secular terms as "king" rather than as "anointed one." Jesus was crucified as "king" (βασιλεύς, מלך, *rex*) and not as "Christ" (Χριστός, משיח, *Christus*). Even if "Christ" had been written on the placard, followers of Jesus would have been unlikely to derive from that point other aspects of his ministry such as his anointing with the Holy Spirit, Davidic descent, divine sonship, and the fulfillment of Jewish hopes for national restoration.[46] The inference that they would have made from the *titulus* (and exactly what the Romans wanted) was that Jesus was actually a failed revolutionary, and they had backed the wrong eschatological horse of the apocalypse. While the *titulus* is undoubtedly part of the overall picture in explaining the grounds for Jesus's death, it alone could not have launched and sustained the messianic faith of the early church.[47]

The Scripturizing of the Tradition

The early Christians ransacked their Scriptures (usually the Septuagint) to find scriptural proof that Jesus was the Messiah and Son of God. Or at least they thought that Jesus emulated scriptural patterns foreshadowing his specific ministry. This was especially important in the context of intra-Jewish debates about Jesus as the Christ and the divisive effects it had in Jewish communities (cf. e.g., Suetonius, *Claud.* 25.4; John 9:22; Justin Martyr, *1 Apol.* 31.5–6; *Dial.* 108). For example, in Matt. 21:5 we have an explicit quotation of Zech. 9:9, which bolsters the perspective that Jesus's triumphal entry is genuinely regal,

45. Davies and Allison, *Saint Matthew*, 2:597.
46. Moule, *Christology*, 33.
47. In this category we can probably add the argument of Klaus Berger ("Zum Problem der Messianität Jesu," *ZTK* 71 [1974]: 15), who argues that the title "king" was applied to Jesus primarily because in the Markan Passion Narrative he does not save himself and he is wholly dependent on God, as Israel's king ought to be. Yet the same could be said of almost any leadership figure from the Jewish Scriptures, not only the king.

royal, and messianic. This was not unique to the early Christian movement, since several other Jewish groups had already engaged in messianic exegesis of texts in Israel's sacred literature. Texts such as Num. 24:17; 2 Sam. 7:14; and Ps. 2 were used to elucidate the role and functions of a coming figure or figures who would execute Yahweh's plan for the rescue of his people from the perils that they faced.

Does this propensity to scripturize the tradition mean that the story of the Messiah's death in the Gospels is a type of midrash on Isa. 53 and the Davidic psalms, which is then retold as a fictitious narrative in aid of Christian apologetics?[48] I find this improbable. To begin with, apart from the lack of clear and widespread expectation for a suffering Messiah in Israel's sacred traditions, the majority of connections between Jesus and the Old Testament either were made by the church in retrospect as a clear addition to what was already evident or were made by Jesus himself. The triumphal entry is a good example with the citation of Zech. 9. Jesus may have consciously entered Jerusalem in order to allude to Zech. 9:9. Mark and Luke either did not make the connection between the action and Zechariah, or else they felt no need to spell it out. Matthew (21:4–5) and John (12:14–15), on the other hand, here find prime evidence of scriptural fulfillment that accords with their own theological interests. Although the evangelists and their sources interpreted Jesus's activities through the lens of Scripture, we have no indication that their reading of Scripture somehow created the story of Jesus's messiahship. Ultimately the Old Testament seems to have formed the interpretive grid through which the story of Jesus's passion was interpreted, rather than comprising the creative pool from which the story was created. Finding in the ancient texts insurmountable proof that Jesus was the Messiah when in fact he never claimed to be so was perhaps an insurmountable task for the bravest and most creative of exegetes. In the words of Dahl: "The application of the title 'Messiah' to Jesus cannot have had its origin in the study of Scripture and in the discussion of the first Christians with Jews. Both are only secondary factors. The messiahship of the crucified Jesus is rather the presupposition that lies at the root of all the scriptural evidence *de Christo*."[49]

What is more, it remains a mystery as to why scholars continue to insist that the evangelists or the early church created stories about Jesus out of Scripture, and yet this same propensity to engage Scripture so creatively is never attributed to Jesus himself. We must wonder why, in principle, Jesus was unable to deliberately act out stories and scriptural patterns that were also creative, innovative, subversive, provocative, and even offensive. In the

---

48. Cf., e.g., John Dominic Crossan, *The Historical Jesus* (San Francisco: Harper Collins, 1991), 368–72.

49. Dahl, "Crucified Messiah," 39–40; cf. Dunn, *Jesus Remembered*, 627; and Craig A. Evans, "The Passion of Jesus: History Remembered or Prophecy Historicized?" *BBR* 6 (1996): 159–65.

absence of explicit indications of post-Easter perspectives in the citations of Scripture found in the Gospels, one should be very careful in denying Jesus the ability to cite, echo, and restate the Scriptures himself. Jesus's riddle of the "Son of David" and "David's Lord" (Ps. 110, cited in Mark 12:35–37) as well as his entry into Jerusalem (Zech. 9) are good examples of texts that, all things being equal, cannot prima facie be rejected as inauthentic. It is simply too one-sided to make the default setting be an approach that attributes all creative exegesis to the minds of the early church and not to Jesus, especially when it comes to the messianic issues that constantly surface in the texts.[50]

Conclusion

Historical Jesus studies have remained fixated on the problem of explaining why the early church venerated and proclaimed Jesus as Israel's Messiah when Jesus himself never set forth an explicit messianic claim. The evidence indicates that while the identification of Jesus as the Messiah has a definite pre-Easter history among his disciples and opponents, his response to this matter remained ambiguous from the very start. Jesus refused to conform to any particular mold or to any one set of eschatological expectations, and yet he acted in such a way as to quite *deliberately* arouse messianic hopes in those around him.[51] In my mind, the real issue is, Why did messianic hopes arise in the pre-Easter period at all if Jesus repudiated the messianic role?[52] This chapter has examined the complicated nature of that problem and has tried to demonstrate that several approaches denying Jesus any messianic self-understanding or vocation are exceptionally problematic. This now paves the way for chapter 4, where I intend to set forth an alternative proposal that sees Jesus as deliberately acting out and playing on messianic motifs in the course of his ministry and teaching.

50. Cf. Brown (*Death of the Messiah*, 1:513–14): "*The perception that OT passages were interpreted to give a christological insight does not date the process.* To prove that this could not have been done by Jesus, at least inchoatively, is surely no less difficult than to prove that it was done by him. Hidden behind an attribution to the early church is often the assumption that Jesus had no christology even by way of reading the Scriptures to discern in what anticipated way he fitted into God's plan. Can one really think that credible?" (with original emphasis).

51. Cf. similarly Dunn, "Messianic Ideas," 372–74.

52. Cf. Vermes, *Jesus the Jew*, 154; W. Manson, *Jesus the Messiah*, 5, 11; M. de Jonge, *God's Final Envoy*, 98.

4

Messiah Jesus—a Role Redefined?

In chapter 3 of this book, I maintained that many of the arguments adduced against Jesus making a messianic claim are lacking in substance. Part of the problem is, as Nickelsburg writes, "The notion that Jesus could not have thought of himself as the 'Anointed One' presumes a set of loaded categories that need to be dismantled and reassembled in the light of the whole range of Jewish texts and a careful study of relevant New Testament passages."[1] That does not mean that postulating a pre-Easter messianic Jesus lacks problems. In the evangelists' narrative, Jesus affirms the application of the title to himself in Mark 8:30/Matt. 16:17; John 4:26; and Mark 14:62. But as we will see, the authenticity of these passages is open to question, and Jesus never once uses the title directly of himself. One possible corollary, taken up by Reginald Fuller, is to posit a halfway position by regarding Jesus as premessianic in that he heightened expectations but did not set out to fulfill them.[2] Yet, that only confuses things further since we are still no closer to finding the smoking gun that explains the rise of messianic beliefs in the pre-Easter period. Is there another way of grappling with this *Messiasfrage* (messiah question) that does better justice to the evidence?

1. Nickelsburg, *Ancient Judaism and Christian Origins*, 116. See also Hofius ("Ist Jesus der Messias?" 103): "Die Erörterung der Frage, ob Jesus der 'Messias' ist, setzt eine präzise Bestimmung des in Frage stehenden Begriffs voraus." [The discussion of the question whether Jesus is "the Messiah" presupposes a precise determination of the term in question.]
2. Fuller, *Mission and Achievement of Jesus*, 108–16.

The Messianic Jesus

In light of the foregoing discussion, I intend to explore the messianic question more broadly by taking into account coded messianic remarks in the tradition, the activation of substories from Israel's sacred traditions in Jesus's teaching, the messianic connotations of several prophetic actions, and the general portrait of Jesus as it emerges in our sources. I will argue that there are sufficient grounds for seeing Jesus as deliberately acting out and identifying with a messianic vocation. That does not require us to believe that Jesus tried to check off a list of messianic expectations from the Jewish Scriptures; it does not suppose that we can penetrate into some kind of messianic consciousness;[3] rather, it means that several sayings and deeds of Jesus suggest that he understood his role and activities in messianic categories. I am pursuing evidence that Jesus's career was "performatively messianic" as opposed to being messianic in the titular sense.[4] What follows is an examination of several types of material drawn from the Gospels that, if authentic, indicate that messianic ideas, symbols, and scriptural echoes were attached to Jesus's activities. That is followed by chapter 5, which looks at the messianic issues surrounding Jesus's death and the subsequent developments in the early Christian communities.

Son of Man as Divine Agent and Messiah

One can scarcely imagine an area of debate more strongly contested than that of the meaning and authenticity of the Son of Man sayings in the Gospels.[5] I admit that it is not the strongest ground upon which to base a messianic claim on the part of Jesus. Nonetheless, it is a piece of scholarly terrain that must be covered in the debate.[6] Moreover, it is my contention that the Son of Man tradition is an important (albeit not uncomplicated) component in the messianism of Jesus.

In the Gospels, the Son of Man tradition is generally stratified into three categories: a present authoritative figure, a suffering figure, and a future escha-

3. Cf. Charlesworth, *Jesus within Judaism*, 131–32; Bockmuehl, *This Jesus*, 55–56; N. T. Wright, *Jesus and the Victory of God*, 489; Dahl, "Messianic Ideas," 403.

4. B. F. Meyer, *Aims of Jesus*, 176; cf. Theissen and Merz, *Historical Jesus*, 538; M. de Jonge, *God's Final Envoy*, 97.

5. For those in want of a short introduction, see Scot McKnight, *Jesus and His Death: Historiography, the Historical Jesus, and Atonement Theory* (Waco: Baylor University Press, 2005), 171–75.

6. For a history of research, see Chrys C. Caragounis, *The Son of Man: Vision and Interpretation* (WUNT 38; Tübingen: Mohr Siebeck, 1986), 9–33; Delbert Burkett, *The Son of Man Debate: A History and an Evaluation* (SNTSMS 107; Cambridge: Cambridge University Press, 1999); Maurice Casey, *The Solution to the Son of Man Problem* (LNTS 343; Cambridge: Cambridge University Press, 2007), 1–55; and Mogens Müller, *The Expression "Son of Man" and the Development of Christology: A History of Interpretation* (CIS; London: Equinox, 2008).

tological figure.[7] In terms of relating these categories to the historical Jesus, the primary options in scholarship (with endless variations, of course) are as follows: (1) The "Son of Man" was an established apocalyptic title in pre-Christian Judaism. The authentic Son of Man sayings are those where Jesus speaks of a future redeemer figure other than himself, and it was the later Hellenistic community that identified Jesus with the coming Son of Man. (2) Jesus combined the title "Son of Man" from Daniel with the roles and function of the Suffering Servant from Isaiah. (3) The Greek expression "Son of Man" is based on an underlying Aramaic idiom meaning either "I," "someone," "human being," or "a man in my position" and is devoid of any allusion to Dan. 7 or a titular sense. (4) Jesus spoke of himself as the Son of Man from Daniel, as an eschatological figure with a messianic function as the representative of Israel.[8] F. Borsch adequately sums up the problem with the debate:

> It is an aspect of our "embarrassment" regarding the Son of Man materials that the evidence seems so open to different misunderstandings by the best trained scholars. People who find good measures of consensus on a number of other New Testament issues can differ widely about the Son of Man. What for one group is early and Aramaic is for another group late and formed in a Greek-speaking milieu, and vice-versa. For some it is eschatology and then reflection on the resurrection and exaltation of Jesus which gave birth to the Son of Man tradition. For others this stage came relatively late in the development.[9]

What will become clear is that I favor option 4 (with a polite nod to option 3) and that when Jesus spoke of himself as the "Son of Man," he was indeed alluding to the enigmatic figure of Dan. 7, who was a corporate figure and representative of Israel. Moreover, while Jesus retreated from use of the title "Messiah," his reference to himself as the "Son of Man" carried a similar eschatological meaning. After clearing the deck on a couple of issues, I return to this subject below.

To begin with, there is the matter of authenticity. Only a few scholars (e.g., Philip Vielhauer and Norman Perrin) are prepared to regard the Son of Man sayings in total as later community formulations.[10] We can respond by suggesting that the sayings meet the indices of (1) multiple attestation, since

7. Bultmann, *Theology*, 1:30.

8. On this view, see the survey of nineteenth-century proponents in Caragounis, *Son of Man*, 11–19.

9. F. H. Borsch, "Further Reflections of 'the Son of Man': The Origins and Development of the Title," in Charlesworth, *The Messiah*, 135.

10. Philip Vielhauer, "Gottesreich und Menschensohn in der Verkündigung Jesu," in *Festschrift für Günther Dehn* (ed. W. Schneemelcher; Neukirchen: Erziehungsverein, 1957), 51–79; Norman Perrin, *Rediscovering the Teaching of Jesus* (London: SCM, 1967); H. de Jonge, "Historical Jesus' View of Himself," 31–37; Michael Goulder, "Psalm 8 and the Son of Man," *NTS* 48 (2002): 18–28. Casey (*Solution*, 29) wryly comments that Vielhauer "borders on the irrational."

the designation occurs in Mark, Q, M, L, John, and Gospel of Thomas; and (2) dissimilarity, since "Son of Man" occurs only four times outside the Gospels (Acts 7:56; Heb. 2:6; Rev. 1:13; 14:14) but never as a form of address or in worship of Jesus.[11] We are then on fairly safe ground in attributing the use of this designation to Jesus. That leads precisely to the problem as to what he meant by it and how it was interpreted in the early church.

A further issue is what to make of the argument concerning the Semitic idiom behind the "Son of Man" based on the Hebrew בן־האדם (*ben hāʾādām*) and the Aramaic בר אנשא (*bar ĕnāšā*).[12] The Aramaic idiom in particular can have the following senses: (1) a generic sense of "human being" or "mankind"; (2) an indefinite sense of "a man" or "someone"; or more disputably (3) as a circumlocution or periphrasis meaning "I."[13] All but the last option have gained support in contemporary scholarship. A generic sense of humanity having authority over the Sabbath is a suitable rendering of "Son of Man" in Mark 2:27–28, where Jesus was remembered as defending the actions of the disciples in plucking grain on the Sabbath as an activity appropriate to the lordship that God had given humankind (or Israel) over all his creation.[14] In the case of Mark 2:10, we have an instance fittingly rendered with the indefinite sense of "a man" who has authority on the earth to forgive sins. That a mere human being can claim to have such an authority raises the scribes' charge of blasphemy and, in the Matthean version, occasions praise from the crowd that God "had given such authority to men" (Matt. 9:8 RSV).[15]

But can one shift from this indefinite and generic usage of "Son of Man" to a titular sense and a connection with Dan. 7:13 in the lifetime of Jesus (and not just in the post-Easter churches)?[16] I believe so. First, the "son of man"

11. See further arguments in Caragounis, *Son of Man*, 147–68.

12. As espoused in various ways by Vermes, *Jesus the Jew*, 163–68, 188–91; idem, *Authentic Gospel*, 234–65; Barnabas Lindars, *Jesus, Son of Man: A Fresh Examination of the Son of Man Sayings in the Gospels in the Light of Recent Research* (Grand Rapids: Eerdmans, 1983); Maurice Casey, *The Son of Man: The Interpretation and Influence of Daniel 7* (London: SPCK, 1979); idem, "General, Generic, and Indefinite: The Use of the Term 'Son of Man' in Aramaic Sources and in the Teaching of Jesus," *JSNT* 29 (1987): 21–56; idem, "Idiom and Translation: Some Aspects of the Son of Man Problem," *NTS* 41 (1995): 164–82; idem, *The Solution to the Son of Man Problem* (LNTS 343; London: T&T Clark, 2007); Bruce D. Chilton, "(The) Son of (the) Man, and Jesus," in *Authenticating the Words of Jesus* (ed. B. D. Chilton and C. A. Evans; Leiden: Brill, 1999), 259–88.

13. According to Fitzmyer (*A Wandering Aramean: Collected Aramaic Essays* [SBLMS 25; Missoula: Scholars Press, 1979], 153), it is open to question whether the circumlocution from Aramaic represents first-century usage.

14. Dunn, *Jesus Remembered*, 741; Casey, *Solution*, 121–25.

15. Dunn, *Jesus Remembered*, 740–41; Casey, *Solution*, 162–66.

16. Cf. Vermes, who overstates his case (*Jesus the Jew*, 188): "It should have also been obvious that the onus of proof that 'the *son of man*' is a title lies squarely on the shoulders of the theologians." Casey (*Solution*, 246–73) offers his own theory of the evolution of the Aramaic idiom into a Greek christological title. In my mind, he begs a number of questions: (1) Why

of Dan. 7 is more of a role than a title.[17] Associations with this role are not dependent upon the use of the article (in Hebrew, Aramaic, and Greek), since Daniel's rendering (7:13 RSV) is "one like a son of man" (כבר אנש) rather than "*the* Son of Man." The human figure of Dan. 7 was a role with which Jesus could easily identify his mission, given that the themes of eschatological authority, enthronement, national vindication, and the triumph of God's kingdom taken from Daniel fit naturally into his proclamation and aims. This is all the more plausible if Jesus drew on Daniel as informing his teaching, ministry, and sense of divine purpose.[18]

Second, the Aramaic idiom may signify a generic designation of "human being" or indefinite sense of "a man," but it is capable of being used with a certain particularizing connotation that alludes to a specific individual.[19] We should keep these categories (generic, indefinite, and circumlocution) fairly flexible. There can be an implied self-reference even in generic forms. For example, in 1QH 12.27–37 "son of man" implies a weakness and frailty that the speaker himself also shares in. Also, in an eighth-century BCE Aramaic inscription, Sefire 3.14–17, the speaker uses "son of man" to refer to himself and to his descendants. Even Casey acknowledges that through the use of this idiom Jesus was communicating something about himself even though the idiom had a broader level of meaning.[20] The force of Mark 2:10 is not just that "a man" can forgive sins but that one specific man has authority to do so. It seems quite likely that a definite sense of "Son of Man" is required in Luke 12:10/Matt.12:32 with "everyone who speaks a word against *the Man* will be forgiven, but whoever blasphemes against the Holy Spirit will not be

---

was it Mark and no one before him who went to Dan. 7:13 in order to embellish or theologize the phrase "Son of Man" (e.g., why not Jesus or the Jerusalem church)? (2) Why would the anarthrous phrase in Dan. 7:13 LXX commend itself to elucidating a double articular title (i.e., is this not a regression back to an indefinite sense)?

17. M. D. Hooker, "Is the Son of Man Problem Really Insoluble?" in *Text and Interpretation* (ed. E. Best and R. McL. Wilson; Festschrift for Matthew Black; Cambridge: Cambridge University Press, 1979), 167.

18. Cf. Craig A. Evans, "Defeating Satan and Liberating Israel: Jesus and Daniel's Visions," *JSHJ* 1 (2003): 161–70.

19. Cf. Richard Bauckham, "The Son of Man: 'A Man in My Position' or 'Someone'?" *JSNT* 23 (1985): 23–33; Douglas A. Hare, *The Son of Man Tradition* (Philadelphia: Fortress, 1990), 241–56; Robert H. Gundry, *Mark: A Commentary on His Apology for the Cross* (Grand Rapids: Eerdmans, 1993), 119; Christopher M. Tuckett, "The Son of Man and Daniel 7: Inclusive Aspects of Early Christologies," in *Christian Origins: Worship, Belief and Society* (ed. Kieran J. O'Mahoney; JSNTSup 241; Sheffield: Sheffield Academic Press, 2003), 182–84; Larry Hurtado, *Lord Jesus Christ: Devotion to Jesus in Earliest Christianity* (Grand Rapids: Eerdmans, 2003), 290–306.

20. Casey, *Solution*, 272. This harks back to the work of Colpe (C. Colpe, *TDNT*, 8:403–4), who pointed out that "a speaker could include himself in ברנש as well as בר נשא, whose generic sense was always apparent, or he could refer to himself in either and yet generalise at the same time."

forgiven." While "Son of Man" in Luke 9:58/Matt. 8:20 can be read as expressing "a man" or "a man like this one," it could also be read generically as a challenge to join Israel (i.e., the Son of Man), who is disinherited and dispossessed from his own land while a puppet king of Idumean stock like Herod Antipas (fox) and the Romans and Gentiles (birds) make themselves at home in Galilee and Judea.[21]

If Son of Man can have a definite meaning, then what lies behind its usage on *some* occasions may be hints of Dan. 7:13. For instance, Mark 14:62 is probably a tacit allusion to Dan. 7:13 via Jesus's own idiom. Bauckham writes: "There seems no reason why Jesus should not have exploited the coincidence between his accustomed form of oblique self-reference and the language of Daniel 7:13, so that *bar enash* in a saying alluding to Daniel 7:13 becomes the same kind of veiled hint of his own status as other authentic Son of Man sayings convey."[22] I would add Mark 8:31 as another example where Jesus's reference to himself as the "Son of Man" is a qualification to Peter's messianic confession rather than a denunciation of it. Jesus is "Messiah" only in the sense that he shares the vocation of the human figure of Dan. 7 (see the first part of chap. 5 below).

Third, while the double articular Greek ὁ υἱὸς τοῦ ἀνθρώπου (lit., "the son of the man") might seem novel or inelegant, it nonetheless is how the transmitters and translators of the Jesus tradition have sought to render Jesus's preferred means of self-reference. This Greek construction cannot be derived exclusively from the Septuagintal version of Dan. 7:13, which uses the anarthrous ὡς υἱὸς

21. Cf. T. W. Manson, *The Sayings of Jesus* (London: SCM, 1949), 72–73. But note the strong criticisms of Casey, *Solution*, 31.

22. Bauckham, "The Son of Man," 29–30; cf. A. Y. Collins ("The Origin of the Designation of Jesus as 'Son of Man,'" in *Cosmology and Eschatology in Jewish and Christian Apocalypticism* [Leiden: Brill, 1996], 154): "If we conclude that Jesus alluded to Dan 7:13 in his teaching, the shift from the indefinite or generic use of the phrase 'son of man' to its definite or quasi-titular use is explained." Casey strenuously objects to the suggestion that Jesus could have connected the Aramaic idiom to Dan. 7:13 on the grounds that כבר אנש is "not really an individual figure, but an abstract symbol of the Saints of the Most High, who are in effect the people of Israel" (Casey, *Solution*, 30, 81–92, 114). Space prohibits me from entering into an extended debate about the nature of the metaphors and symbols of Dan. 7, including the complexity of the imagery and their representations. In any case, Casey's bifurcation between a corporate and individual referent is problematic since the entities in Dan. 7 have both an inclusive and exclusive sense. The text explicitly states in Dan. 7:17 that the "four great beasts are four kings who shall arise out of the earth," and yet in Dan. 7:23 the fourth beast is also representative of the "fourth kingdom." Are the beasts "kings" or "kingdoms"? Is this true also of the "one like a son of man"? Is he a purely "abstract symbol" for the saints of the Most High, or is he also a king who represents the saints of the Most High? Given the royal qualities and royal function of the "one like a son of man," we can hardly dismiss the association with kingship. Kingship was highly symbolic (politically and theologically), and kings were representatives of the people. If one does not concur with an implied reference to an individual Jewish king, some scholars have still seen כבר אנש as a reference to an individual angel, i.e., the archangel Michael (e.g., J. Collins, *Scepter and the Star*, 176). More follows on this below.

ἀνθρώπου (as a son of man). It is plausible that the double articular construction was given in order to reflect the particular emphasis that Jesus himself gave to this expression and its connection with Dan. 7, which embedded the phrase with connotations of eschatological authority.[23]

Fourth, in 1QapGen 21.13 we have one instance in Aramaic where an author uses "one like a Son of Man" of an individual very similar to Dan. 7:13. This indicates that from a linguistic view one could combine an Aramaic idiom in wording close to that of Dan. 7:13.

Fifth, בר־אנשא is a plastic and malleable-enough expression that it is able to accommodate a wide range of usages. It is possible that Jesus detected in Dan. 7:13 a wordplay on the Aramaic idiom that he regarded as a pattern for his own purposes in suffering and vindication. In the words of Matthew Black:

> It is a capital error to assume that Heb. בן־האדם or Aram. בד־(א)נשא, "*the* Son of man," could not be used as a designation or with the titular force for a particular individual, especially for one of a class "where usage has elevated into distinctive prominence a particular individual of the class" [citing A. B. Davidson]. . . . The designation or title "*the* Son of man" to refer to the Daniel figure of "one like a son of man," could as well be used in Aram. or Heb. and with the same force as ὁ υἱὸς τοῦ ἀνθρώπου.[24]

In sum, the Aramaic phrase בר־אנשא certainly does have a generic or indefinite meaning, and this has left its imprint upon the Son of Man tradition in the Gospels. At the same time we should note a connection of the phrase with the language and narrative of Dan. 7, which has also seriously impacted the shape of the Son of Man tradition.[25] The "definite" connotations of the Aramaic phrase make it possible to bridge the Danielic context and the idiomatic significations of the phrase.

If it is possible to associate Jesus's usage of בר־אנשא with "one like a son of man" from Dan. 7,[26] can one associate "son of man" in Dan. 7 with a messianic interpretation?[27] There has been a strong tradition in European scholarship of associating this "son of man" with the Messiah in some sense or another.[28]

23. Cf. Moule, *Christology*, 11–16.

24. Matthew Black, *The Book of Enoch or I Enoch: A New English Edition with Commentary and Textual Notes* (Leiden: Brill, 1985), 206–7.

25. Cf. Caragounis, *Son of Man*, 28.

26. Cf. further (and somewhat overstated) ibid., 168–242.

27. See specific studies by G. R. Beasley-Murray, "The Interpretation of Daniel 7," *CBQ* 45 (1980): 44–58; Brant Pitre, *Jesus, the Tribulation, and the End of the Exile* (WUNT 2.204; Tübingen: Mohr Siebeck, 2005), 54–55; Michael B. Shepherd, "Daniel 7:13 and the New Testament Son of Man," *WTJ* 68 (2007): 99–111.

28. A. Bentzen, "Quelques remarques sur le movement messianique parmi les juifs aux environs de l'an 520 avant Jésus-Christ," *RHPR* 10 (1930): 493–503; M.-J. Lagrange, "La prophétie des soixante-dix semaines de Daniel (Dan. ix, 24–27)," *RB* 39 (1930): 179–98; W. Manson, *Jesus the Messiah*, 15, 101–3; K. Müller, "Menschensohn und Messias," *BZ* 16 (1972): 161–87; 17 (1973):

But before I follow suit, a few caveats are required. To begin with, I am not arguing that "son of man" was a fixed messianic title in pre-Christian Judaism or even that Jesus's self-reference as "Son of Man" was clearly messianic in every utterance. What I am arguing for instead is that the son of man figure of Dan. 7 contributed to the construction of a messianic narrative; it was capable of sustaining a messianic interpretation and was occasionally interpreted as messianic in pockets of pre-Christian Judaism, and Jesus's employment of the phrase taps into this background.

In chapter 7 of the book, Daniel's vision begins with a description of the four beasts who came up out of the sea, and they designate the totality of human kingdoms that oppose and oppress Israel, including the arrogant eleventh horn of the fourth beast (vv. 1–9). The seer then switches perspective and describes the throne and appearance of the "Ancient of Days," who sits ready to render judgment upon the beasts (vv. 9–10 RSV). The beasts, including the boastful horn of the fourth beast, are destroyed, and the dominion of the wicked beasts is taken away from them (vv. 11–12). At this juncture "one like a son of man" comes with clouds before the Ancient of Days,[29] and this human figure is given an everlasting dominion over all peoples, nations, and tongues (vv. 13–14). This everlasting kingdom is identical with the kingdom spoken of earlier in Daniel (2:44–45; 4:3, 17–18; 6:26). When Daniel inquires as to the meaning of this troubling vision, he is told that it refers to the reception of the kingdom by the saints of the Most High, who possess the kingdom despite the evil machinations of the four beasts (vv. 15–18). The rest of chapter focuses on the symbolism of the fourth beast and the horns and how the saints possess the kingdom despite the horn's blasphemous words (vv. 19–28).

I submit that we have here the recapitulation of a narrative that reaches all the way back to both Eden and Sinai. As Dunn puts it: "The implication is clear: that as 'man' = the human being was climax to creation and given dominion over the rest of creation, so Israel was the climax of God's universal purpose and would be given dominion over all other nations."[30] Daniel 7 evokes a series of substories denoted by the "one like a son of man" and his reception of a kingdom over and against the pagan beasts, who ravage the

---

52–66; U. B. Müller, *Messias und Menschensohn in jüdischen Apokalypsen und der Offenbarung des Johannes* (Gütersloh: Mohn, 1972); R. D. Rowe, "Is Daniel's Son of Man Messianic?" in *Christ the Lord: Studies in Christology Presented to D. Guthrie* (London: Inter-Varsity, 1982), 71–96; Seyoon Kim, *The "Son of Man" as the Son of God* (WUNT 30; Tübingen: Mohr Siebeck, 1983), 79–82, 100–101; William Horbury, "The Messianic Associations of 'the Son of Man,'" *JTS* 36 (1985): 34–55; Klaus Koch, "Messias und Menschensohn: Die zweistufige Messianologie der jüngeren Apokalyptik," *JBT* 8 (1993): 73–102; Caragounis, *Son of Man*, 78–81 (with further references at 78n166); I. Howard Marshall, "Jesus as Messiah in Mark and Matthew," in Porter, *The Messiah in the Old and New*, 132–33.

29. On whether the Son of Man comes from earth to heaven or from heaven to earth, see discussion in Dunn, *Jesus Remembered*, 757–58.

30. Ibid., 729.

saints. The authority and reign that God intended for humanity as rulers over all of creation has been granted to Israel, and this function of Israel is carried out by a symbolic figure that represents, and in some sense even is, Israel in person. The problem is that Israel is not currently ruling over creation: instead, they are but prey for the pagan beasts that scour the wilderness in want of flesh to devour. This is the exact line of thought in 4 Ezra, a document much influenced by Daniel's visions, and it depicts Israel as the rightful ruler over the nations, who has become victim for them instead. At one point the seer complains to God that he has chosen one "dove" (Israel) from among all the birds (nations) and one sheep (Israel) from all the flock (nations), on whom God has set his affection, and yet God willingly hands over his people to be dishonored and scattered by those who do not know the promises or the covenant. Would it not have been better to be punished by God himself than by the pagan hordes (4 Ezra 5.24–30)? Similarly in 4 Ezra 6 we find a retelling of the story of creation set in coordinates of Israel's commission to rule over creation like Adam. Here the seer laments that the beasts have overpowered the appointed guardians of the created realm.

> On the sixth day you commanded the earth to bring forth before you cattle, wild animals, and creeping things; and over these you placed Adam, as ruler over all the works that you had made; and from him we have all come, the people whom you have chosen. All this I have spoken before you, O Lord, because you have said that it was for us that you created this world. As for the other nations that have descended from Adam, you have said that they are nothing, and that they are like spittle, and you have compared their abundance to a drop from a bucket. And now, O Lord, these nations, which are reputed to be as nothing, domineer over us and devour us. But we your people, whom you have called your firstborn, only begotten, zealous for you, and most dear, have been given into their hands. If the world has indeed been created for us, why do we not possess our world as an inheritance? How long will this be so? (4 Ezra 6.53–59)[31]

What the throne scene in Dan. 7:13–14 envisages is no less than the vindication of Israel against the pagan oppressors and the return of Israel to its divinely ordained role as custodians of creation. This is accomplished through the enthronement of the mysterious human figure.

That the "one like a son of man" is representative of the "saints" (that is, "Israel" generically or else oppressed Judeans during the Maccabean revolt) is one thing, but it is quite another to establish that he is a messianic figure. In support of a messianic dimension to the narrative we should consider the following:

1. Several commentators have pointed out the *royal* overtones of the Son of Man's coming before the throne of the Ancient of Days. Collins argues:

---

31. For a Christian articulation of a similar theme, see Herm. *Vis.* 2.8.1.

"Rather than messianic expectations, then, what we have in Daniel is a transformation of the royal mythology."[32] Nickelsburg notes that Dan. 7 can be placed between the judicial function of David in traditions from Ps. 2 and Isa. 11 to similar functions that are attributed to the "Chosen One" in 1 En. 48. He writes: "The functions of the Son of Man/Chosen One are primarily judicial, building on the notion that the king is responsible for justice and especially for maintaining and vindicating the rights of the oppressed."[33] The Danielic narrative presents a figure whose ordained purpose includes ruling over the nations on behalf of God (in v. 14, see the reference to "kingship," מלכו). This is, quite naturally, a role that can be predicated of the Messiah. What Dan. 7 does is to take this royal function and place it in an eschatological narrative related to the restoration of Israel. Although the narrative has not arrived at anything we can call messianic in a titular sense, it is certainly at the germinal stages of a messianic trajectory. Collins's perception of the transformation of an ANE royal mythology is correct, with the qualification that the transformation is leading toward the messianic myth of Second Temple Judaism, itself built on the idealization of Davidic kingship.

2. In addition, the one like a son of man is essentially the *representative of Israel*, who comes before the Ancient of Days and receives authority, power, and a kingdom. Put this way, the human figure has the same role as Israel's king, who was the representative ruler of the people before God.

3. The mysterious human appears to be a king since he mirrors the kings represented by the four beasts and the little horn. In Dan. 7:17 the four great beasts are described as "four kings [who] shall arise out of the earth," and the Son of Man by parallel and contrast is the king of Israel, who descends from heaven. What is more, he is also the heavenly counterpoint to the little horn, who is the king and representative of the kingdom designated by the fourth beast in Dan. 7:19–21. The referents of the metaphors seem fluid and oscillate between king, kingdom, and people at various points in the text. The human figure is a similar multivalent metaphor for God's kingdom, God's people, and God's anointed king.[34]

4. Other characteristics of Israel's king can also be related to the Son of Man in Dan. 7. In Ps. 2 the king is the one before whom the *nations* must bow. In Ps. 110 the king is to rule and share the *throne* of the covenant God. The ideas of ruling over the nations and of sharing God's throne that are present in Dan. 7:9, 13–14 can be correlated easily with biblical conceptions of kingship and postbiblical conceptions of the Messiah.

32. J. Collins, *Scepter and the Star*, 37.
33. Nickelsburg, *Ancient Judaism and Christian Origins*, 105.
34. Cf. Pitre, *Jesus*, 54–55.

5. William Horbury makes a comparison between the Son of Man and various words signifying "man" in Num. 24:17 LXX; 2 Sam. 23:1; Zech. 6:12; and also Ps. 80:18, which has בן אדם (*ben 'ādām*) in relation to traditions about David or a future deliverer.[35]

Therefore, we should refrain from reading a full-blown messianic role or messianic title into Dan. 7. But what is apparent is that the contours of Dan. 7 make it "potentially messianic,"[36] a text for which "a messianic interpretation was optional";[37] it provides the "imagistic repertoire" of later messianism.[38] Thus, it makes perfect sense that a text such as this one would lend itself to the formulation of a messianic and cosmological narrative underlying apocalypses such as 1 En. 37–71; 4 Ezra 13; and Rev. 12 and 14.

A further contribution to our study of the quasi-messianic nature of Daniel's Son of Man can be found in the subsequent history of interpretation.[39] This material illustrates good evidence that by the first century CE there were some commonly held assumptions about the figure in Daniel's vision that go beyond what is explicit in the text, and the narrative was taken in a messianic direction.[40]

Dead Sea Scrolls

The Dead Sea Scrolls provide further indication of how Dan. 7 was often given a messianic interpretation.[41] A particular text that concerns us is column two of the Son of God fragment from Cave 4 (4Q246).

He will be called the son of God (ברה די אל), they will call him the son of the Most High (ובר עלין). But like the meteors that you saw in your vision, so will be their

35. Horbury, *Jewish Messianism*, 34. Of further significance is also the use of "man" as a shortened form of "Son of Man" in 4 Ezra 13.3, 25 for a clearly messianic figure.

36. Dunn, "Messianic Ideas," 369.

37. Dahl, "Messianic Ideas," 385.

38. Sabino Chialà, "The Son of Man: The Evolution of an Expression," in *Enoch and the Messiah Son of Man: Revisiting the Book of Parables* (ed. Gabriele Boccaccini; Grand Rapids: Eerdmans, 2007), 158.

39. Horbury (*Jewish Messianism*, 34) asserts in opposition to the angelic interpretation of Dan. 7:13 that "the early messianic interpretation seems more likely to be right." According to J. A. Montgomery (*A Critical and Exegetical Commentary on the Book of Daniel* [ICC; Edinburgh: T&T Clark, 1927], 321): "The strength of the Messianic interpretation arises from the striking impression of the figure of the Son of Man." Burkett (*Son of Man*, 113) notes that "first-century interpreters of Daniel 7:13, in the extant sources at least, assumed that the one like a son of man was an individual, the Messiah."

40. J. Collins, *Scepter and the Star*, 175.

41. Another text of relevance is 4Q243 (= 4QpsDanAᵃ), but unfortunately the text is too fragmentary to be able to make any clear links between "the Son of God" and any messianic figures. See further, Fitzmyer, *Wandering Aramean*, 84–113.

kingdom. They will reign only a few years over the land, while people tramples people and nation tramples nation until there rises the people of God; then all will have rest from warfare. Their kingdom will be an eternal kingdom, and all their paths will be righteous. They will judge the land justly, and all nations will make peace. Warfare will cease from the land, and all the nations shall do obeisance to them. The great God will be their help, he himself will fight for them, putting peoples into their power, overthrowing them all before them. God's rule will be an eternal rule and all the depths of [the earth are his]. (4Q246 2.1–10)

The "Son of God" has been interpreted in various ways, including (1) the Seleucid king Alexander Balas, (2) Antiochus IV Epiphanes, (3) an antichrist figure, (4) the archangel Michael, (5) a collective designation for Israel, (6) a future Jewish king but not necessarily the Messiah, and (7) the Messiah.[42]

Fitzmyer has argued strongly for option 6, which identifies the Son of God as a future Jewish king,[43] perhaps a future Davidide as in Jer. 30:9, but not necessarily the Messiah. In his mind, there may be an allusion to Ps. 2:2, 7, but this is not a messianic text.[44] Likewise, Fitzmyer admits the similarities between 4Q246 and 4Q174 on divine sonship for the "Branch of David," the latter building on 2 Sam. 7:13–16, but maintains that there is no predication of "Son of God" and "Messiah" for one individual as attested in Christian usage. Since Fitzmyer regards this text as an apocalyptic text, the problem remains for him that a coming Davidic figure in an apocalyptic or eschatological setting is by definition or function a Davidic Messiah.[45]

A cohort of scholars has argued for a messianic interpretation of 4Q246 that exhibits some degree of influence from Dan. 7.[46] A link with the vision of Dan.

42. Cf. the short survey of scholarship in J. Collins, *Scepter and the Star*, 155–57; and Craig A. Evans, "Son of God Text (4Q246)," in *DNTB*, 1134–37.

43. Fitzmyer, *The One Who Is to Come*, 104–7; and see his earlier works J. A. Fitzmyer, "4Q246: The 'Son of God' Document from Qumran," *Bib* 74 (1993): 153–74; idem, "The Aramaic 'Son of God' Document from Qumran," in *Methods of Investigation of the Dead Sea Scrolls and the Khirbet Qumran Site: Present Realities and Future Prospects* (ed. M. O. Wise et al.; ANYAS 722; New York: New York Academy of Sciences, 1994), 163–78; idem, "The Palestinian Background of 'Son of God' as a Title for Jesus," in *Texts and Contexts: Biblical Texts in Their Textual and Situational Contexts* (ed. T. Fornberg and D. Hellholm; Festschrift for L. Hartman; Oslo: Scandinavian University Press, 1995), 567–77.

44. Fitzmyer (*One Who Is to Come*, 107) acknowledges the messianic interpretation of Ps. 2:2 in 1 En. 48.10 but pleads that "even such an interpretation in one text does not mean that one can therefore extend it to all contemporary and later texts indiscriminately." While this may be true in principle, we have to reckon that the large number of parallels between 4Q246 and other messianic texts such as 4Q174, 1 En. 48, and Luke 1:32–35 should lead us quite naturally to a messianic association.

45. J. Collins, *Scepter and the Star*, 164.

46. H.-W. Kuhn, "Röm 1,3f und der davidische Messias als Gottessohn in den Qumrantexten," in *Lese-Zeichen für Annelies Findeiss zum 65. Geburtstag am 15. März 1984* (ed. C. Burchard and G. Theissen; DBAT 3; Heidelberg: Carl Winter, 1984), 103–12; J. Zimmermann, "Observations on 4Q246—The 'Son of God,'" in Charlesworth, Lichtenberger, and Oegema,

7 is plausible given that the text is close in genre (eschatological prophecy, vision report), theme (dominion of God, tribulation, kingdom given to Israel), and language to the book of Daniel in general and to Dan. 7 in particular (esp. Dan. 2:4, 9; 4:31; 7:14, 27). The "vision" in question also contrasts human kingdoms with the kingdom of the people of God, much like Dan. 7 (7:18, 22, 27). Karl Kuhn has listed the similarities between Dan. 7 and 4Q246 as in table 2.[47]

Table 2. Similarities between Daniel 7 and 4Q246

Dan. 7		4Q246	
7:4–8	The destruction wrought by the beasts, devouring many bodies.	1.4–6	A great massacre in the province.
7:13–14	The coming of an individual deliverer, "one like a son of man."	1.7–2.1	The coming of an individual deliverer, the Son of the Most High/Son of God.
7:14	Whose dominion is an ever-lasting dominion (שלטנה שלטן עלם).	2.9	Whose dominion is an ever-lasting dominion (שלטנה שלטן עלם).
7:21, 23–24	The trampling (דוש) of the earth by the fourth beast, the conflict between various kings, and subjugation of the people of God "for a time."	2.3	The trampling (דוש) of all by "them" and the mutual trampling of people upon people "for some years."
7:22, 26–27	Until the judgment of the heavenly court, the overthrow of the beast, and the giving over of the kingdom to the people of God.	2.4–6	Until there arises / he raises the people of God, "he shall judge."
7:27	"His/its kingdom will be an everlasting kingdom."	2.5	"His/its kingdom will be an everlasting kingdom."
7:27	"And all dominions shall serve and obey him/them."	2.7	"And all provinces shall pay him homage."

Furthermore, the sequencing of 4Q246, column 2, may be indebted to Dan. 7.[48] The reference to the Son of God, the transient and violent nature of the human kingdoms, and the switch to the people of God show a similar sequence to Dan.

Qumran-Messianism, 175–90; E. Puech, "Les Manuscrits de la Mer Morte et le Nouveau Testament," *Le Monde de la Bible* 86 (1994): 34–41; John J. Collins, "The Son of God Text from Qumran," in *From Jesus to John: Essays on Jesus and New Testament Christology* (ed. M. C. de Boer; Festschrift for Marinus de Jonge; JSNTSup 84; Sheffield: JSOT, 1993), 65–82; idem, "The Background of the 'Son of God' Text," *BBR* 7 (1997): 51–61; idem, *Scepter and the Star*, 163–67; Kim, *Son of Man*, 20–22, 25–26; Karl A. Kuhn, "The 'One Like a Son of Man' Becomes the 'Son of God,'" *CBQ* 69 (2007): 22–42; Chester, *Messiah and Exaltation*, 232–33.

47. K. A. Kuhn, "Son of Man," 27.

48. J. Collins, *Scepter and the Star*, 158–59; K. A. Kuhn, "Son of Man," 28–29.

7. In the Danielic cycle, dominion is given to the one "like a son of man," the kingdom is given to the "saints of the Most High," there is a concentration on the fourth beast and its horns, and references are made to the "people of the saints of the Most High." Both texts present a recapitulation of the malevolent reign of human kingdoms set in opposition to the kingdom given to God's people. In the Son of God/Son of the Most High and the one like a son of man, both texts have figures who are representative of the people of God/saints of the Most High.[49]

In terms of messianic content in 4Q246, ruling and judging is a function of the Davidic king in several places such as Pss. 2:8–12; 72:1–2; and Isa. 11:4; the Psalms of Solomon applies the same function to the eschatological king (Pss. Sol. 17.29). This role is given to the people of God, but it is conceivable that this ruling is exercised by the son of God, who is understood as ruler and representative of the people, and this fits with the representative nature of divinely appointed rulers (Adam, Israel, and king). Within the Qumran writings another text for comparison is 4Q174, where the "son" of 2 Sam. 7:14 is related to the "Branch of David," who is set to arise in the last days; this gives an evidently messianic take on "son." It is quite likely that the son of God in 4Q246 represents an interpretation of the son of man from Dan. 7 similar to that found in 1 En. 37–71 and 4 Ezra 13, which attributes to the son of man figure a clear messianic identity. In addition, there are the similarities between the annunciation to Mary in Luke 1:32–35 and 4Q246 (see table 3).

Table 3. The Annunciation and 4Q246

Luke	4Q246
this one will be great (1:32)	your son will be great (1.7)
Son of the Most High he shall be called (1:32)	Son of the Most High shall he be called (2.1)
he shall be called Son of God (1:35)	he shall be called Son of God (2.1)
he will rule forever (1:33)	his kingdom an everlasting kingdom (2.5)

The Lukan infancy narrative arguably reflects the piety and Christology of a primitive Palestinian Jewish Christianity, whose messianism can be said to correspond with an Aramaic text dated to one generation before the time of

49. The question of how the Son of God relates to the people of God and to the kingdom depends on a number of translation decisions in column 2 of 4Q246. (a) 2.4 could be translated either "until there arises (יקום) the people of God" or "until he raises (יקום) the people of God"; and (b) מלכותה in 2.5 could be rendered as "its kingdom" (= the kingdom of the people of God) or "his kingdom" (= the kingdom of the Son of God). While I favor the corporate interpretation (as do other translators like Vermes), it is important to note the possibility of a metaphorical interchange between the corporate entity (people of God) and a representative individual (son of God).

Jesus. Both texts appear to identify the "Son of God" and "Son of the Most High" with the Messiah.[50] In light of this, it seems that 4Q246 is our first source to place Daniel's "one like a son of man" in the mantle of messianic traditions and attribute uniquely transcendent qualities of sonship to the same figure. Collins's comments are worth citing at length:

> It is difficult to say whether the Son of God figure should be regarded as an interpretation of the "one like a son of man" in Daniel 7. If so, it would probably be the oldest surviving interpretation. No other adaptation or interpretation of that chapter has yet been identified in the Qumran corpus. The two earliest interpretations of Daniel 7 are found in the *Similitudes of Enoch* and *4 Ezra* 13. Both these passages assume that Daniel's "one like a son of man" is an individual, and both use the term "messiah" with reference to him. In both these documents, the Son of Man figure is pre-existent, and therefore transcendent in some sense. The Son of God in the Qumran text is not identical with either of these figures, but he has much in common with them. It should be emphasized that the extant fragment from Qumran lacks clear allusions to Daniel's "one like a son of man" such as we find in the *Similitudes* and in *4 Ezra*. Nonetheless, it is difficult to avoid the impression that the author had Daniel's figure in mind. The Danielic paradigm becomes an important factor in messianism in the first century of the Common Era. The Son of God text suggests that the messianic interpretation of Daniel 7 had begun already in the Hasmonean period.[51]

The Gospels

In the Gospels, "Son of Man" is an obvious title for Jesus and one that is invested with messianic meaning by virtue of its association with their portrayal of Jesus as the Messiah of Israel. In Mark's Gospel, Peter's confession that Jesus is the Messiah is met with Jesus's teaching that the Son of Man must suffer (Mark 8:27–31). During a discussion about kingship and greatness in the kingdom, Jesus teaches that the Son of Man came to serve and to give his life as a ransom for many (Mark 10:45). When Jesus is asked whether or

---

50. Craig A. Evans, "Jesus and the Dead Sea Scrolls from Qumran Cave 4," in *Eschatology, Messianism, and the Dead Sea Scrolls* (ed. C. A. Evans and P. W. Flint; Grand Rapids: Eerdmans, 1997), 94. J. Collins (*Scepter and the Star*, 155) asserts: "The correspondences with Luke might be taken as *prima facie* evidence for a messianic interpretation, but the fragmentary state of the text leaves many points of uncertainty," and later he wrote ("Background," 61) that in light of the parallels with Luke, "the messianic interpretation of 4Q246 remains overwhelmingly probable." For an alternative view, see James D. G. Dunn, " 'Son of God' as 'Son of Man' in the Dead Sea Scrolls? A Response to John Collins on 4Q246," in *The Scrolls and The Scriptures: Qumran Fifty Years After* (ed. S. E. Porter and C. A. Evans; JSPSup 26; Sheffield: Sheffield Academic Press, 1997), 198–210. While Dunn is correct (ibid., 209) that 4Q246 is probably an amalgam of 2 Sam. 7:13–14 and Dan. 7, he overlooks the connection with Luke 1:32–35 in want of more perspicuous evidence of messianism in the language.

51. J. Collins, *Scepter and the Star*, 167.

not he is the Messiah, he responds by way of reference to the vindicated and enthroned Son of Man of Dan. 7 (Mark 14:62).

Perhaps "this presentation of Messiah as suffering-and-vindicated Son of Man expresses Mark's own theological creativity as a Christian."[52] However, this perspective of the suffering/rejected Son of Man as Messiah is not limited to Mark alone. In John 12:34 the crowd asks Jesus: "We have heard from the law that the Messiah remains forever. How can you say that the Son of Man must be lifted up? Who is this Son of Man?" The logic here is as follows: (1) The Messiah is to endure forever; (2) the Son of Man is to die (be lifted up); (3) but the Son of Man is the Messiah, so how can this be? This text suggests that a messianic interpretation of the Son of Man from Dan. 7 was current in the Judaism known to the Beloved Disciple, and one variation of it in his telling could conceivably involve death for the man in question.[53]

In Q we observe elements that relate the Son of Man to rejection (Luke 6:22/ Matt. 5:11; Luke 7:34/Matt. 11:19; Luke 9:58/Matt. 8:20; Luke 12:10/Matt. 12:32; cf. Luke 11:49–51/Matt. 23:34–35; Luke 13:34–35/Matt. 23:37–39) but also with reigning in the messianic kingdom (cf. Luke 22:30/Matt. 19:28; cf. Luke 7:22–23/Matt. 11:4–6).[54] I am not suggesting that Q had an explicit christological conception of Jesus as the Messiah and suffering Son of Man interwoven together (assuming that we can speak coherently of a Christology of Q), but both ideas find parallels in the Q tradition even if they are not specifically integrated together at any particular point in the manner of Mark or John.[55]

Distinctive elements of the Matthean tradition relate the Son of Man to traditions that parallel 1 En. 62–63. The parable of the weeds (Matt. 13:37–43) and last judgment scene (Matt. 25:31–46) include references to the Son of Man's heavenly status and judicial role; God's people are called "righteous" and are promised eternal bliss, there is no mercy for the condemned, there is the summoning of nations before the Son of Man, and angels execute a wrathful judgment.[56] It is quite possible that Matthew's tradition is dependent upon the Enochic material or that both drew from a common pool of traditions concerning the Son of Man, traditions combining messianic and judiciary functions.

I think it entirely plausible that Jesus used the designation "Son of Man" at times to redefine the meaning of messiahship in accordance with the pattern of the enthroned figure of Dan. 7 (more on that later). But even if these units

---

52. Fredriksen, *Jesus of Nazareth*, 142; cf. similarly Jürgen Becker, *Jesus*, 196.

53. Cf. also the close association of "Messiah" with "Son of Man" in John 1:41–51.

54. This is assuming that "Son of Man" in Q^Mt (= Matt. 19:28) is original to Q.

55. Tuckett (*Christology and the New Testament*, 217) states: "Thus the idea of the 'suffering Son of Man' is not confined to Mark: it is implied in both of the earliest strands of the tradition. By the criterion of multiple attestation, it would seem then to have as good a chance as any of being an idea we can confidently trace back to Jesus himself."

56. Leslie W. Walck, "The Son of Man in the Parables of Enoch and the Gospels," in *Enoch and the Messiah Son of Man: Revisiting the Book of Parables* (ed. G. Boccaccini; Grand Rapids: Eerdmans, 2007), 328–31.

are not historically authentic in whole or in part, what is important here is that the canonical Gospels attest to messianic significance being attached to the designation "Son of Man" in the mid to late first century.

Apocalypses

It seems clear that the designation "Son of Man" did not begin as a technical term for a messiah. That notwithstanding, the designation and narrative framework from Daniel was quickly enlisted to aid in constructing messianic narratives, as evidenced by Jewish and Christian apocalypses. This is so much the case that Charlesworth writes: "We professors have been taught and have taught that 'the Son of Man' is a term or title that is to be distinguished from the term or title Messiah. Now, with the recognition that the Parables of Enoch are clearly Jewish, Palestinian, and probably pre-70, we should rethink this assumption."[57] In what follows I give a brief description of the messianic traits of the Son of Man in the Similitudes of 1 Enoch, 4 Ezra 13, and the book of Revelation as they provide a further indication of a messianic interpretation of Dan. 7.

1. The Similitudes of 1 Enoch have been dated variously and, as stated earlier, I favor the view that they were written sometime between the Parthian invasion of 40 BCE and the Jewish war of 66 CE.[58] Although many writings from the Old Testament Pseudepigrapha have a Christian provenance and were created, carried, and copied by Christians, it seems reasonably clear that 1 Enoch does not owe its primary origination to Christian scribes, given the existence of fragments of it (excluding the Similitudes) in the Dead Sea Scrolls, and I doubt that a Christian scribe would make "Son of Man" a circumlocution for Enoch (1 En. 60.10; 70.1; 71.14).[59] The Son of Man[60] figure in the Similitudes is clearly a transcendent and preexistent being, even with a quasi-divine status (esp. 46.1–2; 48.5, 10). He comes to uproot kings, kingdoms, and sinners for their oppression of the elect, for their denial of the "Lord of the Spirits" through idolatry, and because of their failure to realize that the Lord is the "source of their kingship" (46.1–5); these are clearly messianic tasks. The Son of Man is given a name before the creation of the world (48.3; 62.7), and in later rabbinic tradition the name of the Messiah is among the things that preceded the creation of the cosmos (b. Pesaḥ. 54a; b. Ned. 39b). He is also described as being the "light of the Gentiles" (1 En. 48.4; cf. Isa. 42:6; 49:6; Luke 2:32), and he reveals the Lord's wisdom to the righteous and holy ones (1 En. 48.7). Kings and landowners will face grave consequences for their deeds when the

57. Charlesworth, "Messianology to Christology," 31.
58. Hengel, "Effective History of Isaiah 53 in the Pre-Christian Period," 99.
59. On the relationship between Enoch and the Son of Man, see J. Collins, *Scepter and the Star*, 178–81.
60. In Ethiopic, the expressions *walda sab'* (1 En. 46.2, 3, 4; 48.2), *walda be'si* (1 En. 62.5; 69.29; 71.14), and *walda 'egʷāla 'emma-ḥeyāw* (62.7, 9, 14; 63.11; 69.26, 27; 70.1, 17) are used.

Son of Man comes; he is identified also as the "Messiah" (48.8–10). The Son
of Man is mentioned again in a short narrative centered on the reversal of the
status of the elect and the undoing of the ruling class, who are destined for
shame and judgment. The rulers are to behold the "Elect One" (62.1), who
bears the "spirit of righteousness" (62.2; cf. Isa. 11:2) and is later identified
with the Son of Man who shares with the Lord of Spirits the "throne of his
glory" (1 En. 62.5; cf. 69.29; Ps. 110:1; Dan. 7:9). This is followed by a scene of
judgment: rulers grovel before his throne but receive only vengeance. The Son
of Man later presides over what can only be called a messianic banquet: the
elect ones "eat and rest and rise with that Son of Man forever" in a glorious
state (1 En. 62.14). The Similitudes end with Enoch's vision of the heaven of
heavens, and the Lord says: "So there shall be length of days with that Son
of Man and peace to the righteous ones" (71.17); this may be tantamount to
inaugurating a period of peace and prosperity (cf. Isa. 9:7; Zech. 9:10; 4 Ezra
13.12, 39; Pss. Sol. 17.33–35; 4Q246 2.4).

According to Klausner, the evidence from 1 En. 37–71 indicates that "in a
comparatively short time after the composition of the book of Daniel it was
thought among the Jews that this 'son of man' was the Messiah."[61] The "one
like a son of man" in Dan. 7 is developed and transformed into a transcendent
and preexistent individual who effects the Lord of the Spirit's redemption
of the elect, reveals wisdom to the elect, and executes judgment upon their
enemies. Daniel's "one like a son of man" appears after the judgment scene
against the beasts/kingdoms, while in 1 Enoch the "Son of Man" is the very
means by which hostile kingdoms and vicious rulers are destroyed. He is
identified as the Messiah and is even assimilated to the throne of God.[62] The
figure of a human being in Daniel is a symbol for another reality—the saints
of the Most High who are triumphant and vindicated—but in the Similitudes
the other reality is of a messianic figure who is elected to save the Lord of the
Spirit's elect people. This includes a convergence of traditions from Pss. 2 and
110, Isaiah,[63] and Daniel in a creative enterprise of messianic exegesis that is
paralleled by a similar convergence found in the early Jesus movement.

2. Fourth Ezra is probably to be dated to the post–70 CE period and represents a further appropriation of Dan. 7 through its own narration of the
coming eschatological deliverance. The structure of 4 Ezra 13 is similar to

61. Klausner, *Messianic Idea*, 230; idem, *Jesus of Nazareth*, 256.
62. The proximity of the Son of Man to the Ancient of Days in the Similitudes may have been
impacted by the LXX of Dan. 7:13, which has the Son of Man coming ὡς παλαιὸς ἡμερῶν (as/
like the Ancient of Days), whereas in the MT and Theodotion (Θ) he comes ἕως τοῦ παλαιοῦ
ἡμερῶν/ועד־עתיק יומיא מטה (to/as far as the Ancient of Days). In particular, 𝔓967, Codex 88, and
the Syro-Hexapla stress the similarity of the Son of Man with the Ancient of Days. Furthermore,
Rev. 1:13–14 includes a portrayal of the Son of Man taken from the Ancient of Days in Dan.
7:9. See further discussion in Kim, *Son of Man*, 22–26.
63. According to Chialà ("Son of Man," 161), "The language is clearly that of Isaiah, and is
borrowed from those passages of Isaiah that have strongly messianic overtones."

the Danielic account: there is a recounting of a dream/vision, a request for an explanation, and the explanation itself. The text includes these statements (with some emphasis added):

> As I kept looking the wind made something like the *figure of a man* come up out of the heart of the sea. And I saw that *this man* flew with the clouds of heaven; and wherever he turned his face to look, everything under his gaze trembled, and whenever his voice issued from his mouth, all who heard his voice melted as wax melts when it feels the fire. (4 Ezra 13.3–4)

> This is the interpretation of the vision: As for your seeing *a man* come up from the heart of the sea, this is he whom the Most High has been keeping for many ages, who will himself deliver his creation; and he will direct those who are left. (4 Ezra 13.25–26)

> When these things take place and the signs occur that I showed you before, then my *Son* will be revealed, whom you saw as a man coming up from the sea. . . . Then he, my *Son*, will reprove the assembled nations for their ungodliness. (4 Ezra 13.32, 37)

> Just as no one can explore or know what is in the depths of the sea, so no one on earth can see my *Son* or those who are with him, except in the time of his day. (4 Ezra 13.52)

Fourth Ezra is extant predominantly in Latin manuscripts but also in Syriac, Ethiopic, Armenian, and Arabic versions, with additional fragments in Coptic and Georgian. Scholars have concluded that the original version was probably Aramaic or Hebrew as opposed to Greek. That leads to some problems, and we can only guess via the Latin and Syriac (the more reliable witnesses) as to what the original designations were for "figure of a man," "man," and "Son." Regardless of what Semitic idiom for "man" lies beneath the text, a messianic interpretation is certainly given. That is achieved by identifying the "figure of a man" with God's "Son," and earlier in 4 Ezra 7.28–29 the Messiah is designated precisely as "my Son." Thus, 4 Ezra attests to a messianic interpretation achieved by bringing together Dan. 7 and probably Ps. 2:7 and/or 2 Sam. 7:13–14.

3. Revelation is the first extant Christian apocalypse, dated usually to the reign of Domitian in the late 90s of the first century. The book does not use an apocalypticized Son of Man akin to 1 Enoch or 4 Ezra, and there is instead a reversion toward Dan. 7 from both a conceptual and semantic point of view. The "one like a Son of Man" is no longer a symbol for the saints of the Most High but is an encoded title for Jesus of Nazareth.[64] That is partly because the book of Daniel is so formative for the themes, structure, and theology of

---

64. Ibid., 171.

Revelation.[65] Reference to the Son of Man occurs explicitly in only two places in all of Revelation. In the opening vision report in Rev. 1:13, John the Seer declares that among seven lampstands he saw ὅμοιον υἱὸν ἀνθρώπου (one like a son of man). In a subsequent vision detailing the fall of Babylon the Great and the judgment of God, the Seer describes "a white cloud, and seated on the cloud was one like a son of man [ὅμοιον υἱὸν ἀνθρώπου]" (14:14). Both descriptions are distinguished by the absence of the article and by a much closer resemblance to the Greek text of Dan. 7:13. We should also consider the vision recounted in Rev. 12 about a woman giving birth to a "son" who is to "rule all the nations with a rod of iron." The child is snatched away and "taken to God and to his throne" (Rev. 12:5). This reflects an eschatological struggle between the Son and the great red dragon, and heavenly agents like the archangel Michael are enlisted to do battle against the dragon (Rev. 12:1–9).

The Christology of Revelation focuses on Jesus as the crucified, risen, and exalted conqueror of death and of Rome as located in the symbolic universe of this Christian apocalypse. At the same time this Christology has not lost all traces of a titular messianism. At one point the Seer recalls a voice from heaven that announces the news: "Now have come the salvation and the power and the kingdom of our God and the authority of his Messiah [Χριστός]" (Rev. 12:10). This is all the more significant since none of the Son of Man units appear to be directly dependent upon the synoptic tradition.[66] The primary impetus for the Son of Man materials, as well as the narrative of Rev. 12, seems to be Dan. 7 and Joel 3. As in the Similitudes, the Son of Man is primarily a juridical figure in Revelation. He is a judge of the pagan coalition persecuting God's people (Rev. 14:14–20) and also an advocate against the compromised, lethargic, and acculturated churches of Asia Minor (Rev. 1:13–14). The kaleidoscope of military, royal, juridical, and messianic imagery points to Jesus Christ as the one who will punish the wicked rulers of the world, gather together the saints, and rule over God's new creation.

In summary, the evidence gleaned from 1 Enoch and 4 Ezra confirms that "the Son of Man tradition is a transformation of the Davidic messianism."[67]

---

65. Cf. Gregory K. Beale, *The Use of Daniel in Jewish Apocalyptic Literature and in the Revelation of St. John* (Lanham, MD: University Press of America, 1984).

66. Adela Y. Collins ("The 'Son of Man' Tradition and the Book of Revelation," in *Cosmology and Eschatology in Jewish and Christian Apocalypticism* [Leiden: Brill, 1996], 159–97) argues that the tradition behind the Son of Man in Revelation reflects a stage of christological development that is older than the synoptic tradition. This is certainly possible given the lack of references to a suffering, authoritative, or coming Son of Man figure. But I think it very unlikely that the Seer does not know of any synoptic-like traditions about Jesus, since such traditions were available in both written and oral forms in Asia Minor at the end of the first century.

67. Helmut Gese, *Zur biblischen Theologie* (München: Kaiser, 1977), 145: "Die Menschensohnüberlieferung ist eine Transformation des davidischen Messianismus"; cf. J. Collins (*Scepter and the Star*, 189): "What we find in the writings of the first century CE, however, is a tendency to combine traditions about a Davidic messiah with the expectations of a heavenly savior. . . . In

The use of son of man in the Similitudes and 4 Ezra indicates that messianism occurs even when the title "Messiah" does not appear or is seldom used.[68] Revelation continues this interpretive maneuver through its own christologically loaded depiction of a similar eschatological narrative. The Similitudes of 1 Enoch, 4 Ezra, and Revelation represent a wide spectrum of messianic speculation driven by extrapolations from the Danielic narrative about a Son of Man figure who is a heavenly eschatological deliverer. These documents also attest to the abandonment of hopes for an earthly and military Messiah and affirm the need for a transcendent and heavenly one, but they vary considerably in many respects. For example, the Son of Man from 4 Ezra comes to restore Israel; in the Similitudes he delivers the elect wholly apart from a covenantal scheme; in Revelation he is identified as the risen and exalted Jesus. That being said, we cannot speak of a widespread or single concept of messianic interpretation of Dan. 7:13. It was, at most, probably a marginal phenomenon, but one that had utmost significance for the eschatological hopes of certain groups, including those associated with Qumran, Enochic Judaism, the early church, some rabbinic literature,[69] and (perhaps even) the historical Jesus.[70]

Jesus as the Son of Man Messiah

The previous section has tried to establish that Daniel's "one like a son of man" was potentially messianic, and it then became explicitly messianic in the writings of pre-Christian Judaism, in the New Testament, in certain segments of rabbinic literature, and in isolated instances in early patristic writings as well. The question is, Could Jesus have taken a well-known Aramaic idiom for "man" or "someone," used it in connection with Dan. 7, and joined messianic overtones to it? The answer I have reached is in the affirmative.[71]

The phrase "Son of Man" is taken up by Jesus from everyday usage for "human being" and "someone" as well as from Dan. 7:13. It is not un-

---

short 'Davidic messiah' and 'Son of Man' were not mutually exclusive concepts. Each involves a cluster of motifs, which could be made to overlap."

68. Cf. Knight, *Jesus*, 137.

69. Num. Rab. 13.14 reads: "How do we know of the King Messiah (that he will reign supreme on sea and land)? Because it is written 'He shall have dominion also from sea to sea, and from the river unto the ends of the earth' [Ps. 72:8]. How do we know he will hold sway on land? Because it is written, 'All kings shall prostrate themselves before him: all nations shall serve him' [Ps. 72:11], and it also says, 'Behold there came with the clouds of heaven one like unto a son of man . . . and there was given unto him dominion . . . and all the people . . . should serve him' [Dan. 7:13–14]; 'and the stone that smote the image became a great mountain and filled the whole earth' [Dan. 2:35]." Cf. *b. Ḥag.* 14a; *b. Sanh.* 38b.

70. Cf. Kim, *Son of Man*, 25–26.

71. Cf. Russell Morton, "Son of Man," in *EHJ*, 597.

ambiguously messianic in any real sense; if it were, the disciples would have heralded Jesus as Messiah at his very first mention of it.[72] Even so, as Jesus's own idiomatic form of self-reference, the phrase is used as a cipher for the eschatological mystery that surrounds his mission. He can even use it to make tacit references to his divinely given regal-like authority and let the designation link him to a role of suffering and rejection in the divine plan. When framed in the context of his mission to restore Israel, his eschatological teaching on the kingdom, comparisons of himself with David and Solomon, claims to be uniquely anointed with the Spirit for his actions, his symbolic activities and actions—then the vagueness of the designation starts to disappear (for insiders) in favor of a more concrete sense along the lines of messianism (and as we have seen, Jesus was not necessarily the first one who took Dan. 7:13 in a messianic direction, given what has been said about 4Q246 and the traditions behind 1 En. 37–71). The designation, for which the Greek framers of the Aramaic Jesus tradition struggled to find a Greek equivalent, marks Jesus out both as eschatological proclaimer of salvation and arguably as the *messias designatus*.[73] As Theissen and Merz put it:

> At all events, it is certain that Jesus thought in terms of a symbolic representative relationship. When he chose the "Twelve," they represented the twelve tribes of Israel. This presupposes that Jesus himself represents Israel as a whole. He, as a human being, was destined to lead Israel into the kingdom. . . . An everyday expression which simply meant the human being or a human being was evaluated in "messianic" terms by Jesus. Only because of that could it become the characteristic way in which he described himself.[74]

As the *authoritative* Son of Man, Jesus is already exercising the dominion of the Messiah over the affairs of Israel and human beings in general. As the *suffering* Son of Man, Jesus combines the role of the Messiah with the smitten Shepherd of Zech. 13:7 and the Suffering Servant of Isaiah, and he enters the eschatological ordeal on behalf of others. As the *future* Son of Man, Jesus will be vindicated and given a kingdom as Messiah according to the pattern from Dan. 7. Thus, on the lips of Jesus the "term was pregnant with messianic significance."[75]

Jesus as the Anointed One of Isaiah

If Daniel informed a large part of how Jesus understood his mission, purpose, and calling, Isaiah is another text from Israel's sacred traditions that equally informed

---

72. On this point cf. Cadoux, *Historic Mission of Jesus*, 98.
73. Hengel, "Messiah of Israel," 60–61.
74. Theissen and Merz, *Historical Jesus*, 552–53.
75. Matthew Black, "Aramaic Barnāshā and the 'Son of Man,'" *ExpT* 95 (1984): 203.

Jesus's mission and ministry. I am not going to examine the Suffering Servant motif of Isa. 53; rather, I am interested in the significance of the anointed one of Isa. 61 and how it may have affected Jesus's praxis and self-understanding.

In Isa. 61:1 a messenger is anointed (משח) to herald the news of liberation from oppression and of the glorious restoration of Israel to the captives to be released. The text naturally led to reflection about a coming age of deliverance, as evident from 4Q521 and 11QMelch. It thus is unsurprising that a Galilean like Jesus, with eschatological visions, would find Isa. 61 programmatic for his own mission.

One place where an anointed figure from Isaiah (based on Isa. 11:2; 42:1; and 61:1) potentially impacted Jesus is in the baptismal story as narrated in Mark 1:9–11. The episode is normally regarded as authentic, and it may have derived from a vision report stemming from Jesus himself. Jesus's reception of the Spirit would be tantamount to receiving an anointing from God to herald the good news of the kingdom of God and to heal the sick. Jeremias went so far as to link Mark 1:9–11 with Mark 11:27–33, with the result that Jesus based his messianic authority on his commission by God and his reception of the Spirit, both of which took place at his baptism.[76] On the surface of the narrative, that is confirmed by the voice from heaven that declares Jesus to be "my beloved Son," which probably echoes Ps. 2:7 and renders the baptism story as messianic. Although this is indeed a plausible scenario, we must keep in mind that the baptismal story itself merely indicates that Jesus is commissioned and empowered for a charismatic ministry to Israel. Beyond the reference to sonship (which many would attribute to the evangelist), little in the content of the episode necessitates a messianic commissioning.

The Lukan Jesus commences his public ministry in Luke 4:14–30 with a sequence often called the Nazareth Manifesto. In this pericope Jesus returns to his hometown of Nazareth, reads from Isa. 61 in the synagogue, and pronounces its fulfillment; next comes his rejection by the audience. Jesus responds to his rejection by quoting the proverbs of the physician and the rebuffed prophet; then he makes rhetorically loaded allusions to the biblical stories of the widow of Zarephath and Naaman the Syrian (1 Kings 17:1–24; 2 Kings 5:1–14). The account in Luke 4:16–30 probably functions similarly to Mark 1:14–15 as a paradigmatic unveiling of Jesus's ministry; it introduces the various motifs of Luke–Acts: Spirit, mission, Christology, Israel's recalcitrance, and God's acceptance of outcasts.[77] Elsewhere I have argued that Luke 4:16–30 is probably an independent account of the same events recorded in Mark 6:1–6 and is also authentic since the use of Isa. 61 as programmatic for Jesus's ministry is attested also in Luke 7:22–23/Matt. 11:4–6.[78] Is Jesus's reading of Isa. 61 and

76. Jeremias, *New Testament Theology*, 56.
77. Michael F. Bird, *Jesus and the Origins of the Gentile Mission* (LNTS 331; London: T&T Clark, 2006), 64.
78. Ibid., 65–66.

the pronouncement of its fulfillment intended as an announcement that the messianic era has begun? Once more this is plausible, given that kings were anointed figures and Isa. 61:1–3 could certainly be thought to have messianic connotations in the minds of later interpreters.[79] On the other hand, Fitzmyer argues exclusively for a prophetic assignment of this text; this is entirely appropriate since after his rejection by the crowd, Jesus refers to himself as a "prophet without honor" (Luke 4:24; cf. Mark 6:4; John 4:44; Gos. Thom. 31; and P.Oxy 1.6).[80]

What has so far been established is that Isaiah (esp. 42:1; 52:7; 61:1) significantly impacted the historical Jesus's view of his mission along the lines of the Isaianic vision for the restoration of the Jewish nation. Jesus most likely regarded himself as an anointed figure and anointed for a particular office or purpose. As of yet, however, we have not discovered any evidence indicating that he saw himself as "the Anointed One," or "the Messiah," and his anointing may indicate a prophetic commission to speak to Israel on behalf of God. One may reasonably infer that Jesus claimed to be a prophet, Jesus was widely recognized as a prophet, and prophetic figures were common enough in the first century. Hence, several scholars have argued that Jesus appeared as an anointed prophet but not as an anointed king, and belief in him as the anointed king or "the Messiah" was a subsequent development in the early church.[81] Vermes briefly entertains this possibility:

> Is it possible that the recognition of Jesus as the Messiah evolved from his own idiosyncratic resource to the verb, "to anoint"? As a charismatic, he was certainly aware of a divine vocation and need not have objected to the title, the appointed one. But this is no more than a linguistic possibility: the figurative employment of Messiah is not supported on the historico-literary level by any actual evidence in the Greek New Testament.[82]

There are several things that count against this scenario. First, though it is certainly possible that Jesus's identity as the anointed king was inferred from his status as an anointed prophet, the reverse is also possible: that his followers inferred his status as the eschatological prophet of Deut. 18:15 from his messianic identity. This is the impression one gathers from Acts 3:20–22 (cf. 7:37). Second, royal and prophetic traits are not incompatible: it was possible for certain figures (historical

---

79. Cf. David W. Pao and Eckhard J. Schnabel, "Luke," in *Commentary on the New Testament Use of the Old Testament* (ed. G. K. Beale and D. A. Carson; Grand Rapids: Baker Academic, 2007), 290.

80. Joseph A. Fitzmyer, *Luke* (2 vols.; AB; New York: Doubleday, 1983–85), 1:529–30.

81. Cf. W. C. van Unnik, "Jesus the Christ," *NTS* 8 (1962): 101–16; Klaus Berger, "Zum traditionsgeschichtlichen Hintergrund christologischer Titel," *NTS* 17 (1971): 393–400, 424; idem, "Zum Problem der Messianität Jesu," 24; H. de Jonge, "Historical Jesus," 36; Rowland, *Christian Origins*, 182.

82. Vermes, *Jesus the Jew*, 159.

or idealized) to embody both roles. Third, if Jesus was a prophet without royal pretensions, then the Son of David tradition, the messianic charge, and the *titulus* on the cross become more difficult to explain.[83] Fourth, there is one clear instance in Luke 7:22–23/Matt. 11:4–6 where a compilation of texts from Isaiah is clearly employed in the Jesus tradition to show that Jesus is the promised Messiah and not merely an anointed prophet. To this text we now turn.

In this text from Q, we find the novel story about the Baptist's hesitation or doubts about Jesus's status as the eschatological deliverer. The question is quite understandable since Jesus has been proclaiming the good news of the kingdom and yet John the Baptist is languishing in prison. A natural set of questions arises: Are you the one? If so, when is this kingdom coming? John sends his followers to ask Jesus, "Are you the one who is to come, or are we to wait for another?" (Luke 7:19/Matt. 11:3). In Jesus's reply,[84] he answers the question with reference to a compilation of texts drawn from Isaiah that refer to

the blind receiving sight (Isa. 29:18; 35:5; 42:7, 18),

the lame walking (Isa. 35:6),

lepers being cleansed (cf. Isa. 53:4),

the deaf hearing (Isa. 29:18–19; 35:5),

the dead being raised (Isa. 26:19), and

the poor having the good news preached to them (Isa. 61:1).

In response to this messianic question, Jesus answers obliquely but affirmatively with this assortment of texts from Isaiah in order to show that the Baptist need not seek another. Jesus portrays himself as a messianic figure, though not necessarily in the same tradition as the "stronger one" that the Baptist was expecting (Mark 1:7–8). Nonetheless, he should not mismatch his expectation of the kingdom with its reality. What is asserted here is nothing less than the view that Jesus is the Coming One of the Baptist's preaching, the Messiah of Israel's Scriptures, who through his proclamation to the poor, by his miraculous and compassionate deeds, brings to fulfillment the messianic oracles uttered by the prophet Isaiah.[85]

The authenticity of Luke 7:18–23/Matt. 11:2–6 is most probable given the attestation of the Isa. 61 theme elsewhere in Jesus's ministry (e.g., Luke 4:18–21; Luke 6:20/Matt. 5:3). The church would be unlikely to invent a story where the Baptist exhibits doubt in Jesus, since the Baptist was often invoked as a leading

83. Evans, *Jesus and His Contemporaries*, 437.

84. To indicate that Jesus was doing exactly what he goes on to describe himself as doing, Luke provides a setting by adding 7:21, about Jesus providing healing and exorcisms in this very period.

85. Davies and Allison, *Saint Matthew*, 2:242; contrasted with Theissen and Merz, *Historical Jesus*, 272.

witness to indicate Jesus's messianic role and, in the Johannine tradition, his heavenly origins.[86]

More to the point, Is the question put to Jesus messianic, and is Jesus's answer affirmative? I have already indicated my own point of view on this, and now I intend to explicate it further. First, in the wider contexts of both Gospels, it is the activity of Jesus that prompts the Baptist to send a delegation to seek further information from him (Luke 7:18/Matt. 11:2). Matthew even adds the description "When John heard in prison about the works of the Messiah [τὰ ἔργα τοῦ Χριστοῦ], he sent word through his disciples" (Matt. 11:2). Both accounts indicate a question of ambiguity related to Jesus's messianic status as the background for the pericope. Second, the substantive participle ὁ ἐρχόμενος (the coming one) designates a messianic functionary; as will be shown later, this is a common expression for denoting messianic persons (see below, "The 'I Have Come' Sayings"). Third, there is a most intriguing parallel with column 2 of 4Q521, which indicates that a similar range of activities and deeds were predicated of the Messiah.

The Messianic Apocalypse (4Q521) is a fragmentary Hebrew text from Qumran that mentions a messianic figure and is probably best described as an apocalyptic poem with some sapiential characteristics.[87] Column 2 reads as follows:

> [For the hea]vens and the earth shall listen to His Messiah (משיחו) [and all w]hich is in them shall not turn away from the commandments of the holy ones. Strengthen yourselves, O you who seek the Lord, in His service. Will you not find the Lord in this, all those who hope in their heart? For the Lord seeks the pious and calls the righteous by name. Over the humble His Spirit hovers, and He renews the faithful in His strength. For He will honor the pious upon the th[ro]ne of His eternal kingdom, setting prisoners free, opening the eyes of the blind, raising up those who are bo[wed down]. And for [ev]er I shall hold fast [to] the [ho]peful and pious [. . .] [. . .] shall not be delayed [. . .] and the Lord (אדני) shall do glorious things which have not been done, just as He said. For He shall heal the critically wounded, He shall revive the dead, He shall send good news to the afflicted, He shall [. . . the . . .], He shall lead the [. . .], and the hungry He shall enrich.

The publication of this text in 1991 led to comparisons with the Jesus tradition, and the link with Luke 7:22/Matt. 11:5 was immediately noted.[88] According to

86. On various details about the historicity of this text, see W. G. Kümmel, "Jesu Antwort an Johannes den Täufer: Ein Beispiel zum Methodenproblem in der Jesusforschung," in *Heilsgeschehen und Geschichte: Gesammelte Aufsätze 1965–1977* (ed. E. Grässer and O. Merk; 2 vols.; Marburg: Elwert, 1978), 2:177–200. In favor of authenticity are Davies and Allison, *Saint Matthew*, 2:244–46; and Meier, *A Marginal Jew*, 2:130–36.

87. For an introduction, see Daniel Zacharias, "Dead Sea Scrolls: Messianic Apocalypse," in *EHJ*, 138–39.

88. Michael Wise and James Tabor, "Messiah at Qumran," *BAR* 18.6 (1992): 60–65; John J. Collins, "The Works of the Messiah," *DSD* 1 (1994): 98–112.

Klaus Koch, this text lies "closer to the messianic image of the Gospels than does any other Qumran text."[89] But others have pointed out that the text is ambiguous: it is not certain exactly who does the actions described in 2.12–13 and whether the antecedent of "He" is "His Messiah" in 2.1 or "Lord" in 2.11.[90] García Martínez writes:

> But all these speculations [by Wise/Tabor] are unnecessary if one reads the text correctly. It is not the Messiah who awakens the dead and there are no miracles that are not the work of God. What the text teaches us is this: in the last days, the days of "Messiah," God, as promised, will perform miraculous deeds, and the resurrection of the dead (of the faithful, naturally) will be one of those miraculous deeds.[91]

Despite the protests of several scholars, I think it fairly certain that the Messiah is the implied agent here.[92] (1) We must bear in mind that the fragment itself begins with reference to "heaven and earth will listen to His Messiah," which indicates that the Messiah is the one who preaches, heals, and raises the dead; otherwise there is little point in listening to or obeying the Messiah. The extraordinary scale of the obedience he commands pushes his identity in the direction of a royal and ruling Messiah.[93] (2) 4Q521 2.8, 12–13 is indebted to Isa. 61:1–2, and in the Isaianic text it is the anointed one and not the Lord who announces good news to the captives. In addition, in 11QMelch 2.15–25 it is the prophet and not God who proclaims good news. (3) The closest parallel to the use of Isa. 61:1–3 in 4Q521 is Luke 4:18–19 and Luke 7:22/Matt. 11:5, and there the healings refer to those done by a human person, Jesus. (4) While it is possible that the text describes the Lord as doing the various feats in 4Q521 2.4–11, we have to keep in mind that what is envisaged here is probably divine agency: the Lord acting through his messianic deliverer.[94] Many biblical texts have no problem in speaking of what God is doing and then ascribing it to a human entity. Let me give two examples. In Ezek. 34 we observe the promise that God himself will come to shepherd his people

---

89. Klaus Koch, "Heilandserwartungen im Judäa der Zeitenwende," in *Die Schriftrollen von Qumran: Zur aufregenden Geschichte ihrer Erforschung und Deutung* (ed. S. Talmon; Regensburg: Pustet, 1998), 116: "dem Messiasbild der Evangelien näher als jeder andere Qumrantext."

90. Contrast J. Collins, *Scepter and the Star*, 118; with Fitzmyer, *One Who Is to Come*, 96–97.

91. García Martínez, "Messianische Erwartungen in den Qumranschriften," 185: "Doch all diese Spekulationen sind unnötig, wenn man den Text richtig liest. In ihm erweckt nicht der Messias die Toten und gibt es auch keine Wundertaten, die nicht das Werk Gottes sind. Was der Text uns lehrt, ist dies, das in der Endzeit, in der Zeit des 'Messias,' Gott wie versprochen wunderbare Taten vollbringen und die Auferweckung der Toten [natürlich der Treuen] eines dieser Wunderwerke sein wird."

92. What follows is heavily indebted to an email correspondence with Craig Evans dated 11 October 2007.

93. Chester, *Messiah and Exaltation*, 252.

94. Cf. ibid., 314–15.

(Ezek. 34:8–15); yet what in fact is to happen is that God will send a new David to shepherd his people (Ezek. 34:23–24). Similarly, in Luke's version of Jesus's lament over Jerusalem, we are informed that Jerusalem will be destroyed because the inhabitants rejected Jesus and thus the populace "did not recognize your time of visitation [from God]" (Luke 19:44). The presence of God and the presence of his designated functionary become one and the same. As much is true in 4Q521, I maintain, and any strict bifurcation between what the Messiah does and what the Lord does is a distortion of the literary context and neglects the dynamics of divine intermediary agents.

The implication is that 4Q521 2.12–13 and Luke 7:22/Matt. 11:5 both describe the Messiah as doing a series of deeds drawn from Isaiah, in particular from Isa. 35:5–6 and 61:1. Given this understanding of the signs of restoration from Isaiah, it is highly probable that Jesus regarded his ministry as demonstrating that the messianic signs of deliverance were present, and that forms an all-sufficient answer to the question posed to him by followers of John the Baptist. There are apparent differences between 4Q521 and Luke 7:22/Matt. 11:5, not least of which is the realized element of salvation in Luke 7:22/Matt. 11:5.[95] In view of the commonalities, however, Bockmuehl appropriately concludes: "In light of the prophecy of Isa. 61, Jesus's healings and preaching have a self-authenticating messianic significance, especially given the contemporary interpretations of the Isaianic prophecy."[96]

The Kingdom of God Presupposes a King

Closely related to the Isaianic theme of restoration is the coming of God's kingdom or, more properly, the coming of God as King. There can be little doubt that Jesus's central message was the kingdom of God (e.g., Mark 1:15), though what he meant by "kingdom" is open to some question. But if Jesus did proclaim the kingdom, then a further avenue of investigation is to ask, To what degree did Jesus envisage himself as having a role in the future kingdom, and what role would it be? E. P. Sanders rejects the idea that the historical Jesus claimed to be the Messiah on the grounds of the criterion of Jesus's dissimilarity from the early church and because he regards Mark 8:29–30 and 14:61–62 as historically dubious. Instead, Sanders asserts that during Jesus's lifetime his disciples had already begun to think of him as "king" or as a "viceroy" over the future kingdom of God by virtue of Jesus's teaching that he and his disciples would have a position in that coming kingdom. If Jesus was to return in the future to set up this

95. Cf. Michael Labahn, "The Significance of Signs in Luke 7:22–23 in Light of Isaiah 61 and the Messianic Apocalypse," in *From Prophecy to Testament* (ed. C. A. Evans; Peabody, MA: Hendrickson, 2004), 166–67.

96. Bockmuehl, *This Jesus*, 53.

kingdom, then his disciples would have found it appropriate to think of him as the Messiah after their Easter experience.[97]

Sanders is partly correct here, but he does not go far enough. First, if the disciples were able to infer "Messiah" from "king" (and Jesus set out to portray himself as a humble king in his triumphal entry, as Sanders admits), then why could that inference have not been made during the course of his ministry and before the first Easter? Why could the inference be made only after Easter? Sanders never asks such a question. Second, while "king" and "Messiah" are, strictly speaking, not the same thing, messiahs were often thought to rule as kings and kings were themselves anointed figures (e.g., 1 Sam. 10:1; Ps. 2:2). The dividing line between king and messiah is very thin, and the *titulus* hung on the cross is further proof to that fact. Third, interestingly enough, Nickelsburg argues that the "Son of Man" of Dan. 7 functions as "God's vice-regent."[98] If "Son of Man" was the preferred form of self-reference by Jesus and if it carries this viceroy or vice-regent connotations, then it can be correlated to sayings and actions in the Jesus tradition that expect Jesus to be the future king of God's kingdom. Thus, the Son of Man tradition may confirm the view of Jesus as the royal arbiter of God's kingdom.

A pertinent text for this subject is Luke 22:28–30/Matt. 19:28–29, with its claim that in the future age the disciples will sit on thrones, judging the twelve tribes of Israel. This tradition can be safely said to be authentic given its coherence with the theme of restoration in the sayings tradition and with the institution of the circle of the Twelve.[99] The significance of the logion is that it implies a regathering of Israel as symbolized by the Twelve (see the calling of the Twelve in Mark 3:13–19); this corresponds with Pss. Sol. 17.26, where it is part of the messianic task to reconstitute Israel.[100] More to the point, Jesus stood outside the group and was arguably its leader. Davies and Allison contend: "Who then did he take himself to be? It is hard to avoid the inference that he thought of himself as the leader-to-be of the restored people of God, a destined king."[101]

97. Sanders, *Jesus and Judaism*, 234, 307–8; idem, *Historical Figure of Jesus*, 242–43.

98. Nickelsburg, *Ancient Judaism and Christian Origins*, 103.

99. Cf. Bird, *Jesus and the Origins of the Gentile Mission*, 33–34; and more specifically, Volker Hampel, *Menschensohn und historischer Jesu: Ein Rätselwort als Schlüssel zum messianischen Selbstverständnis Jesu* (Neukirchen-Vluyn: Neukirchener, 1990), 140–51.

100. Charlesworth (*Jesus within Judaism*, 155) is willing, albeit hesitantly, to attribute to Jesus a sense of "messianic self-understanding" in light of Jesus's proclamation of the kingdom, his choosing the twelve disciples as symbolic of Israel, and his attempt to establish the messianic age.

101. Davies and Allison, *Saint Matthew*, 2:599–600. On this same text, Theissen and Merz (*Historical Jesus*, 539–60) think that the disciples "form a messianic collective" and that Jesus "gave the status and dignity of the Messiah to others." Accordingly, "He reshaped the messianic expectation which was focused on an individual into a 'group messianism.'" The supposed democratization of kingship is arguably implied in Isa. 40–55 (Chester, *Messiah and Exalta-*

It is worth considering also Mark 10:35–40, which implies that Jesus is king of the coming kingdom. Commentators frequently regard the story as second- ary and suggest that the section was originally made up of two discrete units, 10:35–40 and 10:41–45, which were fused together at some point in the tradition history. Gundry has offered some cogent arguments for the thematic unity of the passage, principally, that the story moves quite naturally from question to criticism to example without any unnatural seams in the material.[102] The unit coheres with the promise of the disciples judging (= ruling benevolently over) Israel in the future age (Luke 22:29–30/Matt. 19:28). Maurice Casey detects some underlying Semitic elements in the Markan text, which may indicate the presence of a primitive tradition.[103] One has to ask whether the early church would really be up to discrediting the disciples in such an abrupt way when they were normally venerated for their role as companions of Jesus and lead- ers of the church (e.g., the "pillars" of Gal. 2:9, the Acts of John, and more generally Acts 1–12).[104] In this pericope, the disciples begin vying for the key positions in the new "cabinet" that they think is about to be put into effect when this kingdom materializes in the near future. This confirms that the disciples were acutely aware of the prospect of Jesus exercising a reign in that kingdom of God. The circle of disciples also appears to have characterized this kingdom principally in political terms and to have perceived Jesus as the acting regent of a new theocracy. Jesus responds to their request by rejecting the self-aggrandizement and tyrannical expression of power and authority epitomized by Gentile rulers (and those who ruled like Gentiles). The model of leadership he set before them is that of humility and servitude, which is epitomized by the Son of Man. Notably, Jesus does not take the political question and spiritualize it so much as he configures what it means to reign and rule with a different set of values and expectations.

If Jesus saw himself in some sense as the king of God's kingdom, and if that role was expressed within the matrix of Jewish restoration eschatology,

---

tion, 227–28), and the idea of other beings human or semidivine as sharing God's throne was not unknown (e.g., Ps. 89:36–37; Dan. 7:9; Rev. 3:21; 20:4; 1 En. 108.12; 3 En. 10.1; *b. Ḥag.* 14a; *b. Sanh.* 38b). The democratization of the Davidic role and its bestowal upon the entire community potentially has connections to Zech. 9–14; see A. Leske, "Context and Meaning of Zechariah 9:9," *CBQ* 62 (2000): 663–68. From some Second Temple texts we can even speak of a corporate messianology; see further M. A. Elliott, *Survivors of Israel*, 569–614. This is an area of research in desperate need of exploration.

102. Gundry, *Mark*, 581–82; cf. Taylor, *Mark*, 442–43; Craig A. Evans, *Mark 8:27–16:20* (WBC 34B; Nashville: Nelson, 2001), 114–15.

103. Maurice Casey, *Aramaic Sources of Mark's Gospel* (SNTSMS 102; Cambridge: Cam- bridge University Press, 1998), 193–218.

104. Cf. Sanders (*Historical Figure of Jesus*, 189): "This cannot be a later invention. Later everyone thought that Peter was the leading disciple, and the possible primacy of James and John would not have arisen. The story is also somewhat discreditable to them, which makes it even less likely that it is a Christian creation."

which could often include messianism, then we must take seriously the claim that sayings and actions of Jesus that point to a royal role for himself are to be understood in a messianic sense. The only way to avoid that conclusion is either to reject Luke 22:29–30/Matt. 19:28; Mark 10:35–45; and the triumphal entry as inauthentic or else to posit a rigid distinction between the roles of king and Messiah, both of which are needless.

Allusions to David and Solomon

Given the prominence of the themes of kingdom and kingship in Jesus's ministry, it is unsurprising that he periodically refers to regal figures from Israel's past in his teaching. Importantly, this may tell us more of Jesus's perception of his own identity and authority in relation to the kingdom. At several places in the synoptic tradition, Jesus compares himself to figures in the royal dynasty of Israel: to David and Solomon. In a saying probably derived from Q, Jesus announces that in his own work something "greater than Solomon is here" (Luke 11:31/Matt. 12:42).[105] When the Pharisees ask Jesus why his disciples pluck grain on the Sabbath, Jesus responds by noting that David and his companions ate "the bread of the presence" to satisfy their hunger (Mark 2:23–28 = 1 Sam. 21:1–6). The justification offered is that Jesus possesses a similar Davidic authority, which is then correlated with the authority of the Son of Man over the Sabbath. During his ministry in Jerusalem, Jesus reportedly asks a riddle as to how the Messiah can also be the Son of David since David calls the Messiah "Lord" (Mark 12:35–37 = Ps. 110:1). While this is a truly enigmatic passage, it is not repudiating the Davidic sonship of the Messiah; rather, it appears to be stating that the Messiah is *more than a* descendant of David. Elsewhere in the tradition, Jesus is announced as a son of David by supplicants of healing (Mark 10:47–48; Matt. 9:27) and by the pilgrims entering Jerusalem for the Passover (Mark 11:10). In Matthew, the crowds ask, "Can this be the Son of David?" in response to his healing of a mute demoniac (Matt. 12:23). As background to this material, expectations of a messiah from the Davidic line figure prominently in Pss. Sol. 17, the Qumran scrolls (e.g., 4Q161, 4Q174, 4Q252, 4Q285), the rabbinic literature (e.g., *y. Ber.* 2.3), and other writings (T. Jud. 24.1–5).

Links between Jesus and David/Solomon can also be made on other grounds as well.[106] One of the distinguishing characteristics of Jesus's exorcisms is that he connected them to the eschatological inauguration of the

---

105. Cf. discussion in N. T. Wright, *Jesus and the Victory of God*, 535.

106. Cf. D. C. Duling, "Solomon, Exorcism, and the Son of David," *HTR* 68 (1975): 235–52; Bruce D. Chilton, "Jesus *ben* David: Reflections on the Davidssohnfrage," *JSNT* 14 (1982): 88–112; James H. Charlesworth, "The Son of David: Solomon and Jesus (Mark 10:47)," in *The New Testament and Hellenistic Judaism* (ed. P. Borgen and S. Giverson; Aarhus: Aarhus University

kingdom (Mark 3:23–27; Luke 11:20/Matt. 12:28).[107] From Qumran, 4Q510 1.1–9 also associates the kingdom of God with exorcisms, underscoring the eschatological significance of exorcisms in some circles. Moreover, it is in response to Jesus's exorcisms that the messianic question is raised in the minds of the crowds (Matt. 12:22–23).[108] The association comports with the tradition of David (Josephus, *Ant.* 6.166–68; L.A.B 60.1–3) and also Solomon (T. Sol. 1.5–7; Wis. 7:17–21; Josephus, *Ant.* 8.45–47; Tg. Pss. 91) as exorcists.[109] There were many Jewish exorcists in the first century (e.g., Luke 11:19/Matt. 12:27; Acts 19:13), and not all of them were claiming through their activities to inaugurate the kingdom of God or to be the long-awaited heir of the house of David. David was regarded as a prophet, or at least as prophetic in his psalms (11QPs[a] 9–11; Josephus, *Ant.* 6.166; Acts 1:16; 2:25, 30–31; Midrash Tehillim), which accords with Jesus's own prophetic claims (Luke 4:24; John 4:44; Gos. Thom. 31; P.Oxy. 1.6; and Luke 13:33) and the crowds' recognition of his prophetic office (Mark 6:15; 8:28; Matt. 14:5; 21:11, 46).

The Branch of David could also be connected with the "spirit of wisdom" in Isa. 11:2, and the Son of Man is a teacher of wisdom and indwelt by the spirit of wisdom in 1 Enoch (48.7; 49.3; cf. 51.3; 48.1; 49.1).[110] The idea of the king or Messiah as sage has obvious affinities with the tradition of Solomon as Israel's legendary wise king. Jesus's teaching often took the form of aphoristic or proverbial wisdom instruction; he was recognized as a sage by others (e.g., Mark 6:2); he referred to his own ministry as greater than that of Solomon (Luke 11:31/Matt. 12:42); and he spoke of his own vindication as the vindication of "Wisdom" itself (Luke 7:35/Matt. 11:19). Thus, the leadership roles of exorcist, prophet, and sage in Jesus's ministry and teaching can all be connected to royal traditions in Israel's sacred writings.

Jesus's Davidic heritage also figured prominently in early Christian writings.[111] It is part of traditional material found in the Pauline corpus (Rom. 1:3; 2 Tim. 2:8; and Paul had met relatives of Jesus [Gal. 1:19]), and it weighs heavily

---

Press, 1995), 72–87; idem, "Solomon and Jesus: The Son of David in Ante-Markan Traditions," in *Biblical and Humane* (ed. L. Bennett Elder et al.; Atlanta: Scholars Press, 1996), 125–51.

107. Cf. Graham H. Twelftree, *Jesus the Exorcist: A Contribution to the Study of the Historical Jesus* (Peabody, MA: Hendrickson, 1993), 217–24; Meier, *A Marginal Jew*, 2:450.

108. This is one episode where M. de Jonge (*Jesus*, 72) is certainly onto something in positing a link between Jesus as teacher, exorcist, prophet and as a "Son of David." In contrast to M. de Jonge, I would not be prepared to make Jesus's perception of himself as a Son of David and, therefore, as the "anointed of the Lord" as exclusively derivative from his status as a prophet and exorcist. More likely, prophecy/exorcism plus Davidic lineage would have enabled him or others to make that claim.

109. Cf. Witherington, *Christology of Jesus*, 189.

110. On Messiah and wisdom, see also Pss. Sol. 17.23, 29, 35, 37; 18.7.

111. Christoph Burger, *Jesus als Davidssohn: Eine traditionsgeschichtliche Untersuchung* (FRLANT 98; Göttingen: Vandenhoeck & Ruprecht, 1970).

in Matthew's Christology.[112] Jesus's Davidic roots figure prominently in the infancy narratives and genealogies of Luke and Matthew. The Davidic theme occurs in the Benedictus of Zechariah, and it indicates that Jesus's Davidic sonship probably figured prominently in the devotional life of Palestinian Christians (e.g., Luke 1:69); it is also part of the kerygma of Acts (2:24–36; 13:22–27). At the same time, Jesus's Davidic status contributed to the eschatological hopes of Revelation (3:7; 5:5; 22:16). While it is undoubtedly true that Jesus's Davidic heritage was part of the christological reflection of the early church, it seems too widespread and too early to attribute it entirely to post-Easter currents. Hence, it probably goes back to (1) common knowledge of Jesus's lineage as a "son of Joseph," who was a son of David;[113] and (2) the title "Son of David" being part of both the deliberate political rhetoric of Jesus's ministry and sometimes assigned to Jesus by crowds or supplicants of healing. In the words of Albert Schweitzer:

> Hitherto the view has been taken that it was the primitive Christian community which made the Lord into the Son of David because it held him to be the Messiah. It is time to consider seriously whether it was not rather Jesus who held himself to be the Messiah because he was descended from David.[114]

In sum, Jesus's exorcisms and healings probably roused hopes that he was a new prophetic Son of David. The repeated reference to royal figures to whom Jesus compared himself certainly was provocative as well. Taken together, all of this suggests that Jesus deliberately touted himself with royal categories; yet we recognize the qualification that monarchic is not necessarily messianic.

The "I Have Come" Sayings

If the kingdom has come and is coming still, then it is coming precisely through the agency of Jesus and his followers (cf., e.g., Luke 11:20). That leads naturally to the issue of the purpose of Jesus's own coming, including its effects and the nature of his task. An additional factor for our inquiry then is the significance of the "I have come" (ἦλθον) sayings as they relate to a messianic task for Jesus. The formula of coming + purpose is multiply attested in Mark, Q, L, M, and John, which should put us on track for regarding this

112. Lidija Novakovic, *Messiah, the Healer of the Sick: A Study of Jesus as the Son of David in the Gospel of Matthew* (WUNT 2.170; Tübingen: Mohr Siebeck, 2003).

113. Cf. Meier, *A Marginal Jew*, 1:216–19; Theissen and Merz, *Historical Jesus*, 194–96.

114. Schweitzer, *Quest*, 319; see also M. de Jonge (*God's Final Envoy*, 103): "Jesus may have understood himself as a prophetic Son of David called to proclaim the gospel and exorcise demons in order to inaugurate the kingdom, and destined to hold full royal power in the near future. If so, he could regard himself as the Lord's anointed like David, not only in the future, but already during his prophetic work in Galilee."

phrase as a way that Jesus was remembered as speaking of himself.[115] Theissen and Merz do not think that the sayings can be derived exclusively from a post-Easter Christology. The "I have come" material can be easily imagined within Judaism, and accordingly they think it is plausible that Jesus spoke of himself in this manner. They regard Mark 2:17; Luke 7:34; and 12:49–51 as authentic and speculate that Matt. 5:17; Mark 10:45; and Luke 19:10 could have developed in analogy to authentic traditions.[116]

To be fair, the meaning of the sayings is disputed. At stake is whether and to what degree they signify the arrival of a prophet, the coming of a preexistent figure, or the advent of the Messiah.[117] Theissen and Merz suppose that all we can infer from the sayings is that "Jesus had a sense of mission," but they do not try to extrapolate from those sayings what that mission was.[118] Though it is a stretch to regard all of the "I have come" sayings as pertaining to a messianic mission, there are at least three factors that count in favor of seeing several sayings as messianic. First, although Harnack seemed to favor a general and prophetic sense for the majority of these sayings, he recognized that some of them might possess messianic connotations: "Whether the verbs for 'being sent' and 'to come' are to be understood as messianic can only be decided by the context (the prophet also 'is sent' and 'came'); but in religious discourse they always express a sending from God or a coming in a mission from God."[119] As such, I believe that the context and content of several of these sayings can be regarded as signifying a messianic task on the part of Jesus:

> Those who are well have no need of a physician, but those who are sick; I have come to call not the righteous but sinners. (Mark 2:17)

This saying occurs in Mark in a setting where Jesus is quizzed as to why he dines with tax collectors and sinners. Jesus's proverbial response about the physician

115. *Mark as source*: Mark 1:38/Luke 4:43; Mark 2:17/Matt. 9:13/Luke 5:32; Mark 10:45/ Matt. 20:28. *Q as source*: Luke 12:51/Matt. 10:34; Luke 7:34/Matt. 11:19. *L as source*: Luke 12:49; 19:10. *M as source*: Matt. 5:17; 10:35. *John as source*: John 5:43; 6:38; 7:28; 8:14; 9:39; 10:10; 12:27, 46–47; 15:22; 16:28.

116. Theissen and Merz, *Historical Jesus*, 525–26; and also Kim, *Son of Man*, 40–43. On inauthenticity, see Rudolf Bultmann (*History of the Synoptic Tradition* [trans. J. Marsh; New York: Harper & Row, 1963], 152–55).

117. On the background to these sayings, see Simon J. Gathercole, *The Pre-existent Son: Recovering the Christologies of Matthew, Mark, and Luke* (Grand Rapids: Eerdmans, 2006), 95–147; A. H. I. Lee, *From Messiah to Preexistent Son: Jesus' Self-Consciousness and Early Christian Exegesis of the Messianic Psalms* (WUNT 2.192; Tübingen: Mohr Siebeck, 2005), 181–201.

118. Theissen and Merz, *Historical Jesus*, 526.

119. Adolf von Harnack, " 'Ich bin gekommen': Die ausdrücklichen Selbstzeugnisse Jesu über den Zweck seiner Sendung und seines Kommens," *ZTK* 22 (1912): 1: "Ob die Verba 'gesandt sein,' 'kommen' messianisch zu verstehen sind, darüber kann nur der Kontext entscheiden (auch der Prophet 'ist gesandt' und 'ist gekommen'); aber immer drücken sie in der religiösen Sprache eine Sendung von der Gottheit her bzw. ein Kommen in ihrem Auftrage aus."

and the sick (variations of which were well known in ancient literature, e.g., Plutarch, *Mor.* 230F; Dio Chrysostom, *Orat.* 8.5) orients his ministry toward those whose covenant membership was thought questionable. At one level this represents a subversion of messianic hopes since the Messiah was supposed to drive out "sinners" (e.g., Pss. Sol. 17.23, 36; 4 Ezra 12.32; 1 En. 48.8), not embrace them in intimate fellowship. On the other hand, Jesus's action can be said to be entirely congruent with such hopes. In 1 Enoch the Messiah is the one in whom the "Gentiles" (the quintessential sinners) and those who are "sick in their hearts" find hope (48.4). The text even relates the Messiah's mission to such activities: "For this purpose he became the Chosen One" (48.6).

The pericope can also be linked to the messianic banquet. It seems that dining with "sinners" was one of the distinguishing features of the ministry of the historical Jesus. These meals were an enacted parable of the openness of the kingdom, and, quite shockingly, they were also an anticipation of the messianic banquet, given the eschatological significance of communal meals in renewal movements. Thus, "Jesus's action in 'reclining' with sinners was much like serving the figurative *hors d'oeuvres* of the messianic feast and foreshadowing exactly who would be vindicated in the renewed Israel that he was creating around himself."[120] Jesus *comes* and he *calls* sinners (i.e., those outside the covenant and scorned by religious leaders) to participate in the messianic feast, and one's participation in it is determined by one's relation to him.[121]

> I came to bring fire to the earth, and how I wish it were already kindled! I have a baptism with which to be baptized, and what stress I am under until it is completed! Do you think that I have come to bring peace to the earth? No, I tell you, but rather division! (Luke 12:49–51; cf. Gos. Thom. 10, 82)

> Do not think that I have come to bring peace to the earth; I have not come to bring peace, but a sword. (Matt. 10:34; cf. Gos. Thom. 16)

Several scholars posit a messianic sense to these logia.[122] The Lukan text is perhaps indebted to Dan. 7:10 and the coming of the "stream of fire," which shows that the eschatological woes must precede the exaltation and vindication of the saints.[123] In Luke 12:49 the reference to "fire" could denote either judgment (e.g., Amos 1–2) or purification (e.g., Mal. 3:2–3). But a reference

---

120. Bird, *Origins of the Gentile Mission*, 105.

121. Cf. François Bovon (*Luke 1* [trans. Christine M. Thomas; Hermeneia; Minneapolis: Fortress, 2002], 190): "The verb ἔρχομαι ('I have come,' 'I am here') has messianic significance here and, in the aorist (Mark, Matthew) as well as the perfect (Luke), looks back over the entire life of Jesus."

122. Cf., e.g., Witherington, *Christology*, 120–24; Hengel, "Messiah of Israel," 68–69; W. Grimm, *Weil ich dich liebe: Die Verkündigung Jesu und Deuterojesaja* (Bern: Herbert Lang, 1976), 85–86.

123. Cf. Pitre, *Jesus*, 395–96.

to the former seems more plausible given that in Matthew's parallel version the judgment associated with the messianic "sword" stands in contrast to the era of messianic "peace" (cf., e.g., Isa. 9:7; 34:5; 66:16; Ezek. 21; 1 En. 63.11; 91.12). Arens detects in the Matthean version

> a Christological outlook wherein Jesus appears as Messiah. His coming was the dawn of the messianic times which are marked by acceptance/rejection and consequent judgment. It is a time of decision. To bring the sword appears as a circumloquium for the end-times which precedes the peace itself. The perspective is therefore highly eschatological. It assumes the understanding of the "who" who speaks and concentrates on the "what" he provokes. With the inauguration of the Kingdom come the adversities: a messianic paradox brought about by a paradoxical figure.[124]

"I have come to cast fire" and (in effect) "I have come with a sword" then have a messianic function. In 4 Ezra similar actions are undertaken by the Son of Man, who "sent forth from his mouth something like a stream of fire" (13.10); in 1 Enoch the Son of Man drives out kings to where the "sword shall abide in their midst" (63.11). It appears that, in continuity with the message of John the Baptist (Luke 3:9, 16–17/Matt. 3:10–12), Jesus believed that it was his role to initiate the coming eschatological judgment.[125] That poses a moment of crisis-decision for the nation as to whether it will choose to accept or reject God's envoy and heed his message.

> For the Son of Man came to seek out and to save the lost. (Luke 19:10)

This logion may or may not be an independent saying that found its place in the narrative about Zacchaeus in Luke 19:1–10. The obvious point of contact that this saying has with messianic hopes is that the devout expected the Messiah to come and regather Israel (e.g., Pss. Sol. 17.26) or expected God to do it at the time of the new Davidic king (Ezek. 34:11–24; Shemoneh 'Esreh 10, 15). In context, the saying is about how "messianic salvation" has come to Zacchaeus and his household.[126]

A second factor in favor of a messianic reading of several of the "I have come" statements is that they can be related to descriptions of the Messiah as "the coming one" (ὁ ἐρχόμενος). The substantive participle is used in the triumphal entry (Mark 11:9/Matt. 21:9/Luke 19:38/John 12:13), in Q in relation to the question put to Jesus by the followers of John the Baptist (Luke

---

124. E. Arens, *The HΛΘON-Sayings in the Synoptic Tradition: A Historio-Critical Investigation* (Göttingen: Vandenhoeck & Ruprecht, 1976), 86.

125. On the continuity between Jesus and the Baptist at this point, see Dunn, *Jesus Remembered*, 368.

126. G. B. Caird, *Saint Luke* (Harmondsworth, UK: Penguin, 1963), 208.

7:19–20/Matt. 11:2–3), in another logion from Q pertaining to Jesus as the rejected prophet (Luke 13:34–35/Matt. 23:37–39), and also in the Johannine tradition (John 1:15, 27; 6:14; 11:27). Only the next to last of these seems devoid of any messianic meaning as it associates Jesus with a line of prophets rejected by the Judean populace.

A messianic meaning is certainly connected to the "coming one" in the triumphal entry and the Q material about Jesus and the Baptist. In the triumphal entry, we have Jesus most probably entering Jerusalem in deliberate fulfillment of Zech. 9:9. The acclamation by the crowd is drawn from Ps. 118:25–26 and includes a reference to "David" in Matthew and Mark's account. In the Lukan version the "one coming" is explicitly defined as the "coming king." John calls this figure quite explicitly "the King of Israel," and in the Markan version the "coming one" stands in parallel to the "coming kingdom." Here the "coming one" is a figure of David's line, a royal king, who establishes God's kingdom and enters Jerusalem as the humble shepherd king promised in Scripture. In material derived probably from Q (Luke 7:19–20/Matt. 11:2–3), a question is put to Jesus by followers of the Baptist: "Are you are the one to come, or should we expect another?" That this is a messianic question seems apparent from the answer, which contains a collection of verses from Isaiah indicating the signs of restoration (26:19; 29:18–19; 61:1). Matthew finds the impetus for the question in the Baptist's hearing about Jesus performing the "deeds of the Messiah" (Matt. 11:2), and we have an analogous description of the blessings of the messianic era in a text from Qumran (4Q521 2.1–14). While "coming one" may not have been a technical title for the Messiah, it was appropriate for referring to the Messiah.

A third factor is evidence from other sources about the Messiah as one who "comes." According to the Greek text of Aquila, ὁ ἐρχόμενος in Hab. 2:3 is a messianic figure. In the version of Dan. 7:13 in Theodotion (Θ), the Son of Man's "coming" is described with the periphrastic construction ἐρχόμενος ἦν instead of the imperfect verb ἤρχετο as found in the LXX. At Qumran, the verb בוא (bôʾ, to come in) can refer to the coming eschatological age, the coming of God, and also to the coming of the Messiahs or the eschatological prophet (4Q252 5.3; CD-B 19.10–11; 1QS 9.11).[127] In Acts 7:52 we have a reference to ἡ ἔλευσις τοῦ δικαίου (the coming of the Righteous One), and "Righteous One" is a title for the Messiah in the Similitudes of 1 Enoch (38.2; 53.6).[128] While not all "coming" figures are the Messiah, the Messiah is a coming figure. The broader contexts of these documents inform us whether the "coming one" or someone who says "I have come" is a messiah or not.

Let me state clearly what I am not arguing for. I am not insinuating that all the "I have come" sayings are essentially messianic. I am not suggesting that "I

127. Gathercole, *Pre-existent Son*, 111–12.
128. There might also be a messianic connotation to δίκαιος in Acts 3:14; 22:14; and 1 John 2:1.

have come" equals "I am *the coming one*" every time. I am not implying that all "coming" figures are necessarily messianic. What I am arguing for is that the Messiah was known as the "one to come," and the "I have come" sayings of Jesus are at least reminiscent of that designation. When Jesus says "I have come," he often sets forth a purpose that could be associated with the "coming one."

Simon Gathercole objects to the messianic interpretation of the "I have come" sayings. He maintains that the "I have come" sayings emphasize the goal of coming rather than the arrival of someone to fulfill expectations about a certain figure who would come. Gathercole acknowledges that there could be some grounds for rooting the sayings in a messianic self-consciousness where a specific purpose is given, such as "to cast fire on the earth" and so forth. But on the whole, he contends that there is little here that points specifically to a messianic function and that it is hard to see how the concept of messiahship could account for all the goals of the advent. On his thinking, the coming from *A* to *B* itself does not have anything specifically to do with a Messiah or tell us anything about the identity of the one who comes. What is more, the purposes for the coming are broad enough to include angelic, prophetic, or divine consciousness too.[129] I concur with Gathercole that the "I have come" sayings are not technical terms for a messianic advent; they can refer to other functions and purposes, and I am willing to posit preexistence as perhaps implied by some of the sayings.[130] Yet I doubt whether there is a lack of specific messianic functions in some of the sayings. In my mind, foreshadowing the messianic banquet (Mark 2:17), inaugurating the final tribulation (Luke 12:49–51/Matt. 10:34), and seeking to save the lost sheep of Israel (Luke 19:10) are not lacking in their messianic specification. Nor does a messianic sense of "I have come" need to emphasize the fact of the coming in order to be messianic. The coming of the coming one only becomes the fulfillment of certain expectations once the purpose is set forth and is related to a messianic function or office. Thus, I am slightly more sanguine than Gathercole in attaching a messianic sense to some sayings.

Conclusion

This chapter has examined several threads and themes from the Jesus tradition that appear to be invested with messianic significance. The overall impression one

---

129. Gathercole, *Pre-existent Son*, 107–8.

130. E.g., a preexistent Messiah could be connected with a number of texts, including Mic. 5:2; Dan. 7:13–14; 1 En. 39.6–7; 46.1–4; 48.3, 6; 62.7; 4 Ezra 7.28; 13.25–26; 2 Bar. 30.1; Odes Sol. 41.15; Justin Martyr, *Dial.* 49; *b. Pesaḥ.* 54a; *b. Ned.* 39b; Pesiq. Rab. 33.6; 36.1. Though the notion of a preexistent Messiah may be a late and Christian idea, Schürer (*History of the Jewish People*, 2:522) wrote: "At the same time, such ideas are fully comprehensible from Old Testament premises." See further Gathercole, *Pre-existent Son*, 234–38; and Lee, *Messiah to Preexistent Son*, 99–114.

gathers is that Jesus possessed an acute sense of his own authority and purpose that clearly edged in the direction of messianic categories. This is all located in a certain underlying story—a story told in action, word, and symbol—concerning the arrival of God's kingdom and the transformation of Israel. His purpose and identity are conveyed through his self-reference as בר־אנשא, which is in some sense particularized and associated with the authority of the enigmatic human figure mentioned in Dan. 7:13.

We have found further grounds for identifying Jesus as an "anointed one" given the strong similarities between 4Q521 and Luke 7:22/Matt. 11:5. Jesus's preaching of the kingdom, the epicenter of his proclamation and praxis, implied his own regal role in the new reordering of power that was being implemented. Jesus also entered into scribal debates about the identity of the Son of David and arguably related the coming Davidide to priestly and monarchic roles. Some of the "I have come" sayings ascribe to Jesus the role of a divine agent that rehearses various messianic traditions.

None of this, in whole or part, establishes beyond all reasonable doubt that Jesus saw himself as *the* Messiah as Christians customarily define the word. Yet umbilically related to each saying and pericope that I have analyzed are the themes of kingship, kingdom, election, and national restoration. Jesus was defining his own role in the saving reign of God that was already bursting in among the political and religious realities of Galilee and Judea. He was also redefining ideas of covenant boundaries, covenant loyalty, and eschatological hopes as held by his contemporaries. The nature and scope of God's kingdom and the concomitant issue of kingship were being delineated in light of a new way of telling Israel's story: where Israel was now, where it was going, and how and by whom the divine promises of deliverance would become a reality.

We thus are firmly in the zone of a messianic claim even if the substance of that claim has not yet been fully verbalized or confronted. As for the moment when the messianic question came to its gripping climax, we must look ahead further in the Gospels to the political, religious, and social issues surrounding Jesus's death in Jerusalem and the riveting aftershocks that it had for the earliest Christian groups.

5

Messiah Jesus—a Crucified Messiah?

T he late Raymond Brown's magisterial work *The Death of the Messiah* is arguably the most thorough and careful examination of the passion narratives in print. Despite the title of the book, however, Brown himself did not think that Jesus claimed to be a messianic figure except perhaps by refusing to deny accusations of having made messianic claims at his trial. Through his seminal essay "The Crucified Messiah," N. A. Dahl was another exegete who reintroduced the issue of messiahship back into the passion narratives for historians of Christianity and made the *titulus* determinative for the origin of a specifically Christian messianism. While I strongly disagree with Dahl and Brown, they are entirely correct to regard the execution of Jesus and the events leading up to it as the definitive point where the topic of Jesus's messianic intentions were brought to the surface by the Jerusalem authorities. In my view, several questions remain to be adequately answered: How did the messianic question arise at Jesus's trial? How did Jesus's actions in Jerusalem relate to his activities in Galilee and Judea? Did Israel's sacred traditions provide any pattern or script that influenced what Jesus thought he was doing in Jerusalem? How did the Christian movement come to venerate someone who, from all legal accounts, was a failed messianic pretender and a false prophet? I shall try to address these questions by moving along chronologically and identifying how Jesus's definition of messiahship overlapped with his conception of the suffering-vindicated Son of Man. A close study of Jesus's final days in Jerusalem enables us to retrieve what Jesus thought God would do for Israel, how God would do it, and Jesus's own role in the divine plan as an anointed agent.

Peter's Confession at Caesarea Philippi

Commentators have long noticed the major turning point that takes place in the Markan narrative when Jesus and his disciples come to Caesarea Philippi (Mark 8:27–30). The climax of the pericope is when Peter replies to Jesus, "You are the Messiah," after which point the whole narrative then becomes oriented toward the Markan Jesus's forthcoming passion. The pressing issue is whether or not Peter did in fact make this confession about Jesus and, if authentic, how Jesus responded to this designation.

First, regarding authenticity, Dahl is one of many scholars who regard the episode as a "secondary interpretation,"[1] and Sanders calls it "dubious historically."[2] Jens Schröter contends that in Peter's confession of Mark 8:29, "Mark ties together two lines of christological development in early Christianity by linking the Christ-confession of the pre-Pauline tradition with the Jesus tradition."[3] This is quite understandable: after all, the episode is integral to the plot and tension that has been developed in the Markan narrative as people ask, "Who is Jesus?" and it accelerates the story to its climactic ending. The confession itself is christologically significant for Mark and for the first Christians (significant both by virtue of the title confessed, "Messiah," and the person who first connected the dots, Peter). Matthew expands the confession, making it far more vivid, triumphalistic, almost iconic, and it explicitly cements Peter's authority in the church (Matt. 16:17–19).[4]

All this must be placed in juxtaposition with further observations pertaining to the possible authenticity of the episode:[5]

1. There is further attestation in the Johannine tradition that appears to be independent of the synoptic accounts, given the differences in setting and contents (John 6:67–71).[6]

2. Questions and conjecture about who Jesus was, or what role in the order of things he was attempting to play, were already raised by his contempo-

---

1. Dahl, "Crucified Messiah," 40.

2. Sanders, *Jesus and Judaism*, 307; idem, *Historical Figure of Jesus*, 241–42.

3. Jens Schröter, *Jesus und die Anfänge der Christologie* (Neukirchen-Vluyn: Neukirchener, 2001), 166: "Indem Mk dies tut, bindet er zwei Linien christologischer Entwicklung im Urchristentum zusammen, indem er das Christusbekenntnis der vorpaulinischen Tradition mit der Jesusüberlieferung verknüpft, die offensichtlich weniger am Christusbekenntnis- als am Menschensohn-Ausdruck orientiert war."

4. For a defense of the authenticity of the Matthean version, see B. F. Meyer, *Aims of Jesus*, 185–97; Davies and Allison, *Saint Matthew*, 2:602–15. See the overall discussion of the text in Stanley E. Porter, *Studies in the Greek New Testament* (New York: Lang, 1996), 102–23.

5. On authenticity, cf. Taylor, *Mark*, 374–75; Gundry, *Mark*, 442–45; N. T. Wright, *Jesus and the Victory of God*, 528–30; Dunn, *Jesus Remembered*, 644–45; Richard Bauckham, *Jesus and the Eyewitnesses: The Gospels as Eyewitness Testimony* (Grand Rapids: Eerdmans, 2006), 165–79.

6. Cf. Gos. Thom. 13, where the central figure in the scene is Thomas and the narration sets Thomas over and against Matthew and Peter in terms of his superior grasp of who Jesus is.

raries (Mark 6:15; 8:27). There remains nothing inherently implausible about the question put to the disciples in Mark 8:27 amid this public speculation about Jesus's perceived role. If, as I have argued, the messianic question has pre-Easter roots, then the question itself would have come up at some point in Jesus's travels and, most likely, in private with his closest followers, who had left families and property to follow him. Along this line, Schweitzer makes an interesting point that the answers given to Jesus's question by the disciples and by Peter were probably spurred on by Jesus's identification of John the Baptist as Elijah (Matt. 11:14; cf. the post-transfiguration question about Elijah in Mark 9:11–13).[7] No one could recognize Elijah in the Baptist unless he knew also of the Messiah as the one coming after Elijah. Someone with such knowledge could easily be suspected of knowing the Messiah or else be the Messiah himself. It thus makes sense that the answer to "Who do men/you say that I am?" has shifted from Baptist/Elijah to Jesus as the Messiah or else from the eschatological forerunner to the eschatological figure.

3. Another factor to add, in terms of plausibility, is that the question and answer about Jesus's identity in Mark 8:27–30 is different from the trial scene in Mark 14:61–62. The trial scene includes a messianic question and a messianic affirmation in a fairly straightforward order, and Jesus is finally revealed as the Messiah. But a much different narrative dynamic occurs in Mark 8:27–30, which runs like this:

a. "Who do men say that I am?"
b. Nonmessianic answers
c. "Who do you say that I am?"
d. Messianic answer
e. Warning not to tell anyone of the messianic answer, and the beginning of the doctrine of the suffering Son of Man

One can imagine the trial scene in 14:61–62 as comprising a creative effort to get Jesus to affirm his messianic identity, especially when posed in the simple question-answer format.[8] However, to have Jesus initiate a nonmessianic question that eventually receives a messianic answer and then to have that answer qualified, the qualification rejected by a venerated apostle, and the same apostle scandalously rebuked and shamed—all this seems to be a rather convoluted path for a makeshift christological confession pressed into a pre-Easter context. There were simpler ways of expressing Jesus's messiahship by Mark or by the originators of the tradition if they had wanted to do so.

7. Schweitzer, *Quest*, 342–44.
8. Cf. the questions put to John the Baptist in John 1:19–28, which has a similar device of simple question and answer to determine the Baptist's identity and eschatological role.

4. While the unique features of the Matthean account may be redactional and dependent upon Mark 8:27–30, there may also be a conflation of traditional material. Matthew conceivably could have combined Mark's account with traditions from Q or M. At any rate the themes of sonship, kingship, and restoring the eschatological people of God generally cohere with the thematic pattern of the historical Jesus's ministry and teaching. Davies and Allison declare: "When Mark, in Mk 14.53–65, and Matthew, in 16.13–20, made Jesus [to be] Son and Christ and builder of a new community or temple, they were not playing fast and loose with the tradition but rather being faithful to it."[9]

Second, according to Mark, Peter's confession is neither lauded nor rejected by Jesus.[10] Charles Moule wrote: "It is frequently said, indeed, that, at Caesarea Philippi, Jesus refused the title Christ. But Mark certainly does not say so."[11] The confession by Peter that Jesus is the Messiah is certainly not rejected, but it is met with an unexpected response as Jesus seeks to redefine the meaning of "Messiah" in line with a different string of values and along the thread of a different messianic story, one related to the enigmatic "Son of Man."[12] The injunction to silence is significant *theologically* because the divinely given secret of the identity of the Messiah has been revealed to the elect circle, and that secret must not be disclosed further until the appointed time. Consequently, those in the Jesus circle are now the custodians of an apocalyptic secret.[13] The injunction to silence is significant *politically* in the sense of Jesus wishing to keep his kingly claims well below the radar of Herod Antipas's security apparatus (which makes sense also for the locale in Caesarea Philippi, in the outer rim of Galilean territory and in the tetrarchy of Philip rather than of Antipas).[14] This is a real messianic secret, not as a Markan or pre-Markan

9. Davies and Allison, *Saint Matthew*, 2:600.

10. Several scholars propose that the rebuke "Get behind me, Satan!" was originally Jesus's response to Peter's confession, "You are the Messiah." In the words of Mowinckel (*He That Cometh*, 449–50), "The Jewish Messianic idea was the temptation of Satan, which he had to reject." For discussion, cf. Cullmann, *Christology*, 122–24; Dinkler, "Peter's Confession and the Satan Saying," 169–202; Charlesworth, "Messianology to Christology," 12; Reginald H. Fuller, *The Foundations of New Testament Christology* (New York: Scribner, 1965), 109; Theissen and Merz, *Historical Jesus*, 539; N. T. Wright, *Jesus and the Victory of God*, 529n182. Yet such a tradition-historical reconstruction is quite unprovable.

11. C. F. D. Moule, *The Origins of Christology* (Cambridge: Cambridge University Press, 1977), 33.

12. Dunn points out that this redefinition goes back to Jesus ("Messianic Ideas," 375–76), and we should admit that redefinition does not require complete repudiation.

13. Cf. Knight, *Jesus*, 138–45.

14. Fredriksen (*Jesus of Nazareth*, 248) asserts that if Jesus did claim the role and title of Messiah for himself while in Galilee, then "Antipas would surely have acted long before Pilate did." While that is perhaps an exaggeration, she is quite right about what Herod Antipas would do if a known messianic contender was in his vicinity. Yet the attempt to seize Jesus is exactly

invention, but as a genuine historical occurrence. What this might suggest is that Jesus identified the role of Messiah with a different set of categories than that of his disciples. One must wonder if ideas from other sacred traditions led him to place the messianic vocation within a matrix of restoration eschatology, vicarious suffering, and the onset of the final tribulation.[15] This is something that became more apparent in the final days of his life.

The Anointing of Jesus at Bethany

The story of the anonymous woman who anoints Jesus at a meal occurs in all four Gospels (Mark 14:3–9; Matt. 26:6–13; Luke 7:36–50; John 12:1–8) and is attested also in Ignatius (Ign. *Eph.* 17.2). All accounts of the story agree that Jesus was anointed with a portion of expensive perfume during a meal. Kathleen Corley argues for the authenticity of this story on the grounds that (1) it has wide attestation in the tradition even if the setting is unclear;[16] (2) it coheres with the tradition of Jesus eating and drinking with "tax collectors and sinners"; (3) Jesus's approval of the woman's actions is consistent with Jesus's compassionate attitude toward women and outcasts, as reported elsewhere in the tradition; and (4) the very presence of a woman at the meal could suggest impropriety or sexual innuendo, which custodians of the tradition would be unlikely to invent.[17]

A pertinent question is whether the anointing was in any sense messianic. A number of scholars answer this question in the negative and point out that Mark's interpretation of the event relates it to Jesus's death, not explicitly to Jesus's messianic identity. Quite legitimately, one can point out that anointing the head was common at banquets, and prophets and priests could also be anointed

---

what we find in Luke 13:31–32. Why were Antipas's security forces after Jesus then? If we follow Fredriksen's line of thought, it was probably because Jesus had made (or was perceived to have made) kinglike claims. Jesus's itinerant movements across various political frontiers (Galilee, Judea, Samaria, Decapolis, Tyre, Sidon, and the tetrarchy of Philip) were probably for the purpose of keeping aloof from crowds and cohorts of infantry. On Jesus as Messiah in Galilee, see Sean Freyne, "A Galilean Messiah?" *ST* 55 (2001): 198–218.

15. Cf. Schweitzer, *Quest*, 347.

16. Mark, Matthew, and John place the story at the beginning of the Passion Narrative, while Luke's setting is indeterminate.

17. Kathleen E. Corley, "The Anointing of Jesus in the Synoptic Tradition: An Argument for Authenticity," *JSHJ* 1 (2003): 61–72. Bultmann (*History of the Synoptic Tradition*, 37) regards the story in Mark as authentic up to v. 8. Vermes (*Authentic Gospel*, 300–301) thinks Luke's account is the most original. Robert W. Funk and Roy W. Hoover (*The Five Gospels: The Search for the Authentic Words of Jesus* [San Francisco: Harper Collins, 1997], 115–16) assert that a female intruder may have anointed Jesus during a symposium, but they doubt whether any of the words preserved can be traced back to Jesus. Similar is Gerd Lüdemann (*Jesus after 2000 Years* [trans. John Bowden; London: SCM, 2000], 94), who regards the historical yield of Mark 14:3–7 as "nil" but says it might reflect the closeness of Jesus to a notorious woman in Galilee (see Luke 7:36–50).

in biblical tradition.[18] Others find reason for supposing that a messianic sense is both the original meaning of the event and what Mark tacitly communicates.[19] It is my contention that the episode makes a furtive connection between Jesus's messiahship and passion at both the horizon of Mark's narrative and in its original historical context.[20] First, Mark places the story in his passion narrative (Mark 14–16), and it should be linked with his theological leitmotiv: the messianic task entails rejection, suffering, and death. By sandwiching the story between the plot of the chief priests against Jesus (Mark 14:1–2) and Judas's promise to betray Jesus to the chief priests (Mark 14:10–11), the political nature of the event becomes apparent. Mark's readers would have assumed the priests' alarm at this act since kings were anointed figures in the Old Testament (e.g., 1 Sam. 10:1; 12:3; 16:1, 13; 1 Kings 1:39; 19:15–16; Pss. 2:2; 89:20). The scene explains why the high priest posed the messianic question to Jesus at his trial (Mark 14:61–62).[21] Second, on the historical horizon, Jesus's anointing, his entry into Jerusalem, his demonstration in the temple—all present a consistent pattern of symbolic messianic actions that were deliberately provocative and confirmed to his followers his messianic status. Moreover, that messianic identity is then linked to a messianic mission that will require suffering on the part of the Messiah (dissimilar to Judaism), and that association is what ultimately triggers Judas's defection (plausibility of consequence).

The most significant objection one can raise against a messianic anointing in Mark 14:3–8 is not whether the anointing took place or whether Mark ascribes an implicit messianic sense to it—I take those points as given—but rather it is the observation that messianic figures appearing on the scene do not have to be anointed: they simply appear as already-anointed persons.[22] That calls into question the rationale for an anointing of Jesus as Messiah because, to his followers at least, he is the "Anointed One" by virtue of his coming as the eschatological deliverer whose activities corresponded *in varying degrees* to known leadership profiles such as the Davidic healer, the postexilic shepherd of Israel, the announcer and chief agent of God's kingdom, the prophet, and perhaps even a priestly anointed one as well. To anoint the "Anointed One" is a metaphorical redundancy; it is something of an anomaly when done outside a prophetic circle (e.g., as Samuel anointed David) and away from the cultus of the temple, where kings were normally anointed. While this objection may

18. Cf., e.g., J. K. Elliott, "The Anointing of Jesus," *ExpT* 85 (1973–74): 105–7; Gundry, *Mark*, 813; R. T. France, *The Gospel of Mark* (NIGTC; Grand Rapids: Eerdmans 2002), 552; Corley, "Anointing of Jesus," 66–67.

19. Cf., e.g., Edwin K. Broadhead, *Prophet, Son, Messiah: Narrative Form and Function in Mark 14–16* (JSNTSup 97; Sheffield: Sheffield Academic Press, 1997), 37n2; Evans, *Mark 8:27–16:20*, 360; Bauckham, *Jesus and the Eyewitnesses*, 191–92.

20. Michael F. Bird, "The Crucifixion of Jesus as the Fulfillment of Mark 9:1," *TrinJ* 24 (2003): 29.

21. Cf. Bauckham, *Jesus and the Eyewitnesses*, 191–93.

22. Jürgen Becker, *Jesus of Nazareth*, 192.

not be insurmountable to an original messianic sense for the anointing, I think it is a significant one.[23]

The Triumphal Entry and Demonstration in the Temple

Historical Jesus studies frequently take greater account of the sayings tradition than of the actions of Jesus as recorded in the Gospels (particularly true of those who focus on a Gospel of Thomas–Q stratum). But roles and actions are just as important if not more so in determining the purposes, aims, and objectives of individuals of antiquity.[24] The most significant event of Jesus's final week was undoubtedly his death. Yet of paramount importance in the lead up to that event was his entry into Jerusalem and his action in the temple, which can be integrated into the historical circumstances surrounding his death. Here I am prepared to argue that it was the implicit messianic nature of these two actions that finally forced the Judean leadership to move against him as they recognized the potential incendiary nature of his claim in their sociopolitical context.

The Triumphal Entry

The authenticity of the triumphal entry is (as with most things in this field) disputed. Bultmann regarded it is as presuppositional absurdity to think that Jesus would set out to deliberately fulfill Zech. 9:9 and that his riding the donkey was immediately perceived as messianic by the crowds.[25] Yet to perceive Jesus as setting out to echo or allude to Zech. 9:9 is no more implausible than the acts of the sign prophets, who tried to emulate signs related to a new exodus beginning in the wilderness and accompanied by divine miracles (*Ant.* 20.167–68 = Exod. 8–16; Ps. 78:15–16; Isa. 40:1–3; 41:18–19; 43:19–21; 51:3; Hos. 2:14–23), starting a new conquest (*Ant.* 20.97–98 = Josh. 3–4), looking for a theophany of the Lord to occur in the temple (*War* 6.285–86 = Ezek. 43:4–5; Mal. 3:1), and expecting the walls of Jerusalem to fall down like those of Jericho (*Ant.* 20.169–72 = Josh. 5:13–6:27). As for the problem of an immediate perception on the part of the crowds, many Galileans and Judeans knew their Scriptures, and many knew their history and could sense the similarity to Maccabean entries into Jerusalem (1 Macc. 4:19–25; 5:45–54; 10:86; 13:49–51; and note the entries of Antigonus [*War* 1.73–74; *Ant.* 13.304–6] and Archelaus [*Ant.* 17.194–239]). The disciples already thought that Jesus was "king" in some sense, and they might have

---

23. A possible counterpoint is that the woman saw her action in anointing Jesus as prophetic. See Elizabeth Schüssler Fiorenza, "Re-visioning Christian Origins: *In Memory of Her* Revisited," in *Christian Origins: Worship, Belief, and Society* (ed. K. J. O'Mahoney; JSNTSup 241; Sheffield: Sheffield Academic Press, 2003), 240–42.

24. Cf. Bockmuehl, *This Jesus*, 52; Knight, *Jesus*, 136.

25. Bultmann, *History of the Synoptic Tradition*, 261–62; cf. Lüdemann, *Jesus*, 75–76.

started the accolades rolling themselves in recognizing the importance of the occasion.

Sanders is slightly more subdued in his doubts. Though entering Jerusalem as king would explain Jesus's execution as "king of the Jews," he objects that if Jesus really did enter Jerusalem in this way, then why did the Roman authorities take several days to move against him. He proposes: "Perhaps the event took place but was a small occurrence which went unnoticed. Perhaps only a few disciples unostentatiously dropped their garments in front of the ass, . . . only a few quietly murmured 'Hosanna.' "[26] Sanders's objections are understandable but not insurmountable. If (as Sanders posits)[27] there were around 300,000 pilgrims entering Jerusalem during that week, Jesus's entry on a donkey might hardly have been noticeable. The Jerusalem Talmud says that before the Passover, ass drivers did a flourishing business in carrying wealthy pilgrims up to the temple mount (*y. Ber.* 13d). The Roman soldiers garrisoned in Jerusalem during the festival were housed in the Antonian fortress and focused on the security of the temple precincts (*War* 5.243–45), which was normally the locus of incidents (e.g., *War* 2.223–27; *Ant.* 20.106–12).

The citation of Zech. 9 in the triumphal entry might seem too good to be true, and one may think that we have here the hand of Christian editors in creating a messianic legend based on archetypes drawn from the Old Testament.[28] Christians certainly did interpret Jesus's actions to suit their own theological and sociological interests. Even so, that interpretive act sometimes consisted of making explicit what was already implicit in the story line, and the triumphal entry is a good example of exactly that, with Matthew (21:4–5) and John (12:14–15) adding explicit quotes of Zech. 9:9, quotes not found in either Mark or Luke's accounts. There can be absolutely no reason why Jesus could not model an action based on events found in Israel's sacred traditions. In fact, several threads from Zechariah may have been programmatic for Jesus. Taken together, the use of Zech. 9:9 (triumphal entry), Zech. 14:21 (temple episode), and Zech. 13:7 (passion prediction) provide a coherent and plausible context indicating that Zechariah was the script that Jesus sought to follow in his final days in Jerusalem.[29]

26. Sanders, *Jesus and Judaism*, 306; idem, *Historical Figure of Jesus*, 254; cf. similarly Fredriksen, *Jesus of Nazareth*, 242–43; John Dominic Crossan and Jonathan L. Reed, *Excavating Jesus: Beneath the Stones, behind the Texts* (San Francisco: Harper Collins, 2001), 262.

27. Sanders, *Historical Figure of Jesus*, 249–51.

28. Cf. Funk and Hoover, *Five Gospels*, 97.

29. F. F. Bruce, "The Book of Zechariah and the Passion Narrative," *BJRL* 43 (1961): 336–53; R. T. France, *Jesus and the Old Testament* (London: Tyndale, 1971), 103–10; N. T. Wright, *Jesus and the Victory of God*, 586–87, 599–600; Craig A. Evans, "Jesus and Zechariah's Messianic Hope," in *Authenticating the Activities of Jesus* (ed. B. D. Chilton and C. A. Evans; Leiden: Brill, 1999), 373–88; Mark J. Boda and Stanley E. Porter, "Literature to the Third Degree: Prophecy in Zechariah 9–14 and the Passion of Christ," in *Traduire la Bible Hébraïque: De la Septante à la Nouvelle Bible Segond / Translating the Hebrew Bible: From the*

If Jesus did enter Jerusalem on a donkey,[30] and if it resulted in fostering hopes of eschatological deliverance with messianic connotations among the accompanying pilgrims, then we have a good indication here that Jesus deliberately set out to follow the script of Zech. 9:9 concerning the arrival of a Davidic shepherd king to Israel (cf. Gen. 49:11; 2 Sam. 16:2).[31]

Did Jesus intend his act to be understood, even obliquely, as messianic?[32] Not all agree that the authenticity of the event necessarily translates into a messianic intent on the part of Jesus. Brent Kinman maintains that the act was royal but not specifically messianic.[33] Gnilka thinks that with the entry into Jerusalem, pilgrims found reasons to rejoice over Jesus's eschatological message of the kingdom.[34] Sanders proposed that the entry depicted Jesus as a king but not necessarily as Messiah.[35] As such, the messianic interpretation was added either by the evangelists[36] or by others during Jesus's final week.[37]

Yet a deliberately messianic act full of symbolism and designed to provoke a response should not be unduly regarded as the imposition of a later perspective onto the event.[38] All of the Gospels have a messianic precursor to

---

Septuagint to the Nouvelle Bible Segond (ed. Robert David and Manuel Jinbachian; Montreal: Médiaspaul, 2005), 215–54.

30. Matthew has a "donkey" and a "colt" in 21:1–7, and this may arise from a misreading of the parallelism of Zech. 9:9 LXX or through a feature of rabbinic exegetical practices that rejected parallelism in interpretation. For discussion, see David Instone-Brewer, "The Two Asses of Zechariah 9:9 in Matthew 21," *TynBul* 54 (2003): 87–99.

31. Schweitzer, *Quest*, 351–52; B. F. Meyer, *Aims of Jesus*, 199; Witherington, *Christology of Jesus*, 107; Bockmuehl, *This Jesus*, 91; Hengel, "Messiah of Israel," 55–56; N. T. Wright, *Jesus and the Victory of God*, 491, 586–87, 599–600; Evans, *Mark*, 400–401; Chester, *Messiah and Exaltation*, 313; and cautiously, Sanders, *Jesus and Judaism*, 235; idem, *Historical Figure of Jesus*, 254. Though Witherington sees Jesus setting himself up as a shepherd king as opposed to a warrior king, it is worth pointing out that shepherd and warrior themes are both applied to God in Isa. 40:10–11. Alternatively, Vermes (*Jesus the Jew*, 145) thinks that Jesus rode a donkey because he found it "more convenient than walking."

32. Cf. Schweitzer, *Quest*, 351–52; B. F. Meyer, *Aims of Jesus*, 168–70; Witherington, *Christology*, 106–7; Bockmuehl, *This Jesus*, 91; Hengel, "Messiah of Israel," 55–56; N. T. Wright, *Jesus and the Victory of God*, 490–91.

33. Brent Kinman, "Jesus' Royal Entry into Jerusalem," *BBR* 15 (2005): 243–44.

34. Joachim Gnilka, *Jesus of Nazareth: Message and History* (trans. Siegfried S. Schatzmann; Peabody, MA: Hendrickson, 1997), 274.

35. Sanders, *Jesus and Judaism*, 235, 306; idem, *Historical Figure of Jesus*, 254.

36. Bultmann, *History of the Synoptic Tradition*, 262; Dunn, *Jesus Remembered*, 641–42. Cf. N. T. Wright, *Jesus and the Victory of God*, 491: "The so-called 'triumphal entry' was thus clearly messianic. The meaning is somewhat laboured by the evangelists, particularly Matthew, but is not for that reason to be denied to the original incident."

37. Fredriksen, *Jesus of Nazareth*, 241–58; Gnilka, *Jesus*, 274; Kinman, "Royal Entry," 248–50.

38. Cadoux (*Historic Mission of Jesus*, 59) called the entry "quasi-messianic." S. G. F. Brandon (*Jesus and the Zealots* [Manchester: Manchester University Press, 1967], 350) regards the entry as a "carefully planned demonstration by Jesus of his assumption of Messiahship" and as a "calculated challenge to both the Jewish leaders and the Romans," by which he means a

Jesus's entry and a series of messianic incidents soon afterward. For instance, while passing through Jericho, Jesus reportedly heals a blind beggar named Bartimaeus (Mark 10:46–52), who calls him "Son of David." Luke's Gospel narrates the parable of the nobleman who goes off to a foreign country to receive a kingdom as a didactic precursor to Jesus's entrance into Jerusalem (Luke 19:11–27). Even John's Gospel prefaces the triumphal entry with a story about the fears of the high priest that Jesus would prompt the Romans to act militarily against Jerusalem (John 11:47–53).[39] The placement of these stories just before the triumphal entry obviously derives from the evangelists, who wanted to emphasize Jesus's messianic identity, but that should not lead us to dismiss the plausible scenario that Jesus himself or even others brought royal, messianic, and eschatological claims and hopes to the surface before the entry.

The reference to Ps. 118 is neither secondary nor incidental to the messianic nature of the event. The targumic version of the psalm historicizes the thanksgiving liturgy into an acclamation of God's choice of David as king. Craig Evans writes:

> The coherence between the Aramaic form of Psalm 118 and Jesus' entry into the city and into the temple precincts, where he engages in polemic with the ruling priests, is impressive. The transformation of the psalm into the story of David's recognition as king of Israel explains the interpretive allusion to Ps 118:25–26 in Mark's account of Jesus' entrance into the city, where people shout, "Blessed is the kingdom of our father David that is coming!" (Mark 11:10). Seen in the light of the Aramaic paraphrase, the allusion now makes sense. The Aramaic speaks of David, who is worthy to be king (מליך); the crowd welcomes the coming of David's kingdom (מלכות).[40]

In addition, Jesus's entry into Jerusalem was followed by his action in the temple (Mark 11:15–17), his teaching there about the riddle of the Son of David's identity (Mark 12:35–37), his instructing the disciples about the coming of the kingdom and the Son of Man (Mark 13:1–32), his facing a messianic question at his trial (Mark 14:61–62), and his crucifixion on a political charge as "king of the Jews" (Mark 15:26). The whole context of Jesus's entry—precursors, content, sequel, result—all point in the direction of a messianic claim.

---

political challenge. According to Moule (*Christology*, 33), the meaning of the entry for Jesus is that "If I *am* Messiah, I am not going to fight the Romans. I am going to fight abuse at the heart of Judaism."

39. A legitimate fear, too, given that priests were customarily deposed after revolts (Josephus, *War* 1.651–55; *Ant.* 17.149–67; 18.85–89). See Fredriksen, *Jesus of Nazareth*, 253.

40. Evans, "Aramaic Psalter," 84.

The Temple Episode

The temple episode contributes further to sewing together the messianic fabric of Jesus's final week. Elsewhere I have argued for the authenticity of the temple episode as a symbolic act of judgment rather than a symbolic act of cleansing.[41] Can Jesus's action then be legitimately called "messianic"? According to Fredriksen, the Messiah battles against Israel's enemies, not against Israel's worship.[42] Dunn is slightly more sanguine in his approach and notes the essential ambiguity of the act but thinks that it could have led to speculation regarding Jesus's own eschatological and messianic status.[43] N. T. Wright confidently states: "Jesus' action in the Temple constitutes the most obvious act of messianic praxis within the gospel narratives."[44]

It is quite possible that Jesus meant the temple episode as a demonstration of prophetic authority rather than an exercise of messianic/royal prerogatives. Still, given the dramatic events surrounding Jesus's last week and textual associations that linked Israel's King and Messiah to the temple, I favor a messianic sense.

First, in 2 Sam. 7:12–14, God promises David that a descendant of his "shall build a house for my name and I will establish the throne of his kingdom forever." At Qumran, 2 Sam. 7:11–14 is cited along with Amos 9:11 as referring to the "Shoot of David, who is to arise with the Interpreter of the Law, and who will [arise] in Zi[on in the La]st Days" (4Q174 3.10–13). In context the new temple is a purified temple, a temple of Adam/humankind (מקדש אדם), that is built by the people in the last days (4Q174 3.3, 6, 10). God promises to build David a house—that is, to raise up a new Davidic deliverer to save Israel once the temple is rebuilt by the people (4Q174 3.10–13).[45] In Zech. 6:12–13 one finds a similar notion that: "Thus says the LORD of hosts: Here is a man whose name is Branch: for he shall branch out in his place, and he shall build the temple of the LORD. It is he that shall build the temple of the LORD; he shall bear royal honor, and shall sit upon his throne and rule." Here it refers to the high priest Joshua son of Jehozadak and/or Zerubbabel the Persian governor; yet the temple built after the return from Babylon turned out to be a false crest in the hope of national restoration since it lacked the grandiosity of Solomon's temple and led to no tangible difference in the state of the Judean nation: they were still dominated by a foreign power.

---

41. Bird, *Origins of the Gentile Mission*, 145–55. See an overview of scholarship in Christina Metzdorf, *Die Tempelaktion Jesu: Patristische und historisch-kritische Exegese im Vergleich* (WUNT 2.168; Tübingen: Mohr Siebeck, 2003), 128–217.

42. Fredriksen, *Jesus of Nazareth*, 251.

43. Dunn, *Jesus Remembered*, 639–40, 650.

44. N. T. Wright, *Jesus and the Victory of God*, 490.

45. On the relevance of 2 Sam. 7:11–14 and 4Q174 to Jesus's "messianic self-consciousness," see Betz, "Die Frage nach dem messianischen Bewusstsein," 24–28; and B. F. Meyer, *Aims of Jesus*, 179–80.

Second, another factor to consider is the relationship of the temple to what William Horbury calls "Herod's Messianism."[46] Much like his appointment of priests, Herod the Great's elaborate reconstruction of the temple was arguably an attempt to cement his status as "king of the Jews" and to make his kingdom a center for Jews of the world. In his rendition of Herod's speech justifying the plan for this momentous project, Josephus has Herod say that the original reconstruction of the temple failed to equal the magnificence of Solomon's temple due to subjection under foreign powers that inhibited them from raising it to its ancient height. This implied that his reign and design would restore the temple to its state of original glory (*Ant.* 15.380–87).

The Roman Senate designated Herod as "king" at the behest of Mark Antony (*Ant.* 14.385). The fact that he wanted to be "king of the Jews" (ruler over an *ethnos*, a people) and not just king of Judea (a location) is strongly suggested by his assembly of the inhabitants of Jerusalem to hear of his trip to Asia Minor: "Appearing before them, he gave an account of his whole journey and told them about the Jews of Asia, saying that thanks to him they would be unmolested in the future" (*Ant.* 16.62–65). That is confirmed by the discovery in an inscription on pottery from Masada reading *Regi Herodi Ioudaic(o)*. Herod was regarded with ambivalence by the populace of Galilee, Judea, and the Jewish Diaspora. He could be revered as a Jewish king and benefactor by the wealthy Jewish inhabitants of Caesarea, who appealed to the fact that their city was Jewish on the grounds that a Jew (Herod) had built it (*War* 2.266). Otherwise Herod could be mocked as an Idumean half-Jew (*Ant.* 14.403); Josephus quotes Strabo as writing that Mark Antony had Antigonus beheaded, but the Jews would not receive Herod as King and "by no torments could they be forced to call him king" (*Ant.* 15.9–10).

Herod's act of rebuilding the temple may thus have been part of his own messianic propaganda to reinforce his claim to be "king of the Jews." This was perhaps moderately successful: "Many Jews would have regarded Herod and his claims with considerable sympathy, perhaps even with a fair amount of eschatological enthusiasm."[47]

Third, there is some evidence (though admittedly post–70 CE and with no certainty of knowing how early such views go back) that the Messiah would build a new temple.[48] In the account of a vision, 4 Ezra reports about the human figure: "I looked and saw that he carved out for himself a great

---

46. Horbury, *Messianism among Jews and Christians*, 83–123.

47. Cf. Steven M. Bryan, *Jesus and Israel's Traditions of Judgment and Restoration* (SNTSMS 117; Cambridge: Cambridge University Press, 2002), 197.

48. Sib. Or. 5.414–33; Lev. Rab. 9.6/Num. Rab. 13.2/Midr. Cant. 4.16; Tg. Isa. 53:5; Tg. Zech. 6:12; Bryan, *Jesus and Israel's Traditions*, 194–95. See further, Chester, *Messiah and Exaltation*, 297–99, 471–96; Jostein Ådna, *Jesu Stellung zum Tempel: Die Tempelaktion und das Tempelwort als Ausdruck seiner messianischen Sendung* (WUNT 2.119; Tübingen: Mohr Siebeck, 2000).

mountain, and flew up on to it" (4 Ezra 13.6). This is an obvious allusion to Dan. 2:34–45, where the mountain is Zion, representing the kingdom of Israel, and 4 Ezra's "man" from the sea arguably remolds the temple city of David. Yet, we cannot confirm if this view of Dan. 2 precedes 70 CE. Similarly, 4Q174 3.1–7 refers to the new eschatological temple and connects it with the promise made to David in 2 Sam. 7:11–12, although who actually builds the eschatological temple is not clear.

Fourth, there is no escaping the point that the charge of speaking against the temple appears at Jesus's trial and leads to a question of his self-claim. At the Markan trial, witnesses report that Jesus said, "I will destroy this temple that is made with hands, and in three days I will build another, not made with hands" (Mark 14:58).[49] Since the statement is quoted by Jesus's opponents, who are described by Mark as "false witnesses," it could lead to the view that Mark regards the accusation as false itself. More likely, Mark thinks that the testimony is only partly false. The error is their assumption that Jesus would build "another [ἄλλον]" temple of *the same kind*, that is, another physical temple.[50] And as we have seen, building of the temple is a legitimate task of Israel's king. B. F. Meyer comments: "We conclude that in the word on building the temple in three days we have found a solid point of departure for dealing with messiahship as a determining factor in Jesus's understanding of himself and his mission."[51] Overall, the progression of thought from temple accusation to messianic question is an entirely natural one. The whole Markan sequence of temple, Messiah, Son of God, enthronement, and execution is premised on Jesus as a messianic claimant.[52] This should lead us to infer that the temple

49. Cf. Mark 15:29; Matt. 26:61; John 2:19; Acts 6:14; Gos. Thom. 71.
50. Bryan, *Jesus and Israel's Traditions*, 231–32.
51. B. F. Meyer, *Aims of Jesus*, 180.
52. Cf. Betz, "Die Frage nach dem messianischen Bewusstsein," 34–36. He writes (ibid., 35–36):

> Nach 2 Sam. vii 13 soll der von Gott erweckte Davidsspross den Tempel erbauen; Sacharja hat diese Forderung für den Davididen Serubbabel wiederholt (vi 13). Wird das Nathanwort endzeitlich interpretiert, so ist die Errichtung des Gotteshauses messianische Pflicht. Umgekehrt erhebt jeder, der sich als Erbauer des Tempels ausgibt, indirekt den Anspruch, der Messias und Sohn Gottes zu sein. Jetzt wird klar, warum der Hohepriester, als das Zeugenverhör beim Tempelwort stockt und der Angeklagte kein Wort dazu sagt, direkt die Messiasfrage stellt und das Bekenntnis Jesu erzwingt. Den messianischen Rang des Tempelwortes enthüllt auch die Verspottung Jesu auf Golgatha. Von Markus wird sie in zwei parallelen Gängen erzählt: eine erste Gruppe höhnt den hilflosen Tempelerbauer, eine zweite den ohnmächtigen Messias und König von Israel (Mk. xv 29–32). Messiaswürde und Tempelbau gehören im Handeln Herodes des Grossen zusammen.

> [According to 2 Sam. 7:13, the shoot of David that God raises up will build the temple; Zech. 6:13 repeats this stipulation for the Davidide Zerubbabel. If Nathan's words are interpreted eschatologically, then establishing God's house is a messianic duty. As such, anyone who comes forth as a builder of the temple indirectly claims

action was at least perceived as messianic by the Judean leadership, probably because Jesus intended it to be so.

I think it unlikely that either the triumphal entry *alone* or the temple episode *alone* can justify the assertion that Jesus sought to exercise a messianic role, given that there are possible nonmessianic interpretations of these events. But taken together, both actions (in addition to the trial, execution, and *titulus*) make the messianic profile of Jesus the most cohesive way of explaining the historical events of his death and the shape of the Gospel narratives as they stand. B. F. Meyer wrote: "The entry into Jerusalem and the cleansing of the temple constituted a messianic demonstration, a messianic critique, a messianic fulfillment event, and a sign of the messianic restoration of Israel."[53]

The Royal Riddle of David's Lord

The triumphal entry and temple episode certainly would have raised the messianic question in the minds of the Judean religious authorities. It thus is unsurprising that Jesus would indulge in a moment of debate and banter about the nature of the Messiah. The royal riddle of Mark 12:35–37 is indicative of this:

> While Jesus was teaching in the temple, he said, "How can the scribes say that the Messiah is the son of David? David himself, by the Holy Spirit, declared, 'The Lord said to my Lord, "Sit at my right hand, until I put your enemies under your feet."' David himself calls him Lord; so how can he be his son?" And the large crowd was listening to him with delight.

This riddle is littered with doubts about its authenticity and meaning.[54] Is this an example of later Christian apologetic exegesis of the Old Testament? Is Mark's Jesus teaching that the Messiah is not from David's line or that he himself (though in fact the Messiah) is not a Davidide?[55] Dahl wrote that

to be the Messiah and Son of God. Now it becomes clear why, when the examination of the witnesses regarding the saying about the temple comes to a halt and the defendant remains silent, the High Priest directly poses the Messiah question and forces Jesus's confession. The mocking of Jesus at Golgotha also reveals the messianic status of the saying about the temple. Mark narrates this mocking along two parallel paths: a first group of people jeers at the helpless temple builder; a second group jeers at the impotent Messiah and the King of Israel (Mark 15:29–32). Messianic honor and the building of a temple are combined together in Herod the Great's accomplishments.]

53. B. F. Meyer, *Aims of Jesus*, 199.

54. Cf. Chilton, "Jesus *ben* David," 92: "The authenticity of our passage seems as open a question as its meaning."

55. Against the second option, given their genealogies and birth stories, Matthew (1:1, 17, 20) and Luke (1:27, 32, 69) evidently do not think this episode contradicts affirmation of Jesus's

this episode is "an indirect messianic claim," and the Christian concept of a Messiah is indeed "presupposed, . . . probably a product of Christian scriptural interpretation. . . . It belongs to those elements of the tradition whose historicity cannot be demonstrated because of their close conformity to the kerygma of the early church."[56] As to its meaning, Paula Fredriksen states: "Mark's Jesus seems to refute as unnecessary the Davidic pedigree of the Messiah. This passage subtly asserts Jesus' messianic status despite his not being David's 'son.' Mark's Jesus cites David himself to make his case."[57] As we will see, both points are contestable.

The authenticity of this text should be affirmed in light of several considerations: (1) In terms of coherence, as we have already seen ("Allusions to David and Solomon" in chap. 4), the use of traditions about David figures prominently in authentic pockets of the Jesus tradition. (2) The early church would be unlikely to invent a pericope that left Jesus's Davidic lineage in ambiguity when it figured so prominently in early tradition (e.g., Rom. 1:3–4; Matt. 1:1; etc).[58] (3) The citation of Ps. 110 seems to presuppose a critical distance between the "Lord" (God) and the "son of David" (the Messiah), which is not characteristic of later exegesis.[59] (4) While Ps. 110 was the centerpiece of early Christian interpretation of Israel's Scriptures,[60] William Horbury has pointed out that Ps. 110 was already part of a messianic narrative and was read messianically in the Targum on the Psalms and possibly by Theodotion.[61] Matthew Black maintains that Jesus used Ps. 110 (both here in Mark 12:35–37 and also in 14:62) as a "messianic *testimonium*."[62] Thus, it is possible to situate Jesus's use of Ps. 110 and the title "son of David" in the context of Jewish interpretation of eschatological deliverers and without having to resort to the *Sitz im Leben* of the early church, with its apologetic and christological readings of Scripture.[63] In

---

Davidic heritage in their telling (Luke 20:41–44; Matt. 22:41–46). However, Barn. 12.10–11 understands Mark 12:35–37 to mean that Christ is the Son of God and not the Son of David, and it also refers to Isa. 45:1 to show that Christ is David's Lord and not David's son.

56. Dahl, "Crucified Messiah," 41.

57. Fredriksen, *Jesus of Nazareth*, 141; which contrasts with Taylor, *Mark*, 491.

58. Cullmann, *Christology*, 131–33; Gundry, *Mark*, 722–23; Evans, *Mark*, 275.

59. Chilton, "Jesus *ben* David," 90.

60. Cf. David M. Hay, *Glory at the Right Hand: Psalm 110 in Early Christianity* (Nashville: Abingdon, 1973).

61. Horbury, *Jewish Messianism and the Cult of Christ*, 34, 58, 96–97, 113; cf. D. M. Hay, *Glory at the Right Hand*, 19–33; J. C. O'Neil, *Who Did Jesus Think He Was?* (Leiden: Brill, 1995), 112–13; Davies and Allison, *Saint Matthew*, 3:254n23. Alternatively others ask whether or not Jesus was the first to interpret Ps. 110 messianically; so C. H. Dodd, *According to the Scriptures* (Digswell Place, UK: Nisbet, 1952), 110, 126; Gundry, *Mark*, 718; N. T. Wright, *Jesus and the Victory of God*, 508n116; Fitzmyer, *Luke*, 2:1311; Jossa, *Jews or Christians?* 56–59.

62. Black, "Aramaic," 205, with original emphasis.

63. The Tg. Pss. 110:4 refers to the Davidic king who is "the appointed leader *in the age to come*," and a similar meaning is applied in Midr. Pss. 110:4–5. In the Targum, the historical David of 110:1 is identified as the eschatological David of 110:4. This is evidence, though perhaps

its original setting the saying may well be a reply to questions based on Jesus's quasi-messianic activity.[64]

It is certainly possible to read this text, as Fredriksen and others do, as repudiating the view that the Messiah must come from the Davidic line. But it seems rather odd for Jesus to do that when, as is taken for granted in the early church, he was from the Davidic line himself. More likely, what we have here is a redefinition of what Davidic sonship means.[65] The use of Ps. 110 could indicate both the priestly function of the Messiah (given the reference to Melchizedek in 110:4) and signify the exaltation of the Messiah to sharing in God's own throne (given the reference to the title "LORD" in 110:1); both themes, priestly Messiah and an exalted Messiah, were current in Second Temple Judaism.[66] Such a claim, though tacitly made, was nonetheless pertinent to a debate with the priestly class over who spoke for God. The fact that, shortly after saying this, Jesus was denounced to Pilate and then crucified as a messianic claimant is further proof that the issue of Jesus's messianic identity was in the air before his death.[67]

On the other hand, there is no escaping the genuinely enigmatic nature of the utterance.[68] This could be a polite debate among religious leaders about who the Messiah will be: Will he be a Davidide?[69] The more one emphasizes the locus of meaning as designating a preexistent and exalted Messiah, the more we have to suspect that what we have here is the hand of early Christian interpreters.[70]

---

late, of Ps. 110:1–4 being interpreted messianically and eschatologically. See Evans "Aramaic Psalter," 66–68, 85–86.

64. Cf., e.g., Barrett, *Jesus and the Gospel Tradition*, 22n36. Schweitzer (*Quest* [2nd ed.; London: Unwin, 1911], 393) stated: "Far from rejecting the Davidic Sonship in this saying, Jesus, on the contrary, presupposes His possession of it"; Darrell L. Bock (*Blasphemy and Exaltation in Judaism: The Charge against Jesus in Mark 14:53–65* [BSL; Grand Rapids: Baker Academic, 1998], 222) comments: "The evidence of Mk 12:35–37 indicates that it is far more likely that Ps 110:1 goes back to a period when the issues surrounding Jesus' identity were surfacing than to roots in a community that was openly confessing him in the midst of dispute."

65. N. T. Wright, *Jesus and the Victory of God*, 509–10. Cf. Jossa (*Jews or Christians?* 57), who states: "I also believe that here Jesus did not contest simply the Davidic origin of the Messiah . . . but instead asserted that this origin was completely insufficient to penetrate the mystery of messiahship."

66. On these themes, see Crispin H. T. Fletcher-Louis, "Jesus as the High Priestly Messiah: Part 1," *JSHJ* 4 (2006): 155–75; idem, "Jesus as the High Priestly Messiah: Part 2," *JSHJ* 5 (2007): 57–79; and Joel Marcus, "Mark 14:61: 'Are You the Messiah-Son-of-God?'" *NovT* 31 (1989): 124–41.

67. Dunn, *Jesus Remembered*, 635.

68. Taylor (*Mark*, 493) calls the saying "allusive" and says that it "half conceals and half reveals the 'Messianic Secret.'"

69. Cf. "If the Messiah-King comes from among the living, his name will be David. If he comes from among the dead, it will be King David himself" (*y. Ber.* 2.3).

70. Cf., e.g., Bultmann, *History of the Synoptic Tradition*, 66, 136–37; Vermes, *Authentic Gospel*, 62–63, 189–90; Funk and Hoover, *Five Gospels*, 105; Lüdemann, *Jesus*, 87.

The Passion of the Shepherd King

A category worth considering is that of the messianic shepherd and its relevance to the Jesus tradition. The familiar image of God as the shepherd of Israel was already in Israel's sacred traditions (Gen. 48:15; 49:24; Pss. 23:1; 28:9; 80:1; Isa. 40:10–11; Jer. 31:10). The image of the king as shepherd was familiar in the ANE[71] and in the Greco-Roman world.[72] Cyrus, the Lord's "anointed one" (משיח), is designated as a shepherd (Isa. 44:28; 45:1). Joshua son of Nun succeeds Moses as the shepherd of Israel (Num. 27:15–19), and the metaphor was frequently applied to David (2 Sam. 5:2; 24:17; 1 Chron. 11:2; Ps. 78:70–72).

In the Hebrew Scriptures, one observes the development of the idea of a coming Davidic shepherd king and the theme of the divine punishment of Israel likened to a flock being scattered. The hope for a new Davidic king who would shepherd Israel was extant in scriptural traditions (Ezek. 34:23–24; 37:24; Mic. 5:4; cf. Jer. 23:3–6). While none of these texts can be regarded as explicitly messianic in the narrower definition of the term,[73] they were interpreted that way, as is evident from the New Testament (Matt. 2:6 = Mic. 5:2–4). Similarly, the language of Israel scattered like sheep without a shepherd was a powerful image for the defeat of its army and death of its king (1 Kings 22:17/2 Chron. 18:16), for those led astray by idols (Zech. 10:2), a catchword denoting exile (Jer. 31:10; 4 Ezra 5:17–18), and a terrible judgment (Zech. 13:7).

A powerful image of restoration was for a Davidic shepherd king to come and rescue Israel from military oppression, exile, and divine judgment (Num. 27:17; Ezek. 34:8, 12; Zech. 10:2; Bar. 4:26; Pss. Sol. 17.40; Tg. Isa. 6:13; 8:18; 35:6; Tg. Hos. 14:8; Tg. Mic. 5:1–3). Josephus reports that after the death of Herod the Great a certain Athronges, a shepherd of no significant social stature, led a revolt in Judea with his brothers, "set himself up as a king," and put a "diadem on his head" (*Ant.* 17.278, 280; *War* 2.60–62). It may have been that Athronges's shepherd vocation actually worked in his favor in propagating his cause and drawing supporters since he was a shepherd making himself king and fighting against foreigners (Rome) and against false shepherds (Archelaus). Perhaps in the eyes of some supporters, Athronges was the shepherd king of Israel.

Jesus as the shepherd over the church became a prominent theme in the Christology of late first-century and early second-century Christianity (Heb. 13:20; 1 Pet. 2:25; 5:4; Rev. 7:17; Ign. *Eph.* 6.2; Mart. Pol. 19.2; Herm. *Vis.* 5.1.1–3). The "Good Shepherd" discourse of John 10 depicts Jesus as the noble shepherd

---

71. Cf. J. Collins, *Scepter and the Star*, 25; and on kings in the ANE more generally, see Day, *King and Messiah in Israel*, 16–90; J.-G. Heintz, "Royal Traits and Messianic Figures: A Thematic and Iconographical Approach," in Charlesworth, *The Messiah*, 52–66.

72. Philo, *Agriculture* 41; *Embassy* 44; Homer, *Iliad* 2.75–109; *Odyssey* 3.156; Dio Chrysostom, *Orat.* 1.13–28; 2.6; 3.41; 4.43–44.

73. Cf. Fitzmyer, *The One Who Is to Come*, 3–7.

king of Israel, and this is related to the theme of Jewish restoration hopes where
the Johannine Jesus intends to bring in "other sheep" so that there might be
"one flock" (John 10:16). While this might conceivably refer to Gentiles, it is
equally possible that it pertains to the Jews of the Diaspora as well (cf. John
7:35; 12:20–23). However, the shepherd theme may have points of contact with
authentic elements of the Jesus tradition since sheep figure prominently in several
parables (Luke 15:1–7/Matt. 18:12–13/Gos. Thom. 107; Matt. 25:31–46), Jesus
likens his followers to sheep or a flock (Luke 10:3/Matt. 10:16; Luke 12:32), and
the mission of Jesus and his disciples is to "the lost sheep of the house of Israel"
(Matt. 10:5b–6; 15:24).[74] If Jesus understood his mission in terms of regathering
and restoring Israel from its exile or dispersion, then by intent or by perception,
he was necessarily committed to a role, as outlined in texts such as Ezek. 34:11–31
and so forth, concerning a divinely sent Davidic figure who shepherds and saves
the scattered sheep of Israel. Does this lead to the conclusion that Jesus sought
to portray himself as a shepherd of Israel, or even a messianic shepherd? Quite
possibly, but further evidence is needed to establish this proposal.

In Mark's passion narrative, a citation of Zech. 13:7 is attributed to Jesus:
"Jesus said to them, 'You will all become deserters; for it is written, "I will strike
the shepherd, and the sheep will be scattered"'" (Mark 14:27). The authenticity
of this citation is obviously disputed as an *ex eventu* Christian interpretation
of Jesus's death.[75] Yet a reasonable case for its authenticity can be made.[76] First,
although the Markan passion predictions are theologically loaded, that Jesus
predicted his death is multiply attested in the tradition in source and form.[77]
In addition, John 16:32 is remarkably similar to Mark 14:27 with regard to a
scattering effected by Jesus's death; it may represent an independent Johannine
tradition of the same saying, transposed to a different literary setting by the
Fourth Evangelist.

Second, for the early church to take a text about a false shepherd from
Zechariah and apply it to Jesus seems at odds with the church's portrayal of
Jesus as the "good," "great," or "chief" shepherd (John 10:11, 14; 1 Pet. 5:4;
Heb. 13:20). What is more, Zech. 13:7 did not come into prominent focus in
early Christian exposition of the Old Testament and is found again only in the
Epistle of Barnabas (5.12), but there it is applied quite differently as referring
to Jesus's opponents rather than to Jesus's disciples.[78]

74. Cf. W. Tooley, "The Shepherd and the Sheep Image in the Teaching of Jesus," *NovT* 7
(1964–65): 15–25; N. T. Wright, *Jesus and the Victory of God*, 533–34.
75. Cf., e.g., Bultmann, *History of the Synoptic Tradition*, 266–67, 306; Vermes, *Jesus the
Jew*, 60–66.
76. For a robust argument for the authenticity of Mark 14:26–28, see Pitre, *Jesus*, 466–78
(and literature cited at 466n229).
77. Michael F. Bird, "Passion Predictions," in *EHJ*, 442–46.
78. Cf. the Fayyum Fragment, a third-century text that parallels Mark 14:26–31, including
agreements with Matthew against Mark on some details and with Mark against Matthew on
other details. This text is probably dependent on one or more of the Synoptic Gospels, given

Third, Jesus's quoting of Zech. 13:7 coheres with his usage of that document elsewhere: it formed part of the prophetic script for his final days, which
he sought to follow.[79] That is hardly a Christian innovation, and it is perfectly
at home in a Palestinian environment. After all, the death of the Teacher of
Righteousness in the Dead Sea Scrolls was associated with Zech. 13:7, and his
death was thought to inaugurate the time of the final testing and the visitation
of the Messiah of Aaron and Israel (CD-B 19.5–11). Rabbinic literature also
interpreted Zech. 13:7 messianically where the Messiah ben Joseph or ben
Ephraim fights Gog and Magog, only to die in the battle; such an approach
is both continuous and discontinuous with Jesus's use of Zech. 13:7.[80] Thus,
applying Zech. 13:7 to the death of a leader, in conjunction with messianic
hopes, and reading it in light of the approaching eschatological ordeal—this
cannot be laid squarely at the feet of the evangelists.

This Markan passion prediction in Mark 14:27–28 was originally a Jesuanic
midrash on Zech. 13:7 that situated his suffering and subsequent vindication
in terms of judgment (v. 27) and restoration (v. 28), or the scattering (v. 27)
and regathering (v. 28) of Israel. In other words, what is going to happen to
Jesus is a microcosm of what has happened or will happen to Jesus's disciples and to Israel. The messianic woes come and judgment is poured out;
in the aftermath, God's people emerge protected from and purified by the
eschatological ordeal. The judgment issued in the striking of the shepherd
results finally in the reconstitution of a remnant of Israel. It was the historical
Jesus's intent that, by death and vindication as the messianic shepherd, he
would effect the eschatological regathering of Israel. Importantly, this mix
of midrash, messianism, apocalypticism, and atonement theology deviates
somewhat from that found in the New Testament; thus it is all the more
likely to be authentic.

If the coming Davidic king was likened to a shepherd (e.g., Ezek. 34:23–24),
if the death of the king meant the scattering of Israel (1 Kings 22:17/2 Chron.
18:16), if there is extant evidence that Zech. 13:7 was already linked to the
coming messianic age and to the great tribulation (CD 19.5–11), then we have
in Mark 14:27 a contextually plausible eschatological scenario comprised of
restoration hopes, kingship, and tribulation. What emerges here is that the
historical Jesus saw himself as the messianic shepherd who would be struck

similarities in the wording between them, rather than being indebted to pre-synoptic sources.
See discussion in Gundry, *Mark*, 852–53; Davies and Allison, *Saint Matthew*, 3:483; J. K. Elliott,
The Apocryphal New Testament (Oxford: Clarendon, 1993), 43–45.

79. Jeremias, *New Testament Theology*, 297–98; N. T. Wright, *Jesus and the Victory of God*,
586–87, 599–600; Pitre, *Jesus*, 475; Evans, *Mark*, 400–401. Gundry (*Mark*, 848) argues that it
was Jesus's use of Zech. 13:7 for both the flight of his disciples and his death that led Christians
to apply to Jesus other passages from Zechariah (e.g., Matt. 21:5 [Zech. 9:9]; 27:9 [Jer. 32:25?];
John 12:15 [Zech. 9:9]; 19:37 [Zech. 12:10]). Note that Matt. 27:9 is a textual problem.

80. Horbury, *Jewish Messianism*, 33.

down in the final days, and his death would protect his scattered followers from the tribulation that is to usher in the new age.[81] The notion of a suffering Messiah is not a pre-Christian theme taken up and applied to Jesus by the early church; instead, it has its roots in Jesus's own interpretation of his death while set in apocalyptic coordinates and in creative contact with Israel's sacred traditions.[82] There is an important qualification to be made: while all messiahs are shepherds since they rule and restore Israel, not all shepherds (political or religious) are messiahs.

The Trial of the Messiah

The trial narratives in the Gospels lend further support to the messianic nature of Jesus's ministry.[83] In the words of Hengel, "We cannot ignore that *the Messiah questions runs through the Passion story of all the gospels like a red thread.*"[84] The problem is, however, that the trial scenes are regarded as historically dubious and loaded with Christian theology, and Jesus's reply to Caiaphas is markedly different in all four Gospels. Thus with good reason the historicity of the scene in Mark 14:61–64 in exegetical studies is disputed.[85] How then does one find a historical kernel let alone evidence of a messianic claim on the part of Jesus in this material? To that task I now turn.

81. Cf. Pitre, *Jesus*, 477–78.

82. It is possible that some Jewish texts refer to a suffering Messiah (Zech 13:7; Dan. 9:26; Tg. Isa. 53; T. Benj. 3.8; 4Q541 frgs. 9, 24; 4Q285 5.4; 4 Ezra 7.29–30; 2 Bar. 30.1; Justin Martyr, *Dial.* 39, 89–90; Tg. Zech. 12:10; Hippolytus, *Haer.* 9.25; *b. Sukkah* 52), and several scholars have inferred from this a form of intertestamental messianic expectation that provides the background for the messianism of Jesus and of the early church (Horbury, *Jewish Messianism*, 33; Hengel, "Messiah of Israel," 37; Markus Bockmuehl, *This Jesus*, 50; idem, "A 'Slain Messiah' in 4Q Serekh Milhamah [4Q285]?" *TynBul* 43 [1992]: 155–69; R. A. Rosenberg, "The Slain Messiah in the Old Testament," *ZAW* 99 [1987]: 259–61). But if there was a well-known tradition about a suffering or dying Messiah, how could the hopes of the disciples be shattered after Good Friday (cf. Luke 24:21)? If such a tradition was extant then, on the contrary, their hope that Jesus was the Messiah would have been confirmed, not dashed. Likewise, the scandal of a crucified Messiah would dissipate if it was thought possible that the Messiah would suffer rather than conquer. Geza Vermes (*Authentic Gospel*, 387) writes: "It should be recalled that neither the death nor the resurrection of the Messiah formed part of the beliefs and expectations of the Jews in the first century AD." Belief in a suffering messiah (Messiah son of Ephraim or Messiah son of Joseph) may have arisen in response to the failed messianic aspirations of Bar Kochba in the post–135 CE period; see also Vermes, *Jesus the Jew*, 139–40; N. T. Wright, *People of God*, 320; idem, *Jesus and the Victory of God*, 488; Theissen and Merz, *Historical Jesus*, 540–41; Stuhlmacher, *Jesus of Nazareth*, 27; Schürer, *History of the Jewish People*, 2:547–49; Evans, "Messianism," 703; J. Collins, *Scepter and the Star*, 123–26.

83. For a survey of the various historical, source-critical, literary, and theological issues, see Theissen and Merz, *Historical Jesus*, 440–73.

84. Hengel, "Messiah of Israel," 45, with original emphasis.

85. Hofius, "Ist Jesus der Messias?" 121.

With regard to the trial itself (Mark 14:53–65; Matt. 26:57–68; Luke 22:63–71), the entire scenario is regarded as a secondary composition by many scholars.[86] The primary objection appears to be that there were no Christian witnesses present to relay accounts of the proceedings.[87] But one can respond by suggesting that there was probably a desperate curiosity among Jesus's followers and the crowds in general as to what actually took place at the proceedings. Part of the trial took place in public, and more information would have been available from attendants, guards, members of the council, and even from sympathizers of Jesus like Nicodemus and Joseph of Arimathea. No one was sworn to secrecy over what transpired.[88] That our sources may contain genuine historical reminiscences of what took place at Jesus's trial should not be ruled out. What seems certain is that Jesus had a prehearing with the Sanhedrin and a formal trial before Pilate.

More problematic is the issue of the messianic question posed to Jesus by the high priest (and later by Pilate [Mark 15:2; Luke 23:2; John 18:33–34]) and his reply.

Again the high priest asked him, "Are you the Messiah, the Son of the Blessed One?" Jesus said, "*I am* [ἐγώ εἰμι]; and 'you will see the Son of Man seated at the right hand of the Power,' and 'coming with the clouds of heaven.'" (Mark 14:61–62, emphasis added)

Then the high priest said to him, "I put you under oath before the living God, tell us if you are the Messiah, the Son of God." Jesus said to him, "*You have said so* [σὺ εἶπας]. But I tell you, From now on you will see the Son of Man seated at the right hand of Power and coming on the clouds of heaven." (Matt. 26:63–64, emphasis added)

They said, "If you are the Messiah, tell us." He replied, "If I tell you, you will not believe; and if I question you, you will not answer. But from now on the Son of Man will be seated at the right hand of the power of God." All of them asked, "Are you, then, the Son of God?" He said to them, "*You say that I am* [ὑμεῖς λέγετε ὅτι ἐγώ εἰμι]." (Luke 22:67–70, emphasis added)

The high priest's question is a flat-out challenge to Jesus to confess to being a messianic claimant. While all three Synoptic Gospels include a conflation of Ps. 110:1 and Dan. 7:13 as part of his answer, the antecedent remark is different and ambiguous. Mark gives the emphatic and affirmative "I am." In Matthew's version we have the ambiguous "You have said so," which is then

---

86. Cf., e.g., Lüdemann, *Jesus*, 100–102; Sanders, *Jesus and Judaism*, 296–99.

87. Bultmann, *History of the Synoptic Tradition*, 270; Sanders, *Jesus and Judaism*, 298; Jürgen Becker, *Jesus of Nazareth*, 197.

88. Bock, *Blasphemy and Exaltation*, 195–97; Dunn, *Jesus Remembered*, 630–31; Hengel, "Messiah of Israel," 53.

contrasted (πλήν) with the Old Testament quotation. In the Lukan account, Mark's single question is split into two questions about the "Messiah" and the "Son of God." When asked if he is the Messiah, Jesus is deliberately evasive; he poses a hypothetical question and answer to the high priest and adds the Old Testament citation. That in turn prompts a further question from council, asking if he is the Son of God. Jesus answers, "You say that I am."

Luke and Matthew change the Markan Jesus's reply "I am" to either "You have said so" (Matthew) or "You say that I am" (Luke). This arguably represents an attempt to tone down the presumption of Jesus's audacious reply to the high priest. Without going into textual issues (notably scribal tendencies to harmonize Jesus's reply to the high priest),[89] I suggest that Luke and Matthew are probably closer to what Jesus actually said. Such a reply is indicative of Jesus's parabolic style of challenge and debate, and such a response corresponds to Jesus's answer to Pilate when asked if he was the "king of the Jews": there Jesus reportedly says in Mark 15:2: "You say so [σὺ λέγεις]." The reply "You say" is probably idiomatic for "That is your way of putting it," "That is how you see it," or perhaps even "You said it, not me." In any case, our sources indicate that when the question was put to Jesus about being the Messiah/Son of God, he answered with an allusive "Yes" and then proceeded to redefine the answer by switching from Messiah to Son of Man.

Jesus adds to his response a conflation of Dan. 7:13 and Ps. 110:1.[90] While this might show the hand of early Christian apologists in embellishing the tradition, the citation corresponds to the Jewish interpretive principle of gĕzērâ šāwâ, of "an equivalent category," since the link between these two texts is that of enthronement with God. Another possible link between them is that both Ps. 110 and Dan. 7 have to do with the subjugation of enemies.[91] John Collins supposes that Ps. 110:1 and Dan. 7:9 both reflect a tradition where beings other than God are said to be enthroned in heaven.[92] Martin Hengel argues that themes from Dan. 7 and Ps. 110 were combined in 1 En. 37–71 (esp. 62.5; 69.29).[93] The two texts are also brought together in the much later

89. A longer reading of "You have said that I am [σὺ εἶπας ὅτι ἐγώ εἰμι]" for Mark 14:62a is attested in Θ 13 472 543 565 700 1071 geo arm Origen. While this might explain the readings in Matthew and Luke, the shorter reading is probably to be preferred. See discussion in Evans, *Mark*, 450; Dunn, "Messianic Ideas," 375n22; Taylor, *Mark*, 568.

90. On a positive case for authenticity, cf. F. H. Borsch, "Mark xiv.62 and 1 Enoch lxii.5," *NTS* 14 (1968): 65–67; David R. Catchpole, *The Trial of Jesus* (Leiden: Brill, 1971), 136–40; Caragounis, *Son of Man*, 224–26; Brown, *Death of the Messiah*, 1:513–15; Bock, *Blasphemy and Exaltation*, 209–37.

91. Davies and Allison, *Saint Matthew*, 3:531n78.

92. J. Collins, *Scepter and the Star*, 142–43.

93. Martin Hengel, " 'Setz dich zu meiner Rechten!' Die Inthronisation Christi zur Rechten Gottes und Psalm 110,1," in *Le trône de Dieu* (ed. M. Philonenko; Tübingen: Mohr Siebeck, 1993), 161–64. Cf. also Johannes Theissen, *Der auserwählte Richter* (Göttingen: Vandenhoeck & Ruprecht, 1975), 94–98. See esp. the echoes of Ps. 110 in 1 En. 61.8; 62.1–5; 69.27, 29.

Midr. Pss. 2:7. That might locate the conflation of texts in Jewish Christianity but not necessarily with Jesus. But if Mark 12:35–37 is authentic, then we already have evidence of Jesus using Ps. 110:1 in response to a messianic question, perhaps even as a messianic testimonium. It is also highly likely that Dan. 7 provided the background for many of the themes of Jesus's message as it related to the kingdom of God and the restoration of Israel.[94] That is of a piece with passages from the Qumran scrolls and Similitudes of 1 Enoch that illustrate the presence of Danielic influences in speculations about regal and intermediary figures in pre-Christian Judaism, in association with the advent of the messianic age. In addition, the reference to himself on a throne at the right hand of God could easily give cause to a charge of blasphemy. That coheres with the rabbinic tradition that Rabbi Akiba was reported to have said that the multiple thrones referred to in Dan. 7:9 include one for God and one for the Son of David, a view that was denounced by Rabbi Yose as profaning God (b. Ḥag. 14a; b. Sanh. 38b). Jesus's audacity in making such a claim is no greater than the claim made in 11QMelch concerning a heavenly enthronement and deification of Melchizedek.[95]

How does one explain the question about destroying the temple, the switch to a messianic question, and a final charge of blasphemy? Is this a smelting pot of Christian exegesis about what *could* have happened at Jesus's trial, or is it based on an authentic tradition history? Widely attested in the tradition (Mark 14:58; 15:29; Matt. 26:61; John 2:19; Acts 6:14; Gos. Thom. 71), the statement that Jesus will destroy and rebuild the temple can be related to royal ideology associated with David. According to 2 Sam. 7:13–14 and Zech. 6:12, the temple is to be built by the Son of David or the "Branch." Temple and Messiah go hand in hand. Thus the switch from a charge of speaking against the temple to a messianic question is inherently plausible and follows conceptually.[96] Jesus's answer to the high priest's question made a messianic claim, placed Jesus in the sphere of divine sovereignty, and sealed a charge of blasphemy. Hofius wisely comments:

> One may question whether Mark 14:62b contains the exact words that Jesus spoke before the Sanhedrin. The formulation, however, does likely reflect that Jesus, when he was interrogated by the High Priest, actually made a claim that exceeded everything messianic by far—that is, qualitatively by far—so that it must have appeared to the Jewish authorities as "blasphemy."[97]

94. Cf. Evans, "Defeating Satan and Liberating Israel," 161–70.

95. Davies and Allison, *Saint Matthew*, 3:532.

96. Cf. Betz, "Die Frage nach dem messianischen Bewusstsein," 34–36; Kim, *Son of Man*, 79–81; Bock, *Blasphemy and Exaltation*, 213.

97. Hofius, "Ist Jesus der Messias?" 121: "Ob Mk 14,62b exakt die Worte wiedergibt, die Jesus vor dem Synhedrium gesprochen hat, wird man fragen dürfen. In der Formulierung dürfte sich aber widerspiegeln, dass Jesus beim Verhör durch den Hohenpriester in der Tat einen

I know that my arguments for the authenticity of Mark 14:62–64 will not convince everyone. What is definitive, though, is the outcome of the trial: Jesus was crucified as a messianic pretender. That is what ultimately leads me to suspect that during the trial (Jewish or Roman) Jesus was (made) party to a messianic claim. While Dahl acknowledged as much, he overlooked the fact that it was Jesus's opponents who made the messiahship question central and forced him to accept the charge.[98] Where did they get that idea from? It is unlikely to have come from nowhere and can confidently be traced back to their suspicion that during his time in Jerusalem (though perhaps even as early as Galilee), Jesus's teaching and actions were soaked in messianic ideas and could potentially lead to an explosion of messianic fervor. Martin Hengel rightly concludes:

> For when Jesus was delivered up and crucified under the charge of being a Jewish messianic pretender—that is, in the political language which only a Roman understood, the "King of the Jews"—then the Messiah question must have already been at the centre of the interrogation by the Jewish authorities. The precautions taken at Jesus' arrest, and the speed with which he was delivered to Pilate, show that the Jewish authorities feared his influence with the people, and thus wished to avoid direct, and public, proceedings. It was his eschatologically based authority, or more precisely, his messianic claim, which finally led, after some wavering by Pilate, to their making short work of him.[99]

The King of the Jews

The most certain fact about the historical Jesus is that he was crucified by the Romans at the behest of the Judean leadership on the charge of being a messianic pretender and was denigrated with the mocking placard "King of the Jews" (Mark 15:26; Matt. 27:37; Luke 23:38; John 19:19).[100] This *titulus* is overwhelmingly regarded as authentic by nearly all commentators.[101] This is

---

Anspruch erhoben hat, der alles messianische weit—und zwar: qualitativ weit—überstieg und den jüdischen Autoritäten notwendig als 'Gotteslästerung' erscheinen musste."

98. M. de Jonge, *God's Final Envoy*, 100–101.

99. Hengel, "Messiah of Israel," 55.

100. On placards in executions, see ibid., 48–50.

101. Cf. Dahl ("Crucified Messiah," 36–37): "The formulation 'King of the Jews' stems neither from proof from prophecy nor from the Christology of the community. . . . The crucified-Messiah motif belongs to the substance of the passion story, though its historicity is still not proved" (ibid., 37). Fitzmyer (*The One Who Is to Come*, 141): "Because that inscription was a Roman formulation, which was contemptuous of the Jewish people, its historicity is scarcely to be contested. If it had been invented by Christians, they may have used Χριστός, but they would scarcely have called their leader 'the King of the Jews.'" Hengel ("Messiah of Israel," 46): "It is improbable in the extreme that the early Church, with no reference to historical reality, introduced of itself the

because: (1) "King of the Jews" occurs both on the cross and in the mocking of Jesus by the Roman cohort and is thus ingrained in the passion story. (2) It is attested also by John's tradition. (3) "King" was not a dogmatic motif in the early church and, apart from Mara bar Serapion, occurs very rarely.[102]

The relationship of the *titulus* to Jesus's own messianism (or lack of it) has been handled differently. Becker, for instance, thinks that "the inscription on the cross is not relevant for the question of the messiahship of Jesus."[103] Dahl maintained that the *titulus* was the grounds upon which the early church inferred that Jesus was the Messiah despite the fact that he never claimed to be so. Another option, the one pursued here, is to follow the trail of evidence back from *titulus* → trial → triumphal entry/temple episode → Jesus. Either we can regard Jesus as the one who got the ball rolling in arousing the messianic hopes of his followers and the messianic suspicions of the Judean authorities, or else we have to revert to other explanations. Those other explanations include the notion that the disciples and pilgrims in Jerusalem believed Jesus to be the Messiah when Jesus gave them only faintly ambiguous reasons for believing so. Jesus then failed to clarify his own eschatological or political role, inflamed the issue through several symbolic actions, and never denied the charge at his trial. These latter options fail to suitably explain the state of the passion narratives as they stand and the messianic nature of early Christianity.

The *titulus* is the smoking gun of the messianic Jesus. The *titulus* was the final verdict of what his ministry meant to the Jerusalemites, a ministry that led to the charge of being a messianic pretender in his final week, and a charge connected to the various themes of his teachings and activities. To varying degrees, further indications of Jesus's messianic mission might also

---

politically (highly) prejudicial expression, 'King of the Jews,' as *causa poenae*, since this would have justified the Roman proceedings against Jesus as a rebel against the ruling state power"; Rudolf Pesch (*Das Markusevangelium* [2 vols.; HTKNT; Freiburg: Basel, 1976–77], 2:484): "On the historical accuracy of our statement no indication of reasonable doubt is possible [ist an der historischen Richtigkeit unserer Angabe kein vernünftiger Zweifel möglich]"; Dunn (*Jesus Remembered*, 628): " 'King of the Jews' was never a Christian title, so the only reason for its appearance in the account of Jesus' execution is that it summed up the charge on which he was executed"; and also Brown, *Death of the Messiah*, 1:476; N. T. Wright, *Jesus and the Victory of God*, 486–89; J. Collins, *Scepter and the Star*, 205; Theissen and Merz, *Historical Jesus*, 458–59; Jürgen Becker, *Jesus of Nazareth*, 353–54; Lüdemann, *Jesus*, 108; Evans, *Mark*, 503–4. For those who doubt the authenticity of the *titulus*, see, e.g., Bultmann, *History of the Synoptic Tradition*, 272, 284; Adela Y. Collins, *Mark* (Hermeneia; Philadelphia: Fortress, 2007), 747–48.

102. Scholars often include the criterion of embarrassment, but I respond: (1) If it was so embarrassing, why does it occur in all four Gospels? (2) The use of irony, especially by Mark and John, was not unknown to the evangelists. Nonetheless, the charge that Jesus was an insurrectionist (and by consequence Christians were a menace to the social order) was something that Christians sought to refute, yet by including such material here, they were potentially hamstringing themselves.

103. Jürgen Becker, *Jesus of Nazareth*, 223n118.

be identified in the sequel to Jesus's life: the testimony, proclamation, social dynamics, and Christology of the early church.

The Messianic Herald of Salvation

In moving now to the post-Easter period, examination of the earliest witnesses to Jesus is important because it tells us something of what was *believed* about Jesus and what was *remembered* of Jesus after his death. Premised on the two-source theory, our earliest sources, Mark and Q, arguably contribute to an overall picture of Jesus as the messianic herald of salvation.[104]

Before launching into a brief description of Mark's titular Christology, it is worth drawing attention to the caveats of H. C. Kee. According to Kee, one approach to Markan Christology seeks to investigate how Mark ascribed existing messianic titles to Jesus and what other redemptive categories were extant in pre–70 CE Judaism. Another approach seeks to describe the function of the messianic secret in Mark and, on the assumption that messiahship was a known category, show that Jesus tried to keep this secret away from the public in general and from his opponents in particular. Kee's objection to these approaches is, first, that it assumes that messianic titles and concepts were fixed entities in Judaism in the Second Temple period. Second, the primary disagreement between the Markan Jesus and the Judean leaders was over his messianic claim.[105] In response to Kee, to regard Mark as attempting to portray Jesus as the Messiah does not require him to be presupposing fixed messianic titles and concepts. (1) As I argued in chapter 2, messianic expectations of the era were indeed *fluid*, but I also pointed out that there could be recurring or *familiar* themes that often reemerged and were sometimes associated with certain figures or titles, especially in the interpretation of key texts. (2) Though there was a diverse range of divine agents in Judaism, this does not negate the fact that some titles or patterns were already known to support messianic interpretations. For instance, "son of God" is a not a technical term for "Messiah," since it can refer to Israel, Israel's earthly monarch, and even angels. Yet "son" was already a recognized way of designating the Messiah (e.g., 1QSa 2.11–12). And again, "christ" or "anointed one" could potentially describe a prophet, a king, or a priest; but when placed in a certain context, it could clearly denote a coming messianic figure (e.g., Pss. Sol. 17.32; 1 En. 48.10; 52.4; 1QSa 2.12). (3) Fixation on the title to at least some degree is assumed by Paul's remark that "we preach Christ crucified, a stumbling to

---

104. My line of argumentation here is inspired by and partly dependent upon Edward P. Meadors, *Jesus the Messianic Herald of Salvation* (Peabody, MA: Hendrickson, 1997).

105. H. C. Kee, "Christology in Mark's Gospel," in *Judaisms and Their Messiahs at the Turn of the Christian Era* (ed. J. Neusner, W. S. Green, and E. Frerichs; Cambridge: Cambridge University Press, 1987), 187.

Jews" (1 Cor. 1:23 RSV) and Justin's Trypho, who claims, "But this so-called Christ of yours was dishonourable and inglorious, so much so that the last curse contained in the law of God fell on him, for he was crucified" (*Dial.* 32). In the Johannine literature, confession of Jesus as the Messiah led to one's being "put out of the synagogue" (John 9:22; 12:42; 16:2). Without some clear delineation of what a messiah was and what titles appropriately described him, the early Christian proclamation would have been strangely innovative but not necessarily offensive. Thus, Mark does not presuppose a fixed set of messianic titles; rather, he takes titles that are *potentially* messianic (Son of Man), *occasionally* messianic when placed in an eschatological framework (Son of God, Son of David), and *explicitly* messianic when tied to political realities (King of the Jews)—in order to redefine the role of Messiah and to proclaim Jesus as Messiah.

In Mark's Gospel, the designation Χριστός occurs at several points, including the incipit with "Jesus Christ" at the beginning of the Gospel (1:1), Peter's confession of Jesus as the "Messiah" at Caesarea Philippi (8:29), the description of those who are "of Messiah" (9:41), the Messiah-David pericope (12:35), the prediction of false Messiahs (13:21), the high priest's asking Jesus if he is the "Messiah" (14:61), and finally the mocking scorn of the crucified Jesus as "the Messiah, the King of Israel" (15:32). Other titles are used in Mark's Gospel, and they are integral to Jesus's identity as the Messiah.[106]

In its Markan usage, the title "Son of God" espouses both Jesus's unique filial relationship with Israel's God and also his messianic identity. "Son of God" was a designation for Israel's king as evident from Ps. 2:7 and in 2 Sam. 7:14. In the trial narrative, the high priest asks Jesus, "Are you the Messiah, the Son of the Blessed One?" (Mark 14:61). The description "Blessed One" is a circumlocution for "God," and "Son of the Blessed One" is tantamount to "Son of God." In this position "Messiah" and "Son of God/Blessed One" are synonymous. That is confirmed by the messianic exegesis of Qumran, which correlated the Son of God with a coming messianic figure (e.g., 4Q174 3.10–11; 4Q246).[107] The demons declare Jesus to be the Son of God, who vanquishes them and thus carries out the messianic role of defeating the powers of the evil age (Mark 3:11; 5:7). Elsewhere Jesus is called the "beloved Son" at his baptism (1:11) and at the transfiguration (9:7). These are moments of divine revelation concerning the nature of Jesus's sonship. The voice heard in the baptismal story echoes the passages concerning the Servant of Isa. 42:1, who has the Spirit placed upon him, and the royal son of Ps. 2:7, who is designated king. The voice from heaven hails Jesus in terms of both the conquering Messiah

---

106. For a similar point, see recently Herbert W. Bateman, "Defining the Titles 'Christ' and 'Son of God' in Mark's Narrative Presentation of Jesus," *JETS* 50 (2007): 537–59.

107. On Son of God as Messiah, see 4 Ezra 7.28–29; 13.32, 37, 52; 14.9; 1 En. 105.2.

and the Suffering Servant of Isaiah.[108] This event represents the commissioning of the royal son for his redemptive mission. In Mark 9:7, the words from the cloud, "This one is my beloved Son," are a divine confirmation of Jesus's teaching in Mark 8:27–9:1 that the Messiah, the Son of Man, must suffer. Hence the royal and redemptive roles of Jesus are merged together. The Son is also a suffering figure, just like the Son of Man, in the parable of the wicked tenants, where the Son is killed and cast out of the vineyard (12:1–11). All this illustrates that the ruling and redemptive roles of the Son of God and Son of Man overlap. The climax of Mark's Christology is probably the confession of the centurion at the cross, "Truly this man was a Son of God!" (15:39).[109] In having a Roman centurion confess Jesus by a title normally used to describe Roman emperors, the confession represents a mocking jibe at the imperial cult and the emperors' pretentious claims to kingship and divinity. In the confession of the centurion, Jesus is made worthy of divine honor despite the dishonor of the cross, and he is validated as the king of Israel by a non-Jew.

With regard to the "Son of Man" title in Mark, there appear to be three different usages of this designation in the narrative: an authoritative figure (2:10, 28), a suffering figure (8:31; 9:9, 12, 31; 10:33, 45; 14:21, 41), and a future judge (8:38; 13:26; 14:62). This title is clearly indebted to Dan. 7:13–14 and had already become a messianic designation in some quarters of Judaism. In Mark, it functions as a messianic title stripped of its nationalistic and political underpinnings; it is invested with a rich array of theological meanings anchored in apocalypticism and combined with notions of the royal son of Israel (e.g., Mark 14:62) and the Suffering Servant from Isaiah (Mark 10:45). As *the* Son of Man, Jesus is the generic human, the representative of Israel, the bearer of divine authority, who comes for a redemptive purpose.

Two minor titles in Mark are "Son of David" and "King of the Jews," yet they are significant for the messianic dimension of Mark's Christology. In the controversy story about plucking grain on the Sabbath, the example of David that Jesus cites stands in correlation with the authority of the Son of Man, who has authority over the Sabbath (2:23–28). On the way to Jerusalem, blind Bartimaeus seeks mercy from Jesus as the "Son of David" (10:46–52). In the triumphal entry, Jesus, as the Coming One, gives the crowds cause to celebrate the coming kingdom of David. In the debate about David's son and David's Lord (12:35–37), we find that "the messianic figure does not merely model the Davidic paradigm but surpasses David in a transcendent manner."[110] While Jesus rejects the ploy to press him into either the cause of revolution or the cause of political collaboration with regard to Roman taxation (12:13–17), he nonetheless experiences the charge of being an insurrectionist (15:9, 12, 18,

---

108. France, *Mark*, 80–81; A. Collins, *Mark*, 150–51.

109. Regarding the anarthrous character of υἱὸς θεοῦ ἦν ("*a* Son of God"), see the discussion in A. Collins, *Mark*, 766–69.

110. Kee, "Christology in Mark's Gospel," 203.

26, 32). In a dramatic irony, Mark's Messiah is none other than the crucified King of the Jews who refuses to save himself (15:32) and is confessed as a Son of God by a centurion (15:39).

By way of summary, in Mark's Christology Jesus is portrayed as the Servant Messiah who exchanges his divine honor as "Son" for human ignominy on the cross as the crucified king. As such, the christological titles, though not necessarily synonymous, are mutually interpretive, and the functions of ruling and redeeming clearly overlap between them.[111] Mark's story of Jesus essentially unpacks the designation "Jesus Christ" from the incipit (1:1) so as to show that the Messiah whom Christians confess is made known as

- The Son of God, who is beloved by the Father, commissioned for his messianic mission by reception of the Spirit, and exercising command over God's enemies, be they demons or the armies of Rome.
- The Son of Man, who is authorized to speak for God, appointed to suffer and rise from the dead, and destined to judge the inhabited world.
- The Son of David, who heals the afflicted of Israel, is greater still than David himself and ushers in David's coming kingdom.
- The King of the Jews, who in an ironic twist, at the end of his triumph, is enthroned as the King of Israel on the cross and there reveals the true power of his kingship by refusing to save himself.

In one sense this is a fairly radical reinterpretation of messiahship, but in another sense it is also an apology for Jesus as the Messiah. The crucifixion is not thrust upon Jesus as a pure accident of unfortunate events; rather, he deliberately embraces it as part of a larger redemptive purpose. Mark's Gospel is fundamentally an apology for a crucified Messiah, something that was pertinent theologically, sociologically, and culturally for Christians in the Greco-Roman world. In other words, Mark's Jesus is not the Messiah despite the cross, but precisely because of it.[112]

On Q and messianism, the subject is, as with anything to do with Q, shrouded in debate and indecision. The Christology of Q and tradition-historical reconstructions of the Q material are all open to question. For instance, James Robinson notes: "Nowhere in the Sayings Gospel Q is Jesus

111. Bird, "Mark 9:1," 30; W. Grundmann, "Χριστός," *TDNT*, 9:528–29; Chialà, "Son of Man," 164; Marshall, "Jesus as Messiah in Mark and Matthew," 131.
112. Gundry, *Mark*, 1022–26; Evans, *Mark*, lxxxi–xciii; Michael F. Bird, "Jesus Is the Christ: Messianic Apologetics in the Gospel of Mark," *RTR* 64 (2005): 1–14. Cf. Leander E. Keck (*Who Is Jesus? History in Perfect Tense* [Columbia: University of South Carolina, 2000], 144): "For Christians, Jesus is not the messiah despite Golgotha but because of it, since after Easter it was Golgotha that redefined *messiah*. In retrospect, this may have been the most important result of the Golgotha hermeneutic."

referred to as Messiah, 'Christ.' "[113] Robinson acknowledges that Q contained reference to Jesus as the "one to come," but he does not think that that designation was part of the original layer of Q.[114] Hence Edward Meadors asks: "Is Q's omission of the term 'Messiah/Christ' forceful evidence of its transmitters' ignorance, disinterest, or perhaps even rejection of Jesus' 'messianic' identity[?]" Meadors himself thinks not and prefers to speak of a messianic "profile," "implications," "endowments," and "functions" of Q material.[115] He then proceeds to identify several messianic texts in Q, including the following: Luke 4:1–13/Matt. 4:1–11; Luke 6:20/Matt. 5:3; Luke 7:22/Matt. 11:5; Luke 10:22/Matt. 11:27; Luke 11:20, 31b/Matt. 12:28; Luke 13:34–35/Matt. 23:37–39; Luke 22:28–30/Matt. 19:28.

Meadors's study is quite maximalistic, and I doubt whether several of the texts he alludes to really are clear and lucid evidence of a messianic portrayal of Jesus. For instance, I am hesitant to ascribe a "messianic authority" to Jesus based on the Beatitudes and woe oracles contained in Q simply for the fact that the eschatological does not equate to the messianic. That Jesus is anointed with the Spirit, as implied by Luke 11:20/Matt. 12:28, could mean that he is a prophetic figure and not necessarily a messianic figure. Despite that, there are at least two elements of Q that contribute to a messianic portrait of Jesus: Luke 7:22/Matt. 11:5 and Luke 22:28–30/Matt. 19:28.

On Luke 7:22/Matt. 11:5, we have already seen ("Jesus as the Anointed One of Isaiah," in chap. 4) that Jesus is approached by followers of John the Baptist with a messianic question, and he answers with a string of citations from Isaiah that parallel 4Q521 regarding the works of the Messiah. Here Jesus is portrayed as the divine agent who is anointed with the Spirit and empowered to bring salvation to the poor and oppressed. Jesus identifies himself as a messianic figure who fulfills the Isaianic script in the execution of his ministry.[116] On Luke 22:28–30/Matt. 19:28, I have already shown ("The Kingdom of God Presupposes a King," in chap. 4) that this text lends itself to a messianic interpretation in which Jesus is a king over Israel in the coming kingdom, while his disciples rule as judges over the twelve tribes. The disciples sit with Jesus in the messianic kingdom and share in the messianic feast.[117]

---

113. James M. Robinson, *Jesus according to the Earliest Witness* (Minneapolis: Fortress, 2007), ix. Similar is Walter Grundmann ("Χριστός," *TDNT*, 9:537): "The Gospel witness does not offer incontestable proof of the Messianic consciousness of Jesus. This observation is supported by the fact that the sayings source does not contain an unequivocal Messianic designation." For a list of scholars who say similar things, see Edward P. Meadors, "The 'Messianic' Implications of the Q Material," *JBL* 118 (1999): 254.

114. Robinson, *Jesus according to the Earliest Witness*, 5.

115. Meadors, "Messianic Implications," 255, 257.

116. Cf. Meadors, *Messianic Herald*, 162–68.

117. While one might be tempted to add Luke 13:28–29/Matt. 8:11–12, this passage refers to a patriarchal banquet rather than to a messianic banquet since it is hosted by the patriarchs and not the Messiah.

The single greatest challenge to using this material as evidence for the historical Jesus being a messianic claimant is the argument that this eschatological and messianic material is part of a later accretion to Q. One might well heed John Kloppenborg's point that "literary history is not convertible with tradition history," so material that belongs to (say) Q^3 is not necessarily inauthentic.[118] Be that as it may, Kloppenborg is not certain of the historical utility of Q, and elsewhere he has exhibited his own suspicions of the theological reasons for positing an eschatologically laden historical Jesus.[119] In response, I side with Helmut Koester, who writes: "The original version of Q must have included wisdom sayings as well as eschatological sayings. It cannot be argued that Q originally presented Jesus simply as a teacher of wisdom without an eschatological message."[120] And also: "The reconstruction of a Jesus who is purified from all eschatological elements finally would make the beginnings of Christianity as a movement with a pervasive eschatological message a complete conundrum."[121]

This view is valid for the following reasons: (1) Eschatological material is strewn throughout all sources of the Jesus tradition, and eschatology links Jesus to John the Baptist and to the early church. (2) Luke 7:22/Matthew 11:5 belongs to a string of similar sayings in Q associated with Isaianic imagery (Luke 3:16–17/Matt. 3:11–12; Luke 6:20–23/Matt. 5:3–12; Luke 13:34–35/ Matt. 23:37–39), and Luke 22:28–30/Matt. 19:28 can also be situated beside Q material that looks forward to the restoration of Israel (Luke 13:28–29/Matt. 8:11–12). (3) The attempt to reconstruct developmental stages in Q is about as futile as using the Gospels of Matthew and Luke to reconstruct the composition history of the Gospel of Mark. Thus, assigning Luke 7:22/Matt. 11:5 and Luke 22:28–30/Matt. 19:28 to the final stages of Q's redaction is unlikely given its correlation with similar themes in Q that are quite probably relatively early in the compositional history of Q. One final caveat on Q: the very nature of the Q document is shrouded in a web of uncertainty (including the valid question of its actual existence), which means that we should be extremely hesitant in thinking that tradition-historical judgments can reasonably rest on theories that build hypothesis on hypothesis regarding Q's development. Any approach to the historical Jesus should not be married to any single theory of the compositional history of Q.

118. John S. Kloppenborg, *The Formation of Q: Trajectories in Ancient Wisdom Collections* (Philadelphia: Fortress, 1987), 287.

119. John S. Kloppenborg, "The Sayings Gospel Q and the Historical Jesus," *HTR* 89 (1996): 344; idem, "As One Unknown, without a Name? Co-opting the Apocalyptic Jesus," in *Apocalypticism, Anti-Semitism and the Historical Jesus: Subtexts in Criticism* (ed. J. S. Kloppenborg and J. W. Marshall; JSNTSup 275; London: T&T Clark/Continuum, 2005), 1–23.

120. Helmut Koester, *Ancient Christian Gospels: Their History and Development* (London, SCM: 1990), 150.

121. Helmut Koester, "The Historical Jesus and the Cult of the Kyrios Christos," *Harvard Divinity Bulletin* 24 (1995): 14.

While Q lacks the messianic title Χριστός, it clearly places Jesus in a messianic role. In light of that, what I regard as *probably* messianic in Q is the following:

> Jesus is an eschatological figure who enacts the Isaianic signs of restoration associated with the deeds of the Messiah (Luke 7:18–22/Matt. 11:2–5).
>
> Jesus will reign in the coming kingdom as king with his twelve disciples as his vice-regents, who exercise justice over a restored Israel (Q [cf. Luke] 22.28–30/Matt. 19:28).

What I regard as *possibly* messianic in Q is the following:

> Jesus is the one to come who initiates the eschatological judgment (Luke 3:16–17/Matt. 3:11–12).
>
> Jesus is greater than Solomon, is the temple builder, and is the son of David (Luke 11:31/Matt. 12:42).
>
> Jesus as the Son of Man is the representative of dispossessed and disinherited Israel (Luke 9:57–60/Matt. 8:19–22).
>
> Jesus is the eschatological prophet who is associated with the messianic age (Luke 13:34–35/Matt. 23:37–39).[122]

Both Q and Mark are important witnesses in plotting the origin of New Testament Christology.[123] There is undoubtedly a disparity between Q and Mark on matters of genre, themes, and even contents. Yet what binds them together is their portrayal of Jesus as a divine agent whose role can be described in categories related to Israel's Messiah.[124] It is surely significant that two of our earliest sources (three if we include Paul [e.g., Rom. 1:3–4; 9:5]) attest to Jesus as a messianic figure.

Crucified Messiah, Not Crucified Martyr

In terms of the effective history of Jesus, the first significant feature that we come across is that, despite the fact that he was crucified as a messianic pretender, he was quickly proclaimed as Messiah by his original followers. The title Χριστός (Christ) is ubiquitous in early Christian usage.[125] The phrase Ἰησοῦς Χριστός probably stands for "Jesus is the Christ" and represents one of the most basic Christian confessions. However, when we reach Paul, Χριστός

---

122. Cf. the eschatological prophet of the messianic age from Qumran in 1QS 9.11.
123. Cf. Schröter, *Jesus und die Anfänge der Christologie.*
124. Cf., with some overstatement, Meadors, *Messianic Herald,* 317–42.
125. Cf. Hengel, "Messiah of Israel," 1–15.

has become a true name, and only a few texts retain titular use in the sense of המשיח. A shift from the titular meaning to a cognomen probably occurred in transmission from Aramaic to Greek as the medium of expressing devotion to Christ.[126] Even so, Χριστός was not a "colorless proper name, however, but an honorific designation."[127] Dahl wrote:

> Thus from the beginnings of Greek-speaking Christianity (within a few years of the crucifixion), the name "Christ" as applied to Jesus must have been firmly established. But this presupposes that Jesus was already designated "the Messiah" and "Jesus the Messiah" in Aramaic-speaking regions. To this extent the Christology of the primitive community from the very first must have been a Messiah Christology.[128]

While Dahl is able to link the messianic title to Jesus's death, he is unwilling to push it back any earlier than that. But I wonder whether Dahl's messianic inference would actually be able to engender a messianic faith—of the variety that we find in the New Testament—in the disciples and into the communities that they formed. Could such an inference, in the face of the historical Jesus's own apparent rejection, discomfort, ambivalence, or alarm toward the title, really make messianism the distinctive mark of their movement and lead them to radically transform certain pillars of Jewish belief? I doubt it. As N. T. Wright puts it: "If Jesus did *not*, in any way, give the impression that he thought he was Israel's Messiah, that merely increases the puzzle still further. Where did the sudden burst of Messiah-belief come from?"[129]

---

126. Ibid., 1, 7; Meier, *A Marginal Jew*, 1:206; K. Rengstorf, "Jesus Christ," *NIDNTT*, 2:338. Alternatively, for Χριστός as "Messiah" in Paul, see N. T. Wright, *Climax of the Covenant* (Edinburgh: T&T Clark, 1991), 41–56; and also Gordon D. Fee, *Pauline Christology: An Exegetical-Theological Study* (Peabody, MA: Hendrickson, 2007), 536.

127. Dahl, "Crucified Messiah," 37.

128. Ibid., 37–38.

129. N. T. Wright, *Resurrection of the Son of God*, 557; cf. Jeremias, *New Testament Theology*, 255: "Finally, the early church's belief in the Messiah may also suggest that Jesus believed himself to be the bringer of salvation. From the beginning it regarded Jesus as the Messiah. It is hardly possible that this belief should have emerged without some starting point from before Easter, because for two reasons it cannot be derived from the Easter faith. Faith in the resurrection of a murdered messenger of God certainly does not amount to a belief in his messiahship (cf. Mark 6:16). Furthermore, the scandal of the crucified Messiah is so enormous that it is hardly conceivable that the community should have presented itself with such a stumbling block"; J. Collins, *Scepter and the Star*, 204: "It is unlikely that Jesus' followers would have given him such a politically inflammatory title after his death if it had no basis in his life. . . . The messianic identity of Jesus must be grounded in some way before his crucifixion"; Allison, *Jesus of Nazareth*, 67: "For no persuasive purely post-Easter explanation for confession of Jesus as 'the Messiah' has been forthcoming. If, however, Jesus' followers already, in his own lifetime, identified him as an eschatological figure 'anointed' by God (Isa 61:1), then the step to confession of him as 'the Anointed One' would not have been large"; Evans, "Messianic Hopes and Messianic Figures," 37: "But there is another factor that strongly supports the probability of Jesus'

The confession that "Jesus is the Messiah" was maintained with such rigor, with deep commitment, and at grave personal expense in the early churches. Χριστός was an honorific title for Jesus, expressing his historical fulfillment of Jewish hopes; yet Χριστός was not merely an honorific title like ἀρχηγός (prince) or πρωτότοκος (firstborn) and given to make Jesus into a "somebody." Nor was it the highest designation that Jesus could be afforded (e.g., Κύριος [Lord] and ὁ υἱὸς τοῦ θεοῦ [the Son of God] are far more elevated terms for attributing transcendent identity and divine function to Jesus). Thus, a desire to address Jesus in honorific terms would not necessarily lead to Jesus being called Χριστός.[130]

The messianism of the early church was not an impromptu add-on to disappointed hopes; instead, it issued forth in a comprehensive reconfiguration of the Jewish belief mosaic on topics such as kingship, vindication, eschatology, restoration, and the fate of the nations. The messianism of the first Jesus followers was not merely the Christianization of a homogeneous and extant Jewish messianic myth; rather, it involved the redefinition and transformation of a selection of pluriform exegetical traditions and apocalyptic narratives around Jesus. Even the highest Christology of the New Testament exhibits connections with its Jewish context. The Christian conception of a crucified but glorious Messiah is best interpreted by Jewish representations of the Messiah as embodying superhuman qualities as a preexistent being who even participates in the reign of God.[131] While messianism developed in different ways by different Jesus-believing groups, adherence to Jesus as messiah was primitive and pervasive. The conviction that Jesus was/is the Messiah was at the root of the proclamation, apologetics, and self-definition of the early Christian communities. Let me explore that more fully.

---

messianic self-identity. Everywhere in early Christian literature Jesus is called the Messiah (or, in Greek, Christ). There is no doctrine of Jesus in which Jesus is understood in non-messianic terms. Even the Ebionites, who rejected the divinity of Jesus, viewed him as Israel's Messiah and as the fulfilment of messianic prophecies. Only certain Gnostics in the second century and later denied Jesus' messianic identity, but these denials were rooted in dogma, not primitive historical tradition. This early, widespread recognition of Jesus by his followers as Israel's Messiah can most plausibly be explained as owing its origin to Jesus and his disciples, not to post-Easter faith superimposed upon an otherwise non-messianic dominical tradition. It would be almost impossible to explain the lack of diversity in opinion on the identity of Jesus if his messiahship did not in fact derive from the pre-Easter ministry."

130. Contra Sanders, *Historical Figure of Jesus*, 242. Note also Berger ("Zum Problem der Messianität Jesu," 25–29), who suggests that the christological interest of the church in applying the messianic title to Jesus was to underscore the nearness of the kingdom associated with his person and Jesus's unique soteriological role for the future of God's people. Once more, titles other than "Messiah" can have a similar effect.

131. Cf. William Horbury, "Jewish Messianism and Early Christology," in *Contours of Christology in the New Testament* (ed. R. N. Longenecker; Grand Rapids: Eerdmans, 2005), 23.

First, a messianic faith was formed and fostered during heightened opposition with religious competitors and rivals.[132] A singular issue was the Christians' appropriation of Scripture in aid of their messianic proclamation, which
seems to have created immediate disputes and divisions where Jesus-believers
were in proximity to other Jewish groups. As Berger puts it: "The difference
between (non-Christian) Judaism and Christianity is sufficiently summarized
by the statement 'Jesus is the Messiah' (or the 'last' messenger of God). At
the same time, this is also the key to the early Christians' use of Scripture, for
this is always designed to show that Jesus is 'the Christ.' "[133] That is verified by
Paul, who indicates that a crucified Messiah was a point of contention with
his Jewish compatriots and a point of compromise with his Jewish Christian
opponents (Rom. 9:32–33; 1 Cor. 1:18–23; Gal. 5:11; 6:12–14; Phil. 3:18). In
fact, the Christ element of Christianity proved to be a point of lasting division
between Jews and Christians (cf., e.g., John 9:22; 12:42; Justin Martyr, *1 Apol.*
31.5–6; *Dial.* 108).[134] A crucified Messiah was far more than an "insufferable
paradox."[135] The scandal erupts because the Messiah was meant to be the
representative of Israel par excellence, and thus "the cross is offensive to Jews
because a crucified Messiah implies a crucified Israel."[136]

Second, Jesus as Messiah constituted a fundamental way of connecting
the story of the church to the story of Israel.[137] The messianic Christology
(tautological as it sounds) of the early church was the central means through
which it related its own claims to be the people of God in *continuity with* and
as the *climax to* Israel's sacred traditions. The confession that "Jesus is the
Messiah" becomes shorthand for a whole set of conclusions about promise and

132. Vermes (*Jesus the Jew*, 155) tries to turn this into a reason for maintaining the title when
he states that retention of "the Messianic idea is chiefly due, it seems, to its psychological and
polemical value in the Jewish-Christian debate." I respond by pointing out that the Christian interpretation of the messianic idea was at the root of the division rather than a response to it.

133. Klaus Berger, *Theologiegeschichte des Urchristentums* (Tübingen and Basel: Francke,
1994), 19: "Die Differenz zwischen (nichtchristlichem) Judentum und Christentum ist auf die
Aussage 'Jesus ist der Messias' (bzw. der 'letzte' Bote Gottes) vollständig und zureichend zurück-
zuführen. Zugleich liegt hier auch der Schlüssel für die Besonderheiten des frühchristlichen
Schriftgebrauchs. Denn dieser ist, wie es immer wieder heisst, darauf ausgerichtet zu zeigen,
dass Jesus 'der Christ' sei."

134. Cf. Michael F. Bird, "The Historical Jesus and the 'Parting of the Ways,' " in *The Handbook of the Study of the Historical Jesus* (ed. T. Holmén and S. E. Porter; 4 vols.; Leiden: Brill,
forthcoming).

135. Jacob Neusner, "Varieties of Judaism in the Formative Age," in *Jewish Spirituality* (ed.
A. Green; London: SCM, 1989), 190.

136. N. T. Wright, "The Paul of History and the Apostle of Faith," *TynBul* 29 (1978): 68. On
the Messiah as fulfilling the task of Israel, see Cullmann, *Christology*, 126–27, 133.

137. Cf. Cullmann (*Christology*, 126–27): "Despite all its inadequacies, therefore, the idea
of the Messiah is important to the extent that it establishes a continuity between the work of
Jesus and the mission of the chosen people of Israel."

fulfillment as this confession relates to eschatology and exegesis and signifies a particular way of reading Scripture.

Third, the messianic theme has widespread permeation and elaboration in the New Testament; this fact underscores the extent to which messianism determined the contours of beliefs, practices, and social relationships for the first Christians. In Matthew's Gospel and the network of churches that this Gospel represented, the messianic identity of Jesus and the messianic mission of Jesus were axiomatic. Matthew amplifies the son of David theme at almost every opportunity (e.g., 1:1; 9:27; 12:23; 15:22; 21:15), and he commends to his audience the Messiah as the "only teacher" (23:10). The Matthean genealogy, birth narrative, and temptation story have the purpose of laying out the credentials for Jesus to be the Messiah of Israel. The fact that Jesus goes "only to the lost sheep of the house of Israel" (15:24) means that Jesus is the Davidic shepherd king who comes to restore and regather Israel.[138]

Mark's Gospel is largely an apology for a crucified Messiah.[139] Though Mark 8:31 represents a sharp transition in the Markan story and propels Jesus to the cross, the passion theme is present much earlier, in 2:19–20; 3:6; and 6:14–29. The Jesus of Mark is the Son of God, Son of Man, and Messiah, who is crucified by his own people. In the end the second evangelist has composed what Jack Kingsbury calls "the Gospel of the Cross."[140]

In Luke–Acts is further emphasis on Jesus as Messiah.[141] In the Lukan writings, Jesus is the Spirit-anointed prophetic Messiah promised by Israel's Scriptures (e.g., Luke 4:18–21; 7:22). In Luke 1–2, Jesus is the Davidic deliverer who comes to save his people from oppression. The Nazareth manifesto at the commencement of the Galilean ministry (4:16–21) makes the work of the anointed prophet of Isa. 61 programmatic for Jesus's own ministry, so much so that he emerges as the anointed prophet of the last days. Peter's confession of Jesus as the "Messiah of God" (9:20) means that Davidic elements are also added to the portrayal of Jesus. The narrative Christology of Luke's Gospel gives way to a mostly titular Christology in the Acts of the Apostles. Peter's Pentecost speech in Acts 2 draws on an explicitly messianic exegesis of Ps. 16 so that Jesus is "Lord and Christ" (Acts 2:36), and this becomes programmatic for the rest of the book. In light of Acts 3:18, 20, Χριστός must mean "Messiah," given the association of fulfillment, divine design, and national renewal:

138. Joel Willitts, "Matthew's Messianic Shepherd-King: In Search of 'the Lost Sheep of the House of Israel,'" *HTS* 63 (2007): 365–82.

139. Gundry, *Mark*, 1022–26; Evans, *Mark*, lxxxi–xciii; Bird, "Jesus Is the Christ," 1–14.

140. Jack Dean Kingsbury, "The Significance of the Cross within Mark's Story," in *Gospel Interpretation: Narrative Critical and Social-Scientific Approaches* (ed. J. D. Kingsbury; Harrisburg, PA: Trinity, 1997), 95.

141. Michael F. Bird, "Jesus Is the 'Messiah of God': Messianic Proclamation in Luke-Acts," *RTR* 66 (2007): 69–82; Stanley E. Porter, "The Messiah in Luke and Acts: Forgiveness for the Captives," in Porter, *The Messiah in the Old and New*, 144–64.

"the Messiah appointed for you."[142] A major fixture in the proclamation of the Lukan Paul is that Jesus is the Christ (Acts 9:22; 17:3; 18:5; 24:24; 26:20, 23; 28:31). Based on this, Rebecca Denova states: "Luke-Acts, we may conclude on the basis of a narrative-critical reading was written . . . to persuade other Jews that Jesus of Nazareth was the messiah of Scripture and that the words of the prophets concerning 'restoration' have been 'fulfilled.' "[143]

The question of whether Jesus is the Messiah dominates the Fourth Gospel too.[144] John parades an ensemble of witnesses and wonders to show his audience that Jesus is the Messiah (John 20:31). The excited report of Andrew to Peter in John's narrative was also the testimony of the Johannine network of churches: "We have found the Messiah" (1:41). In one sentence, Nathanael calls Jesus "Rabbi," "King of Israel," and "Son of God" (1:49). Belief in Jesus as the Messiah is the confession of true discipleship and what marks out the distinctive identity of followers of Jesus amid intra-Jewish debates over the limits of Jewish belief (9:22; 12:42; 16:2; 1 John 3:23–34; 4:2; 5:1–6, 20) and within the Johannine network itself over and against the secessionists (1 John 2:22; 2 John 7). Later Martha confesses Jesus to be "the Messiah, the Son of God, the one coming into the world" (John 11:27). The Johannine Jesus combines the prophetic-Messiah (6:14) and royal-Messiah categories in his own work and person (6:15).

In Paul's letters, while Χριστός may be a cognomen, Paul has not forfeited all traces of the titular usage. In Romans he writes of national Israel: "Theirs are the patriarchs, and from them is the Messiah according to the flesh, who is God over all, forever praised! Amen" (9:5). The Pauline Jesus is no cosmic redeemer sent to awaken the divine spark within individuals; he is none other than the Messiah of Israel (see too 15:8). Paul was also more than aware of the scandal of the cross and the offense that it evoked for his Jewish interlocutors. Yet Paul was adamant that he would not remove this stumbling block, because that would jeopardize the very gospel he had been sent to preach (1 Cor. 1:18–2:5; Gal. 5:11; 6:12–15; Phil. 2:8). The rubric of Paul's Christology is the identification of the human life of "Jesus the Messiah" with the risen and exalted "Lord Jesus Christ."[145]

142. N. T. Wright, *Resurrection of the Son of God*, 555.

143. Rebecca I. Denova, *The Things Accomplished among Us: Prophetic Tradition in the Structural Pattern of Luke-Acts* (Sheffield: Sheffield Academic Press, 1997), 230–31.

144. Rudolf Schnackenburg, "Die Messiasfrage im Johannesevangelium," in *Neutestamentliche Aufsätze* (ed. J. Blinzler, O. Kuss, and F. Mussner; Festschrift for Joseph Schmid; Regensburg: Friedrich Pustet, 1963), 240; see more recently Richard Bauckham, "Messianism according to the Gospel of John," in *Challenging Perspectives on the Gospel of John* (ed. J. Lierman; WUNT 2.219; Tübingen: Mohr Siebeck, 2006), 34–68.

145. Contra Fredriksen, *Jesus of Nazareth*, 135: "Jesus' first appearance had not been messianic, and Paul knew it"; and Bultmann, *Theology*, 1:27: "Paul, like others [the Synoptics], also did not understand it [Jesus's ministry] as messianic." J. Collins (*Scepter and the Star*, 2) writes in contrast: "On the Christian side, we have had the astonishing claim

To many, a crucified Messiah was utter madness (e.g., Acts 26:23–25), but it is precisely what Christians maintained under trying and difficult circumstances. As Joachim Jeremias put it, "Furthermore, the scandal of the crucified Messiah is so enormous that it is hardly conceivable that the community should have presented itself with such a stumbling block."[146] Thus, Jesus as "Messiah" held manifold significance for the early church as its constituting principle (Matthew, John), the object of apologetics (Mark), a mark of distinctive theological and social identity (Johannine literature), and the root of proclamation (Luke, John, and Paul).

The Origins of the *Christianoi*

A second highly significant feature of Jesus's effective history is that eventually his disciples were given (or took) the name Χριστιανοί ("Christians," or "Messianists") as a way of distinguishing them from other religious groups. The early church, in addition to having a messianic proclamation, eventually came to be regarded as a messianic sect. What then does the origination of the term Χριστιανοί tell us of the Jesus movement and perhaps even of the historical Jesus?

The Jesus movement already had their own set of names to identify themselves, including "the Way," "disciples," "saints," "believers," "brothers," and "church."[147] Non-Christian Jews in Palestine, it seems, referred to this group as a αἵρεσις (sect); Ναζωραῖοι, or *Nasrayya* (Nazarenes); and eventually as *minim*, or heretics.[148] It is reported by Luke that, in the ethnically mixed congregation of Antioch, this group was first called Χριστιανοί (Acts 11:26). The issues here are, Is Luke's narration accurate? If so, who designated the followers of Jesus with this term?

First, the use of Χριστιανοί as a self-designation does not occur until the time of Clement, the Didache, Polycarp, and most clearly in Ignatius of Antioch.[149] Before that, Χριστιανοί appears to be a designation used by pagans

---

that Paul, the earliest Christian writer, did not regard Jesus as the messiah [footnote to John Gager and Lloyd Gaston]. The ecumenical intentions of such a claim are transparent and honorable, but also misguided since the claim is so plainly false." Noteworthy is H. C. Kee's comment (*The Beginnings of Christianity: An Introduction to the New Testament* [New York: T&T Clark, 1995], 97): "In the Pauline letters, the primary interest in Jesus is his role as God's Messiah."

146. Jeremias, *New Testament Theology*, 255.

147. Cf. Lee Martin McDonald and Stanley E. Porter, *Early Christianity and Its Sacred Literature* (Peabody, MA: Hendrickson, 2001), 233–34.

148. Acts 24:5, 14; 28:22; Justin Martyr, *Dial.* 108; Tertullian, *Adv. Marc.* 4.8; *m. Sanh.* 10.1; and obviously the *birkat ha-minim* (benediction against the heretics), regardless of its provenance. Cf. Richard Bauckham, "Why Were the Early Christians Called Nazarenes?" *Mishkan* 38 (2003): 80–85.

149. 1 Clem. 3.4; Did. 12.4; Mart. Pol. 10.1; 12.1; Ign. *Eph.* 9.2; 11.2; 14.2; 15.1; *Magn.* 4.1; *Rom.* 3.2–3; *Pol.* 7.3.

or Jews for Jesus believers.[150] Several scholars think that applying the designation Χριστιανοί to the Jesus movement in this early period as Luke does is an anachronism.[151] The vast majority of scholars do not take this view and think that the designation is original and Luke depicts it correctly.[152] Second, was the designation Χριστιανοί first created by Jesus-followers themselves[153] or by outsiders like pagan authorities?[154] The name Χριστιανοί could refer to any number of Jewish groups with messianic aspirations. What is more, the -ιανοί (Greek) suffix is a Latinism (-*iani*) and points to a non-Jewish origin by pagans. It was used predominantly of political groupings around figures like Herod ('Ηρῳδιανοί)[155] and Caesar (Καισαριανοί) and for other groups such as the *Galbiani, Pompeiani,* and *Augustiani.*[156] While Nero was surrounded by his clique of sycophants known as *Augustiani,* for the arson of Rome he punished a group known as the *Christiani.* Yet we have no indication that

150. Cf. Acts 26:28; 1 Pet. 4:16; Tacitus, *Annals* 15.44; Suetonius, *Nero* 16.2; Pliny, *Epistle* 10.96.1–5; Josephus, *Ant.* 18.64; Lucian, *Alexander* 25, 38; *Peregr.* 11–13, 16; and see the inscription in *CIL* 4.679.

151. Helmut Koester, *Introduction to the New Testament* (2 vols.; Philadelphia: Fortress, 1982), 2:92; Dieter Georgi, *The Opponents of Paul in Second Corinthians* (Philadelphia: Fortress, 1986), 348; Gerd Lüdemann, *Early Christianity according to the Traditions in Acts: A Commentary* (trans. John Bowden; London: SCM, 1989), 138–39; C. K. Barrett, *Acts 1–14,* vol. 1 of *A Critical and Exegetical Commentary on the Acts of the Apostles* (ICC; London: T&T Clark, 1994), 1:556.

152. Johannes Weiss, *Earliest Christianity: A History of the Period A.D. 30 to 150* (2 vols.; New York: Harper, 1959), 1:175–76; Henry J. Cadbury, "Names for Christians and Christianity in Acts," in *The Beginnings of Christianity* (ed. F. J. Foakes-Jackson and Kirsopp Lake; 5 vols.; New York: Macmillan, 1920–33), 5:282–86; Martin Hengel, *Acts and the History of Earliest Christianity* (Philadelphia: Fortress, 1980), 103; Wayne A. Meeks and Robert L. Wilken, *Jews and Christians in Antioch in the First Four Centuries of the Common Era* (Sources for Biblical Study 13; Missoula, MT: Scholars Press, 1978), 16.

153. Paul Zingg, *Das Wachsen der Kirche: Beiträge zur Frage der lukanischen Redaktion und Theologie* (Göttingen: Vandenhoeck & Ruprecht, 1974), 217–22; Helge Botermann, *Das Judenedikt des Kaisers Claudius: Römischer Staat und Christiani im 1. Jahrhundert* (Hermes Einzelschriften 71; Stuttgart: Steiner, 1996), 144–88.

154. F. Hahn, "Χριστός," *EDNT* (ed. H. Balz and G. Schneider; ET; 3 vols.; Grand Rapids: Eerdmans, 1990–93), 3:478; W. Grundmann, "Χριστός," *TDNT* 9:536–37; Alexander J. M. Wedderburn, *A History of the First Christians* (UBW; London: T&T Clark, 2005), 69–70; Eckhard J. Schnabel, *Early Christian Mission* (2002; repr., Downers Grove, IL: InterVarsity, 2004), 1:794; Rainer Riesner, *Paul's Early Period: Chronology, Mission Strategy, Theology* (trans. D. Scott; Grand Rapids: Eerdmans, 1998), 112; Martin Hengel and Anna Maria Schwemer, *Paul between Damascus and Antioch* (trans. John Bowden; London: SCM, 1997), 203, 225–30; Adolf von Harnack, *The Mission and Expansion of Christianity in the First Three Centuries* (trans. James Moffatt; 1904–5; repr., New York: Harper & Brothers, 1961), 1:53–54, 411–12; E. A. Judge, "Judaism and the Rise of Christianity: A Roman Perspective," *TynBul* 45 (1994): 355–68; Lüdemann, *Early Christianity according to the Traditions in Acts,* 138.

155. Cf. Matt. 22:16; Mark 3:6; 12:13.

156. Cf. Martin Hengel, "Das früheste Christentum als eine jüdische messianische und universalistische Bewegung," in *Judaica, Hellenistica et Christiana: Kleine Schriften 2* (WUNT 109; Tübingen: Mohr Siebeck, 1999), 200–218; Hengel and Schwemer, *Paul,* 228–29.

followers of Jesus were ever called the Ἰησουιανοί (Jesuians).[157] Tacitus and
Tertullian both point out that Christians take the name from their founder.[158]
There might also be a pejorative sense to the term as "partisan of Christ,"
"client of Christ," or perhaps even "sycophant of Christ."[159]

It is my assessment that the title Χριστιανοί arose when an ideological and
praxis-related divide opened up between Jewish followers of Jesus with their
Gentile clientele and other Jews of Antioch. As such, sooner or later a name
had to be given that designated this group as distinct from other religious
associations in Antioch. The Antiochene Jesus movement had its own range
of vocabulary for self-identification as "the Way" or "brothers," but that
was either too generic or lacked any vituperative connotation to be of use
to outsiders. The application of the label Χριστιανοί would fill this void and
achieve this purpose: the designation and denigration of messianic enthusi-
asts who had taken to the affronting act of breaking down the barriers that
separated Jews and Gentiles in their fellowship and in venerating a crucified
pseudomessiah.

The naming of the "Christians" in Antioch is significant for three reasons:
(1) It designated a group that was at once Jewish and part of the Jewish network
of Antioch, but the term also differentiated these persons from other Antiochene
Jews, especially with regard to their reception of Gentile adherents into their
midst.[160] (2) It implied the political alignment of this group as being oriented toward the restoration of a Jewish kingdom through a Jewish ruler (which perhaps
brought them to the attention of the authorities since pagans knew of Jewish
hopes for a future king; e.g., Tacitus, *Hist.* 5.13; Suetonius, *Vesp.* 4.5).[161] (3) It
demonstrates the very early association of the name Ἰησοῦς with Χριστός and
also the identification of the Jesus movement as a messianic faction. Hence, by
the early to mid-40s of the Common Era, "Christ" has become a name in the
eyes of pagan authorities, and on top of that, the Jesus movement is discernible
from other Jewish groups most of all by its messianic ethos.

To bring these last two sections to a close, let us face a question: Why
did the first Christians preserve the memory of Jesus as Messiah and not
merely as a righteous martyr who had been assumed into heaven and was

157. Hengel, "Messiah of Israel," 8.
158. Tacitus, *Annals* 15.44; Tertullian, *Apology* 3.6.
159. The context of 1 Pet. 4:16 gives the impression that "Christian" is a term of derision
that has been used to designate the audience of the author, and the audience is urged to embrace
the term.
160. Cf. Riesner, *Paul's Early Period*, 112; Meeks and Wilken, *Jews and Christians in Antioch*,
15–16. The important qualification to make is that Jewish synagogues and gatherings probably
had Gentile adherents/sympathizers as well. The difference between them was that the Jewish
Christians in Antioch, at least according to Gal. 2:11–14, accepted Gentiles as full and equal
members of the Israel of God without having first to become proselytes to Judaism.
161. Philo (*Against Flaccus* 36–39) tells of a mob of Alexandrians who ridiculed the notion
of a Jewish king.

now in the bosom of Abraham? Why not venerate him as a prophet who had been morphed into an angelic being? "Messiah" was a politically charged designation that evoked suspicion from Roman authorities and protest from Jewish leaders who regarded a crucified messiah as an oxymoron at best and blasphemous at worst. Abandonment of the title would have assuaged some opposition to their preaching; it would have enabled many to keep their places in Jewish communities of the Diaspora and even allowed them to remain a *religio licita*. However, despite grave adversity, the maintenance of the designation was highly robust and survived under difficult conditions. The widespread adherence to Jesus as the Christ and its function as an integral component of Christian proclamation and identity is surely telling of something. This forces us, I think, to come close to what Cullmann said: "The early Church believed in Christ's messiahship only because it believed that Jesus believed himself to be Messiah."[162]

None of this proves that Jesus claimed to be the Messiah, but we must reckon with the fact that the messianic character of the Jesus movement is surely the most enduring feature of the *effective history* of the historical Jesus. In other words, some way or somehow that effect has to be mapped out in relation to Jesus. Although historical study of Jesus undoubtedly sheds light on early Christology, the converse is equally true.[163] That is not to say that the continuity between Jesus and the church is simple and complete. As James Charlesworth writes, "There is no smooth transition from messianology to Christology."[164] While movements can change radically and depart from the vision and goals of their founder, for the most part, continuity is the norm in the early years.[165] Bockmuehl writes that "it can be historically legitimate to see Jesus of Nazareth in organic and causal continuity with the faith of the early Church."[166] If one

162. Cullmann, *Christology*, 8.

163. Bockmuehl, "Resistance and Redemption," 77.

164. Charlesworth, "Messianology to Christology," 29.

165. We might say that the discontinuity between Jesus and the early church on the role of the "Messiah" is that some of the first Christians universalized the vocation because "according to the New Testament witness Jesus is the Messiah *for* Israel and *for* the Gentile nations [nach dem neutestamentlichen Zeugnis ist Jesus der Messias *für* Israel und *für* die Heidenvölker]" (Hofius, "Ist Jesus der Messias?" 128). Nevertheless, I think it worth pointing out that Jewish conceptions of the Messiah were to some degree already universalized since several expressions of messianism expected the Messiah to rule the earth. See, e.g., Philo, *Rewards* 95; 1QSb 5.27; and Schürer, *History of the Jewish People*, 2:493: "The earlier ideal kingdom of the future did not reach beyond the actual boundaries of the holy land; the later kingdom of God was seen to contain all those who, willingly or by force, were united within one kingdom of the world under the sceptre of Israel. The Messiah was therefore to be judge and ruler of the earth. Even the animals of the earth—i.e., the whole universe in the strict sense—were to be transformed; the old creation was to be destroyed and replaced by the new and the lovely." On Jesus as movement founder, see Michael F. Bird, "The Purpose and Preservation of the Jesus Tradition: Moderate Evidence for a Conserving Force in Its Transmission," *BBR* 15 (2005): 161–85.

166. Bockmuehl, *This Jesus*, 8.

places the historical Jesus between the messianic character of the early church on the one hand and the messianic testimony of the Gospels on the other hand, and if we note the explicit absence of credible witnesses to a nonmessianic Jesus,[167] then this scene surely shows good prima facie evidence for ascribing a messianic role to Jesus.

The alternative is to regard the messianic Jesus as a post-Easter creation or else to postulate a very comprehensive and creative tradition history that renders all of the messianic elements of the tradition as later accretions. The first option has already been rejected; the second option requires far too many steps in the evolution of the tradition, none of which can be proved. In contrast, I think that Jesus's deliberate attempt to act out a messianic vocation is the smoking gun that explains the messianic testimony of the early church (i.e., the theology of early Christianity) and their eventual designation as "Christians" as summarizing negatively the constitutive element of their identity and praxis (i.e., the sociology of early Christianity). It is a reading of early Christian history that has a great deal of explanatory power. What is more, it is a particular reading that does not need to introduce fanciful tradition-historical judgments as to how events of Jesus's life warped from nonmessianic to messianic in the space of a few years or months.

Conclusion

David Flusser asked: "Can one, following the belief of the Church, think that Jesus regarded himself as the Messiah, or must one agree with those who suggest that Jesus's life was 'non-messianic'?"[168] In this study I have chosen the former option. Early Christianity has a testimony, that testimony is based on a memory, and the memory is of one who had who sought to enact a specific vocation as Israel's Messiah. I have deliberately avoided the question of a "messianic consciousness." Instead, I have chosen to speak of messianic claims, messianic actions, evoking messianic hopes, and a career that could be designated as performatively messianic. In this study I have presented a broad cross section of materials based on several patterns and themes from the Jesus tradition (in chap. 4), a series of linear events from Jesus's ministry in Galilee to his final days in Jerusalem (in chap. 5), and the aftereffects of

---

167. While Q does not include the title "Christ," it does include material that can be categorized as messianic (e.g., Q [cf. Luke] 4.1–13; 6.20; 7.22; 10.22; 11.20, 31b; 13.34–35; 22.29–30). According to Schröter (*Jesus und die Anfänge der Christologie*, 166), the Q tradition had no need to reinterpret the title "Christ" since the title "Son of Man" remained the essential aspect of its christological focus, which still overlaps at several points with Mark's Christology. The Gospel of Thomas, though I suspect it to be mostly second century and dependent upon the canonical Gospels, itself has materials that could be categorized as messianic, e.g., logia 10, 16, 66, 98, 107.

168. Flusser with Nutley, *Sage from Galilee*, 109.

Jesus's life and death as evidenced by the messianism contained in some early Christian sources and in the proclamation and social dynamics of the nascent church (late in chap. 5)

What has become evident is that Jesus's career centered on several messianic scenarios based upon the themes of victory, temple, and enthronement, and these were related to the sociopolitical circumstances of Palestine in the first century. His proclamation of the kingdom—with its roots in Isaianic material, his entrance and actions in Jerusalem, and his claim to operate as God's vice-regent—are all de facto messianic claims when seen in light of Israel's sacred traditions.[169] The various units that associate Jesus with messianic ideas are rooted in patterns and paradigms from the Hebrew Bible that were often played out in contemporary messianism as well. It overlaps with them and at the same time often exceeds them.

Jesus's own self-designation takes an Aramaic idiom and combines it with Dan. 7:13 in order to indicate his role as "the man" who will be vindicated and receive a kingdom. The Isaianic program for Israel's new exodus includes good news being preached to the poor and healings by an anointed one. The coming kingdom requires a king to act as God's vice-regent in ruling over a restored Israel. Jesus likens himself to the figures of David and Solomon from Israel's royal dynasty. Jesus announces himself as coming for certain tasks that can be characterized as messianic. Peter's confession of Jesus at Caesarea Philippi confirms the pre-Easter belief in Jesus as the Messiah, and it is abruptly redefined by Jesus along the lines of the suffering Son of Man tradition developed from Dan. 7. Jesus's being anointed at Bethany may be a symbolic and oblique gesture affirming his status as the "anointed one." His final week brings an underlying messianic question to the surface through the triumphal entry and episode in the temple, which alarmed the Judean authorities about his messianic pretensions. Jesus is eventually executed on a messianic charge after facing a messianic question at his trial, to which he answers enigmatically but positively. The *titulus* that mocks Jesus as "king of the Jews" is surely historical and stands as the end result of the messianic career of one who considered himself to have been anointed by God for his task.

Though his earliest followers should have been convinced by an ignominious death that Jesus was a false prophet and pseudo-messiah, they quickly came to the conviction that he was not only the Messiah, but was more than the Messiah and was now to be identified with the Lord in some way. Significant elements of the primitive church not only held to the rather odd belief of a crucified Messiah, but they did so at great cost. The fact that they were given the name "Christians" as opposed to "Jesuians" suggests that the messian-

---

169. Cf. Cynthia Long Westfall, "Messianic Themes of Temple, Enthronement, and Victory in Hebrews and the General Epistles," in Porter, *The Messiah in the Old and New*, 210–29.

ism of this group located on the fringe of Jewish synagogues was perceived by outsiders as one of its distinguishing tenets. The confession that "Jesus is the Christ," which eventually became abbreviated in the name "Jesus Christ" or "Christ Jesus," implies some degree of continuity between the mission of Jesus and the developing Christologies of the early church.

6

Toward a Messianic Christology

According to Amy-Jill Levine: "Whether Jesus *was* a or the messiah is another question, and that can be answered only by the voice of faith, not by the voice of the historian."[1] I am not so sure that I would want to push the messianic question away from history and place it exclusively in the realm of faith and theology. Nonetheless, I do want to ask, What is the theological significance of identifying Jesus as the Christ? Such an overtly theological question might seem out of place in a book about the "historical Jesus." I can only say that the quest for Jesus is theologically motivated by some of its practitioners, and it has huge theological consequences.[2] No doubt some will infer that my historical venture is a purely dogmatic Christology in disguise. I can only respond by saying that my faith would not be particularly impaired or revised if Jesus had not claimed to be the Messiah and the early church had attached this title to him as merely one way of explicating his significance. The early church did, after all, attach certain roles and functions to Jesus—such as "Righteous One," "Prince," and "Firstborn"—that Jesus did not claim for himself. I for one feel no compulsion to project those roles and titles into the ministry of the historical Jesus so as to somehow validate them, and I am not particularly bothered by the fact that they are purely post-Easter formulations

1. Amy-Jill Levine, *The Misunderstood Jew: The Church and the Scandal of the Jewish Jesus* (San Francisco: Harper One, 2006), 85–86.
2. Cf. Michael F. Bird, "The Peril of Modernizing Jesus and the Crisis of Not Contemporizing the Christ," *EQ* 78 (2006): 291–312.

of the early church's faith in Jesus. So I would not be bothered at all if the historical Jesus never claimed to be the Messiah.[3]

Even so, I am convinced, based on a careful review of the evidence, that the historical Jesus did in fact engage in a career that was performatively messianic and that he referred to himself as the quasi-messianic figure of the Son of Man. Now I wish to ask, What is the theological significance of this conclusion? In my reckoning, the answer can be described in three main categories: eschatological finality, continuity between the church and Israel, and the offices of Jesus Christ.

Eschatological Finality

If Jesus is the Messiah, then he is the eschatological deliverer that some Jewish groups were expecting and can even be identified with prophecies and patterns in Israel's sacred traditions. Calling Jesus "the Messiah" does more than identify him as another anointed figure like a prophet, priest, or a king; rather, he is the definitive revelation of God's eschatological deliverance. He is the anointed figure from which none other follows and the Savior that none can exceed. In other words, he is "the One." Jesus becomes the final mediator of the Father's kingdom. One might add that the final inauguration of the messianic kingdom will represent the day when God is finally all in all (1 Cor. 15:27–28). This "day" constitutes the ultimate future of God, who will dwell fully and finally with his people in the new creation. This future has begun in the messianic ministry of Jesus.

The Church and Israel

To use Χριστός as a title or as a name would inevitably require one to relate Jesus to Israel's Scriptures and to Israel itself.

To confess that Jesus is God's "Messiah" was to claim that he was a key figure as he relates to Israel's sacred traditions.[4] Paul's gospel, which he himself received and passed on to the Corinthians, is that "Messiah died for our sins according to the Scriptures, and that he was buried, and that he was raised on the third day in accordance with the Scriptures" (1 Cor. 15:3–4). In the opening state-

---

3. In this regard, I agree completely with Marcus Borg ("An Appreciative Disagreement," in *Jesus and the Restoration of Israel: A Critical Assessment of N. T. Wright's* Jesus and the Victory of God [ed. Carey C. Newman; Downers Grove, IL: InterVarsity, 1999], 235): "Importantly, I do not see the truthfulness of the claim that Jesus is the Messiah as being dependent upon his having said so or thought so himself. . . . To illustrate that principle, I do not think that the truth of 'Jesus is the light of the world' or 'Jesus is the Word made flesh' is dependent on Jesus having thought of himself or spoken of himself in these terms."

4. Cf. Cullmann, *Christology*, 126–27.

ment of Romans, Paul regards the gospel as being about God's Son, who is also David's son, and this gospel is that which God "promised beforehand through the Holy Scriptures" (Rom. 1:1–4). The sacred traditions of Israel provide the authorizing narrative for Paul's story of the crucified and risen Messiah. On the road to Emmaus the risen Jesus informs the two travelers: " 'Oh, how foolish you are, and how slow of heart to believe all that the prophets have declared! Was it not necessary that the Messiah should suffer these things and then enter into his glory?' Then beginning with Moses and all the prophets, he interpreted to them the things about himself in all the scriptures" (Luke 24:25–27). The statement that "Jesus is the Messiah" presupposes a certain way of reading Israel's Scriptures and assumes a certain hermeneutical approach that finds in Jesus the unifying thread and the supreme goal of Israel's sacred literature.

A messiah can only be a messiah *from* Israel and *for* Israel. The story of the Messiah can only be understood as part of the story of Israel. Paul arguably says as much to a largely Gentile audience in Rome: "For I tell you that Christ [Messiah] has become a servant of the circumcised on behalf of the truth of God in order that he might confirm the promises given to the patriarchs, and in order that the Gentiles might glorify God for his mercy" (Rom. 15:8–9). For Paul, then, the Gentiles who enjoy the blessings of Israel must remain in heartfelt gratitude to the Judean nation even if they find themselves, tragically, at odds with them over their own torah and traditions. Although the evangelists all present Jesus as rejected by the Judean populace to some degree or another, they are unanimous in claiming that he came to Israel. This is made explicit in Matthew (15:24; cf. 10:5b–6) and John (1:11). Jesus was not a timeless heavenly redeemer imparting esoteric truths to receptive human vessels.[5] The vision of the New Testament authors and of proto-orthodox Christianity is that the day of salvation has been brought to the world through the Messiah of Israel. Though Gentile Christians could malign and mock Israel for its rejection of the Messiah, the door nonetheless remained open for Israel to enjoy the times of refreshing that God has provided for them through his anointed Son (e.g., Acts 3:20). What is more, it is only because Jesus is the Messiah of Israel that Israel still has an irrevocable calling and a certain place in the divine design (Rom. 11:1–32). In the words of Wolfhart Pannenberg:

5. That stands in contrast to several versions of Christianity in the second century that deliberately cut off Jesus as Christ to Israel and saw this link as a rude embarrassment to the idealization of Jesus as one who stood opposed to the things of the Hebrew race (e.g., Gos. Phil. 51.29–52.24). As such, "Christ" is not the King of Israel but regarded as the ultimate heavenly redeemer (e.g., Gos. Phil. 56.3–15; 61.27–35; 62.7–17). Even the proto-orthodox Epistle of Barnabas appears to devalue messianism in favor of a purely divine Christology (Barn. 12.10–11). In other words, Barnabas considers "Son of God" to be exclusively a divine title rather than a messianic one. This of course reflects the anti-Judaism of the Epistle of Barnabas. Barnabas's anti-messianic remarks, born out of Jewish-Christian disputes in Egypt, can be contrasted with Ignatius (*Trall.* 9.1–2; cf. *Smyrn.* 1.1), who uses Jesus's Davidic heritage ("of the family of David, who was the son of Mary") to counter a docetic Christology.

This connection remained constitutive for the Gentile Christian church. Jesus is what he is only in the context of Israel's expectation. Without the background of this tradition, Jesus would never have become the object of Christology. Certainly this connection is also clear in other titles and generally throughout the New Testament, especially in Jesus' own message. His message can only be understood within the horizon of apocalyptic expectations, and the God whom Jesus called "Father" was none other than the God of the Old Testament. This context is concentrated in a most particular way in the title *Christos*. This title brings into view the whole arc of suspenseful development of traditions from ancient Israel to the Gentile Christian church. This justifies the formulation of the content of the confession of Jesus at the beginning of this chapter: he is the Christ of God.[6]

Prophet, Priest, and King

Christian theology has often expressed its Christology through the *munus triplex Christi*, where the person and work of Jesus Christ are described in terms of the threefold offices of prophet, priest, and king (or more properly the threefold office of "Christ"). These three offices are all messianic in a sense since all three functionaries were anointed with oil, according to the Old Testament. Modern expression of this theological construct is indebted to the Reformation. During the Reformation period, Andreas Osiander is usually credited with popularizing the scheme, which was subsequently taken up and used by Calvin extensively in the *Institutes of the Christian Religion*.[7] The French Reformer wrote: "Therefore, that faith may find in Christ a solid ground of salvation, and so rest in him, we must set out with this principle, that the office which he received from the Father consists of three parts. For he was appointed both Prophet, King, and Priest."[8] I want to advocate that the *munus triplex* goes back even earlier, into early patristic Christology; it has antecedents in Second Temple Judaism and is even consistent with New Testament witness to Jesus.

The notion of a threefold office of Christ reaches back into the ancient church. Eusebius stated that the heavenly Logos is "the only high priest of the universe and the only king of creation and the Father's only archprophet of prophets."[9] In the Pseudo-Clementine *Recognitions* the work of Christ as anointed by God is related to his function as king, prophet, and priest:

> He set, therefore, an angel as chief over the angels, a spirit over the spirits, a star over the stars, a demon over the demons, a bird over the birds, a beast over the

6. Wolfhart Pannenberg, *Jesus, God and Man* (trans. L. L. Wilkins and D. A. Priebe; London: SCM, 1968), 32.
7. Calvin, *Institutes*, 2.15.1–9.
8. Ibid., 2.15.1.
9. Eusebius, *Hist. eccl.* 1.3.8.

beasts, a serpent over the serpents, a fish over the fishes, a man over men, who is Christ Jesus. But He is called *Christ* by a certain excellent rite of religion; for as there are certain names common to kings, as Arsaces among the Persians, Caesar among the Romans, Pharaoh among the Egyptians, so among the Jews a king is called *Christ*. And the reason of this appellation in this: Although indeed He was the Son of God, and the beginning of all things, He became man; Him first God anointed with oil which was taken from the wood of the tree of life: from that anointing therefore He is called *Christ*. (1.45)[10]

Then, however, a priest or a prophet, being anointed with the compounded ointment, putting fire to the altar of God, was held illustrious in all the world. But after Aaron, who was a priest, another is taken out of the waters. I do not speak of Moses, but of Him who, in the waters of baptism, was called by God His Son. For it is Jesus who has put out, by the grace of baptism, that fire which the priest kindled for sins; for, from the time when He appeared, the chrism has ceased, by which the priesthood or the prophetic or the kingly office was conferred. (1.48)[11]

The offices here are related to Jewish-Christian debates on whether Jesus is the Christ of Israel's Scriptures and why the Jews persist in unbelief (*Recog.* 1.43–50). Similar descriptions can be found in Lactantius, Gregory of Nyssa, and John Chrysostom.[12] This is indicative of the early theologizing of the early church as identifying in Jesus the exemplary example of Old Testament patterns and types.

In postexilic Judaism the offices of priest and king were closely related through the "sons of oil," which probably refers to the Persian governor Zerubbabel and the high priest Joshua (Zech. 4:14). Philo could also portray Moses simultaneously as a prophet, priest, and king (Philo, *Moses* 2.1–6). To the consternation of many of their fellow Judeans, the Hasmoneans combined priesthood and kingship. Josephus writes how all three ministrations were present in John Hyrcanus, of whom Josephus states, "[He was] accounted by God worthy of three of the greatest privileges, the ruler of the nation, the office of high-priest, and the gift of prophecy" (*Ant.* 13.299). The Hasmonean usurpation of the priesthood arguably led to the construction of diarchic messianism, or the hope for a royal and priestly Messiah to replace them, as indicated by the Qumran scrolls and the Testaments of the Twelve Patriarchs.

A case can be made that Israel was considered to have a role vis-à-vis the nations as prophet, priest, and king. In certain apocalyptic hopes for restoration, Israel was often conceived of as ruling over the nations (e.g., Jub. 26.23; Sib. Or. 3.49; 1 En. 48.7–10). As a kingdom of priests (Exod. 19:6), Israel could medi-

10. *The Ante-Nicene Fathers* (ed. A. Roberts and J. Donaldson; repr., Peabody, MA: Hendrickson, 1994), 8:89.

11. Ibid., 90.

12. Pannenberg, *Jesus*, 213.

ate between God and the nations (e.g., Philo, *Moses* 1.149). Julius Wellhausen thus summed up Israel's mission to the nations: "There is no God but Yahweh, and Israel is his prophet."[13] In the Old Testament, the anointed functionaries of prophet, priest, and king were the prominent leadership positions of the covenant community. The reconstitution of the Jewish nation would therefore require the renewal of these offices in the new eschatological scenario. In several places in the later prophetic writings, a prophet, priest, or king is described as a "messenger" (מלאך; e.g., Hag. 1:13, prophet; Mal. 2:7, priest; Zech. 12:8, king). In the renewal of the nation, the offices of king, prophet, and priest must be represented in the new age.[14] The Christologies of the New Testament that depict Jesus as prophet, priest, and king remain firmly implanted in their Jewish milieu. Anna Maria Schwemer rightly points out that the rediscovery of the triple office by the Reformation was a theological necessity and was broadly based on the New Testament itself.[15]

In sum, to label Jesus as the Messiah or "Anointed One" is to say something about his role and relation to God and to humanity. He is anointed and set apart for his threefold function: (1) as *prophet* he is a *messenger* from God and is the one who *reveals* God, (2) as *priest* he is a *mediator* between God and human beings and so *reconciles* human beings to God, and finally (3) as *king* he is a *monarch* beside God and *rules* with God.

Conclusion

Jesus undoubtedly had a particular view of himself. Though it is perhaps a little anachronistic, I have no problem in speaking of the "Christology of Jesus," to quote the title of Ben Witherington's useful book. I have no problem either in speaking of the messianism of Jesus as a more specific expression of Jesus's own convictions about himself and his mission. That is not to say, however, that the path from Jesus's messianic aspirations to the description of Jesus as prophet, priest, and king was a straight and short line.

There is no reason to make Jesus out to claim everything that the New Testament writers and patristic authors ascribed to him. We cannot say for certain all the things that a historical figure of antiquity thought or did not think of himself regardless of whether we are talking about Jesus, Josephus, John Calvin, or a Napoleon. At any rate I am convinced that Jesus's own conception

---

13. Cited in Robert Martin-Achard, *A Light to the Nations: A Study of the Old Testament Concept of Israel's Mission to the World* (trans. John Penney Smith; Edinburgh: Oliver & Boyd, 1962), 9.

14. Dunn, "Messianic Ideas," 368.

15. Anna Maria Schwemer, "Jesus Christus als Prophet, König und Priester: Das *munus triplex* und die frühe Christologie," in *Der messianische Anspruch Jesu und die Anfänge der Christologie: Vier Studien* (ed. M. Hengel and A. M. Schwemer; WUNT 138; Tübingen: Mohr Siebeck, 2001), 230. For a critique of the *munus triplex*, see Pannenberg, *Jesus*, 212–25.

of his mission, work, and ministry was indeed formative and constitutive for the primitive christological reflection of the early church. Question, debate, and reflection on who Jesus was probably started during Jesus's own lifetime with his first disciples, continued in the immediate post-Easter setting, and has indeed continued unabated to this very day. That led to the confession that Jesus is the Christ.

Jesus is the goal and fulfillment of the Jewish Scriptures. The person of Jesus links the story of the church to the story of Israel. He is the supreme mediator between God and humanity. Furthermore, Jesus is for the Gentiles only because he was first (and continues to be!) a servant to Israel. He is the royal and divine Son of God only because he is also the suffering Son of Man. Here is the confession not only of the Johannine network but of all Christians: "We have found the Messiah!"

Bibliography

Primary Sources

Aland, B., et al., eds. *The Greek New Testament*. 4th rev. ed. Stuttgart: United Bible Societies, 1994.

Charlesworth, J. H., ed. *The Old Testament Pseudepigrapha*. 2 vols. Anchor Bible Reference Library. New York: Doubleday, 1983–85.

Colson, F. H., et al., translators. *Philo*. 12 vols. Loeb Classical Library. Cambridge, MA: Harvard University Press; London: Heinemann, 1929–53.

Elliott, J. K., ed. *The Apocryphal New Testament: A Collection of Apocryphal Christian Literature in an English Translation Based on M. R. James*. Oxford: Clarendon, 1993.

Epstein, I., ed. *The Babylonian Talmud*. 18 vols. London: Soncino, 1948.

Harden, J. M., ed. *The Ethiopic Didascalia*. Translations of Christian Literature. London: SPCK, 1920.

Holmes, M., ed. *The Apostolic Fathers*. 3rd ed. Grand Rapids: Baker Academic, 2007.

The Holy Bible: New Revised Standard Version; Containing the Old Testament and the New Testament with Apocrypha. Nashville: Nelson, 1993.

Neusner, J., ed. *The Mishnah: A New Translation*. New Haven: Yale University Press, 1988.

Roberts, A., and J. Donaldson, eds. *The Ante-Nicene Fathers*. 10 vols. Reprint, Peabody, MA: Hendrickson, 1994.

Robinson, J. M., ed. *The Nag Hammadi Library*. Leiden: Brill, 1988.

Thackeray, H. St. J., et al., translators. *Josephus*. 9 vols. Loeb Classical Library. Cambridge, MA: Harvard University Press, 1929–53.

Wise, M., M. Abegg, and E. Cook, translators. *The Dead Sea Scrolls: A New Translation*. Sydney: Hodder & Stoughton, 1996.

Secondary Literature

Abegg, M. G., and C. A. Evans. "Messianic Passages in the Dead Sea Scrolls." Pp. 191–203 in *Qumran-Messianism: Studies on the Messianic Expectations in the Dead Sea Scrolls*. Edited by J. H. Charlesworth, H. Lichtenberger, and G. S. Oegema. Tübingen: Mohr Siebeck, 1998.

Ådna, J. *Jesu Stellung zum Tempel: Die Tempelaktion und das Tempelwort als Ausdruck seiner messianischen Sendung*. Wissenschaftliche Untersuchungen zum Neuen Testament 2.119. Tübingen: Mohr Siebeck, 2000.

Allison, D. C. *Jesus of Nazareth: Millenarian Prophet*. Minneapolis: Fortress, 1998.

———. *The Jesus Tradition in Q*. Harrisburg, PA: Trinity, 1997.

Arens, E. *The ΗΛΘΟΝ-Sayings in the Synoptic Tradition: A Historio-Critical Investigation*. Göttingen: Vandenhoeck & Ruprecht, 1976.

Aune, D. "The Problem of the Messianic Secret." *Novum Testamentum* 11 (1969): 1–31.

Barnett, P. "The Jewish Sign Prophets—A.D. 40–70: Their Intention and Origin." *New Testament Studies* 27 (1980–81): 679–97.

Barrett, C. K. *Acts 1–14*. Vol. 1 of *A Critical and Exegetical Commentary on the Acts of the Apostles*. International Critical Commentary. Edinburgh: T&T Clark, 1994.

———. *Jesus and the Gospel Tradition*. London: SPCK, 1967.

Barton, J. *The Nature of Biblical Criticism*. Louisville: Westminster John Knox, 2007.

Bateman, H. W. "Defining the Titles 'Christ' and 'Son of God' in Mark's Narrative Presentation of Jesus." *Journal of the Evangelical Theological Society* 50 (2007): 537–59.

Bauckham, R. *Jesus and the Eyewitnesses: The Gospels as Eyewitness Testimony*. Grand Rapids: Eerdmans, 2006.

———. "Messianism according to the Gospel of John." Pp. 34–68 in *Challenging Perspectives on the Gospel of John*. Edited by J. Lierman. Wissenschaftliche Untersuchungen zum Neuen Testament 2.219. Tübingen: Mohr Siebeck, 2006.

———. "The Son of Man: 'A Man in My Position' or 'Someone'?" *Journal for the Study of the New Testament* 23 (1985): 23–33.

———. "Why Were the Early Christians Called Nazarenes?" *Mishkan* 38 (2003): 80–85.

Beale, G. *The Use of Daniel in Jewish Apocalyptic Literature and in the Revelation of St. John.* Lanham, MD: University Press of America, 1984.

Beasley-Murray, G. R. "The Interpretation of Daniel 7." *Catholic Biblical Quarterly* 45 (1980): 44–58.

Becker, J. *Jesus of Nazareth.* Translated by J. E. Crouch. New York: de Gruyter, 1998.

———. *Messianic Expectation in the Old Testament.* Translated by D. A. Green. Philadelphia: Fortress, 1980.

Bentzen, A. "Quelques remarques sur le movement messianique parmi les juifs aux environs de l'an 520 avant Jésus-Christ." *Revue d'histoire et de philosophie religieuses* 10 (1930): 493–503.

Berger, K. *Die Auferstehung des Propheten und die Erhöhung des Menschensohnes: Traditionsgeschichtliche Untersuchung zur Deutung des Geschickes Jesu in frühchristlichen Texten.* Studien zur Umwelt des Neuen Testaments 13. Göttingen: Vandenhoeck & Ruprecht, 1976.

———. "Die königlichen Messiastraditionen des Neuen Testaments." *New Testament Studies* 20 (1973–74): 1–44.

———. *Theologiegeschichte des Urchristentums.* Tübingen and Basel: Francke, 1994.

———."Zum Problem der Messianität Jesu." *Zeitschrift für Theologie und Kirche* 71 (1974): 1–30.

———. "Zum traditionsgeschichtlichen Hintergrund christologischer Hoheitstitel." *New Testament Studies* 17 (1971): 391–425.

Betz, O. "Die Frage nach dem messianischen Bewusstsein Jesu." *Novum Testamentum* 6 (1963): 24–48.

———. *Jesus der Messias Israels.* Vol. 1 of *Aufsätze zur biblischen Theologie.* Wissenschaftliche Untersuchungen zum Neuen Testament 42. Tübingen: Mohr Siebeck, 1987.

———. *What Do We Know about Jesus?* Philadelphia: Westminster, 1968.

Bird, M. F. "The Crucifixion of Jesus as the Fulfillment of Mark 9:1." *Trinity Journal* 24 (2003): 23–36.

———. "The Historical Jesus and the 'Parting of the Ways.'" In *The Handbook of the Study of the Historical Jesus.* Edited by T. Holmén and S. E. Porter. 4 vols. Leiden: Brill, forthcoming.

———. "Is There Really a 'Third Quest' for the Historical Jesus?" *Scottish Bulletin of Evangelical Theology* 4 (2006): 195–219.

———. *Jesus and the Origins of the Gentile Mission.* Library of New Testament Studies 331. London: T&T Clark, Continuum, 2006.

———. "Jesus and the Revolutionaries: Did Jesus Call Israel to Repent of Nationalistic Ambitions?" *Colloquium* 38 (2006): 127–39.

————. "Jesus Is the Christ: Messianic Apologetics in the Gospel of Mark." *Reformed Theological Review* 64 (2005): 1–14.

————. "Jesus Is the 'Messiah of God': Messianic Proclamation in Luke-Acts." *Reformed Theological Review* 66 (2007): 69–82.

————. "Passion Predictions." Pp. 442–46 in *Encyclopedia of the Historical Jesus*. Edited by C. A. Evans. New York: Routledge, 2008.

————. "The Peril of Modernizing Jesus and the Crisis of Not Contemporizing the Christ." *Evangelical Quarterly* 78 (2006): 291–312.

————. "The Purpose and Preservation of the Jesus Tradition: Moderate Evidence for a Conserving Force in Its Transmission." *Bulletin for Biblical Research* 15 (2005): 161–85.

Black, M. "Aramaic Barnāshā and the 'Son of Man.'" *Expository Times* 95 (1984): 200–206.

————. *The Book of Enoch or I Enoch: A New English Edition with Commentary and Textual Notes*. Leiden: Brill, 1985.

Blevins, J. L. *The Messianic Secret in Marcan Research, 1901–1976*. Washington, DC: University Press of America, 1981.

Blomberg, C. L. *The Historical Reliability of John's Gospel*. Downers Grove, IL: InterVarsity, 2002.

————. "Messiah in the New Testament." Pp. 111–41 in *Israel's Messiah in the Bible and the Dead Sea Scrolls*. Edited by R. Hess and M. D. Carroll R. Grand Rapids: Baker Academic, 2003.

Bock, D. L. *Blasphemy and Exaltation in Judaism: The Charge against Jesus in Mark 14:53–65*. Biblical Studies Library. Grand Rapids: Baker Academic, 1998.

Bockmuehl, M. "Resistance and Redemption in the Jesus Tradition." Pp. 65–77 in *Redemption and Resistance: The Messianic Hopes of Jews and Christians in Antiquity*. Edited by M. Bockmuehl and J. C. Paget. London: T&T Clark, 2007.

————. "A 'Slain Messiah' in 4Q Serekh Milhamah (4Q285)?" *Tyndale Bulletin* 43 (1992): 155–69.

————. *This Jesus: Martyr, Lord, Messiah*. Edinburgh: T&T Clark, 1994.

Bockmuehl M., and J. C. Paget, eds. *Redemption and Resistance: The Messianic Hopes of Jews and Christians in Antiquity*. London: T&T Clark, 2007.

Boda, Mark J. "Figuring the Future: The Prophets and Messiah." Pp. 35–75 in *The Messiah in the Old and New Testaments*. Edited by S. E. Porter. Grand Rapids: Eerdmans, 2007.

Boda, Mark J., and Stanley E. Porter. "Literature to the Third Degree: Prophecy in Zechariah 9–14 and the Passion of Christ." Pp. 215–54 in *Traduire la Bible Hébraïque: De la Septante à la Nouvelle Bible Segond / Translating* the Hebrew Bible: From the Septuagint to the Nouvelle Bible Segond. Edited by R. David and M. Jinbachian. Montreal: Médiaspaul, 2005.

Borg, M. "An Appreciative Disagreement." Pp. 228–43 in Jesus and the Restoration of Israel: A Critical Assessment of N. T. Wright's Jesus and the Victory of God. Edited by Carey C. Newman. Downers Grove, IL: InterVarsity, 1999.

————. Conflict, Holiness, and Politics in the Teachings of Jesus. Harrisburg, PA: Trinity, 1998.

Borgen, P. " 'There Shall Come Forth a Man': Reflections on Messianic Ideas in Philo." Pp. 341–61 in The Messiah: Developments in Earliest Judaism and Christianity. Edited by J. H. Charlesworth. Minneapolis: Fortress, 1992.

Bornkamm, G. Jesus of Nazareth. Translated by I. McLuskey et al. London: Hodder & Stoughton, 1973.

Borsch, F. H. "Further Reflections on 'the Son of Man': The Origins and Development of the Title." Pp. 130–44 in The Messiah. Edited by J. H. Charlesworth. Minneapolis: Fortress, 1992.

————. "Mark xiv.62 and 1 Enoch lxii.5." New Testament Studies 14 (1968): 65–67.

Botermann, H. Das Judenedikt des Kaisers Claudius: Römischer Staat und "Christiani" im 1. Jahrhundert. Hermes Einzelschriften 71. Stuttgart: Steiner, 1996.

Bovon, F. Luke 1: A Commentary on the Gospel of Luke 1:1–9:50. Hermeneia. Translated by Christine M. Thomas. Minneapolis: Fortress, 2002.

Brandon, S. G. F. Jesus and the Zealots. Manchester: Manchester University Press, 1967.

Broadhead, E. K. Prophet, Son, Messiah: Narrative Form and Function in Mark 14–16. Journal for the Study of the New Testament: Supplement Series 97. Sheffield: Sheffield Academic Press, 1997.

Brown, R. E. The Death of the Messiah. 2 vols. Anchor Bible Reference Library. New York: Doubleday, 1993.

————. The Gospel according to John 1–12. Anchor Bible. New York: Doubleday, 1966.

Bruce, F. F. "The Book of Zechariah and the Passion Narrative." Bulletin of the John Rylands Library 43 (1961): 336–53.

Bryan, S. M. Jesus and Israel's Traditions of Judgment and Restoration. Society for New Testament Studies Monograph Series 117. Cambridge: Cambridge University Press, 2002.

Bultmann, R. Theology of the New Testament. Translated by K. Grobel. 2 vols. London: SCM, 1952.

Burger, C. *Jesus als Davidssohn: Eine traditionsgeschichtliche Untersuchung.* Forschungen zur Religion und Literatur des Alten und Neuen Testaments 98. Göttingen: Vandenhoeck & Ruprecht, 1970.

Burkett, D. *The Son of Man Debate: A History and an Evaluation.* Society for New Testament Studies Monograph Series 107. Cambridge: Cambridge University Press, 1999.

Cadbury, H. J. "Names for Christians and Christianity in Acts." Pp. 282–86 in vol. 5 of *The Beginnings of Christianity.* Edited by F. J. Foakes-Jackson and K. Lake. 5 vols. New York: Macmillan, 1920–33.

Cadoux, C. J. *The Historic Mission of Jesus: A Constructive Re-examination of the Eschatological Teaching in the Synoptic Gospels.* London: Lutterworth, 1941.

Caird, G. B. *New Testament Theology.* Edited by L. D. Hurst. Oxford: Clarendon, 1994.

———. *Saint Luke.* Harmondsworth, UK: Penguin, 1963.

Caragounis, C. C. *The Son of Man: Vision and Interpretation.* Wissenschaftliche Untersuchungen zum Neuen Testament 38. Tübingen: Mohr Siebeck, 1986.

Casey, M. *Aramaic Sources of Mark's Gospel.* Society for New Testament Studies Monograph Series 102. Cambridge: Cambridge University Press, 1998.

———. "General, Generic, and Indefinite: The Use of the Term 'Son of Man' in Aramaic Sources and in the Teaching of Jesus." *Journal for the Study of the New Testament* 29 (1987): 21–56.

———. "Idiom and Translation: Some Aspects of the Son of Man Problem." *New Testament Studies* 41 (1995): 164–82.

———. *The Solution to the Son of Man Problem.* Library of New Testament Studies 343. London: T&T Clark, 2007.

———. *The Son of Man: The Interpretation and Influence of Daniel 7.* London: SPCK, 1979.

Catchpole, D. R. *The Trial of Jesus.* Leiden: Brill, 1971.

Charlesworth J. H. "From Messianology to Christology: Problems and Prospects." Pp. 3–35 in *The Messiah: Developments in Earliest Judaism and Christianity.* Edited by J. H. Charlesworth. Minneapolis: Fortress, 1992.

———. *Jesus within Judaism: New Light from Exciting Archaeological Discoveries.* London: SPCK, 1989.

———, ed. *The Messiah: Developments in Earliest Judaism and Christianity.* Minneapolis: Fortress, 1992.

———. "Solomon and Jesus: The Son of David in Ante-Markan Traditions." Pp. 125–51 in *Biblical and Humane.* Edited by L. B. Elder et al. Atlanta: Scholars Press, 1996.

————. "The Son of David: Solomon and Jesus (Mark 10.47)." Pp. 72–87 in *The New Testament and Hellenistic Judaism*. Edited by P. Borgen and S. Giverson. Aarhus: Aarhus University Press, 1995.

Charlesworth, J. H., H. Lichtenberger, and G. Oegema, eds. *Qumran-Messianism: Studies on the Messianic Expectation in the Dead Sea Scrolls*. Tübingen: Mohr Siebeck, 1998.

Chester, A. *Messiah and Exaltation: Jewish Messianic and Visionary Traditions and New Testament Christology*. Wissenschaftliche Untersuchungen zum Neuen Testament 207. Tübingen: Mohr Siebeck, 2007.

————. "The Parting of the Ways: Eschatology and Messianic Hope." Pp. 239–313 in *Jews and Christians: The Parting of the Ways, A.D. 70 to 135*. Edited by J. D. G. Dunn. Grand Rapids: Eerdmans, 1992.

Chialà, S. "The Son of Man: The Evolution of an Expression." Pp. 153–78 in *Enoch and the Messiah Son of Man: Revisiting the Book of Parables*. Edited by G. Boccaccini. Grand Rapids: Eerdmans, 2007.

Chilton, B. D. "Jesus *ben* David: Reflections on the Davidssohnfrage." *Journal for the Study of the New Testament* 14 (1982): 88–112.

————. "(The) Son of (the) Man, and Jesus." Pp. 259–88 in *Authenticating the Words of Jesus*. Edited by B. D. Chilton and C. A. Evans. Leiden: Brill, 1999.

Cohn-Sherbok, D. *The Jewish Messiah*. Edinburgh: T&T Clark, 1997.

Collins, A. Y. *Mark*. Hermeneia. Philadelphia: Fortress, 2007.

————. "The Origin of the Designation of Jesus as 'Son of Man.'" Pp. 139–58 in *Cosmology and Eschatology in Jewish and Christian Apocalypticism*. Leiden: Brill, 1996.

————. "The 'Son of Man' Tradition and the Book of Revelation." Pp. 159–97 in *Cosmology and Eschatology in Jewish and Christian Apocalypticism*. Leiden: Brill, 1996.

Collins, J. J. "The Background of the 'Son of God' Text." *Bulletin for Biblical Research* 7 (1997): 51–61.

————. " 'He Shall Not Judge by What His Eyes See': Messianic Authority in the Dead Sea Scrolls." *Dead Sea Discoveries* 2 (1995): 145–64.

————. "Messianism in the Maccabean Period." Pp. 97–109 in *Judaism and Their Messiahs at the Turn of the Christian Era*. Edited by J. Neusner, W. S. Green, and E. S. Frerichs. Cambridge: Cambridge University Press, 1987.

————. *The Scepter and the Star: The Messiahs of the Dead Sea Scrolls and Other Ancient Literature*. Anchor Bible Reference Library. New York: Doubleday, 1995.

————. "The Son of God Text from Qumran." Pp. 65–82 in *From Jesus to John: Essays on Jesus and New Testament Christology*. Edited by M. C. de

Boer. Festschrift for Marinus de Jonge. Journal for the Study of the New Testament: Supplement Series 84. Sheffield: JSOT Press, 1993.

———. "The Works of the Messiah." *Dead Sea Discoveries* 1 (1994): 98–112.

Colpe, C. "ὁ υἱὸς τοῦ ἀνθρώπου." Pp. 400–477 in vol. 8 of *Theological Dictionary of the New Testament*. Edited by G. Kittel and G. Friedrich. Translated by G. W. Bromiley. 10 vols. Grand Rapids: Eerdmans, 1964–76.

Corley, K. E. "The Anointing of Jesus in the Synoptic Tradition: An Argument for Authenticity." *Journal for the Study of the Historical Jesus* 1 (2003): 61–72.

Crossan, J. D. *The Historical Jesus*. San Francisco: HarperCollins, 1991.

Crossan, J. D., and J. L. Reed. *Excavating Jesus: Beneath the Stones, behind the Texts*. San Francisco: HarperCollins, 2001.

Cullmann, O. *The Christology of the New Testament*. Translated by S. C. Guthrie and C. A. M. Hall. 2nd ed. London: SCM, 1963.

Dahl, N. A. *The Crucified Messiah and Other Essays*. Minneapolis: Augsburg, 1974.

———. "Messianic Ideas and the Crucifixion of Jesus." Pp. 382–403 in *The Messiah*. Edited by J. H. Charlesworth. Minneapolis: Fortress, 1992.

Davies, W. D., and D. C. Allison. *The Gospel according to Saint Matthew*. 3 vols. International Critical Commentary. Edinburgh: T&T Clark, 1988–97.

Day, J., ed. *King and Messiah in Israel and the Ancient Near East*. Journal for the Study of the Old Testament: Supplement Series 270. Sheffield: Sheffield Academic Press, 1998.

Denova, R. I. *The Things Accomplished among Us: Prophetic Tradition in the Structural Pattern of Luke-Acts*. Sheffield: Sheffield Academic Press, 1997.

Dinkler, E. "Peter's Confession and the Satan Saying: The Problem of Jesus' Messiahship." Pp. 169–202 in *The Future of Our Religious Past: Essays in Honour of Rudolf Bultmann*. Edited by J. M. Robinson. New York: Harper & Row, 1971.

Dodd, C. H. *According to the Scriptures*. Digswell Place, UK: Nisbet, 1952.

———. *The Founder of Christianity*. London: Collins, 1971.

———. *Historical Tradition in the Fourth Gospel*. Cambridge: Cambridge University Press, 1963.

Duling, D. C. "Solomon, Exorcism, and the Son of David." *Harvard Theological Review* 68 (1975): 235–52.

Dunn, J. D. G. *Jesus Remembered*. Vol. 1 of *Christianity in the Making*. Grand Rapids: Eerdmans, 2003.

————. "Messianic Ideas and Their Influence on the Jesus of History." Pp. 365–81 in *The Messiah*. Edited by J. H. Charlesworth. Minneapolis: Fortress, 1992.

————. "The Messianic Secret in Mark." *Tyndale Bulletin* 21 (1970): 92–117.

————. *Romans 1–8*. Word Biblical Commentary 38A. Dallas: Word, 1988.

————. " 'Son of God' as 'Son of Man' in the Dead Sea Scrolls? A Response to John Collins on 4Q246." Pp. 198–210 in the *Scrolls and the Scriptures: Qumran Fifty Years After*. Edited by S. E. Porter and C. A. Evans. Journal for the Study of the Pseudepigrapha: Supplement Series 26. Sheffield: Sheffield Academic Press, 1997.

Ebeling, H. J. *Das Messiasgeheimnis und die Botschaft des Markusevangelium*. Berlin: Töpelmann, 1939.

Eco, U. *The Limits of Interpretation*. Bloomington: Indiana University Press, 1990.

Elliott, J. K. "The Anointing of Jesus." *Expository Times* 85 (1973–74): 105–7.

Elliott, M. A. *The Survivors of Israel: A Reconsideration of the Theology of Pre-Christian Judaism*. Grand Rapids: Eerdmans, 2000.

Evans, C. A. "The Aramaic Psalter and the New Testament: Praising the Lord in History and Prophecy." Pp. 44–91 in *From Prophecy to Testament: The Function of the Old Testament in the New*. Edited by C. A. Evans. Peabody, MA: Hendrickson, 2004.

————. "Defeating Satan and Liberating Israel: Jesus and Daniel's Visions." *Journal for the Study of the Historical Jesus* 1 (2003): 161–70.

————, ed. *Encyclopedia of the Historical Jesus*. New York: Routledge, 2008

————. *Jesus and His Contemporaries*. Leiden: Brill, 1995.

————. "Jesus and the Dead Sea Scrolls from Qumran Cave 4." Pp. 91–100 in *Eschatology, Messianism, and the Dead Sea Scrolls*. Edited by C. A. Evans and P. W. Flint. Grand Rapids: Eerdmans, 1997.

————. "Jesus and Zechariah's Messianic Hope." Pp. 373–88 in *Authenticating the Activities of Jesus*. Edited by B. Chilton and C. A. Evans. Leiden: Brill, 1999.

————. *Mark 8:27–16:20*. Word Biblical Commentary 34B. Nashville: Nelson, 2001.

————. "Messianic Hopes and Messianic Figures in Late Antiquity." *Journal of Greco-Roman Christianity and Judaism* 3 (2006): 9–40.

————. "Messianism." Pp. 698–707 in *Dictionary of New Testament Background*. Edited by C. A. Evans and S. E. Porter. Downers Grove, IL: InterVarsity, 2000.

————. "The Passion of Jesus: History Remembered or Prophecy Historicized?" *Bulletin for Biblical Research* 6 (1996): 159–65.

————. "Qumran's Messiah: How Important Is He?" Pp. 135–49 in *Religion in the Dead Sea Scrolls*. Edited by John J. Collins and Robert A. Kugler. Grand Rapids: Eerdmans, 2000.

————. "Son of God Text (4Q246)." Pp. 1134–37 in *Dictionary of New Testament Background*. Edited by C. A. Evans and S. E. Porter. Downers Grove, IL: InterVarsity, 2000.

Fee, G. D. *Pauline Christology: An Exegetical-Theological Study*. Peabody, MA: Hendrickson, 2007.

Fiorenza, E. S. "Re-visioning Christian Origins: *In Memory of Her* Revisited." Pp. 240–42 in *Christian Origins: Worship, Belief, and Society*. Edited by K. J. O'Mahoney. Journal for the Study of the New Testament: Supplement Series 241. Sheffield: Sheffield Academic Press, 2003.

Fishbane, M. A. *Biblical Interpretation in Ancient Israel*. Oxford: Clarendon, 1985.

Fitzmyer, J. A. "The Aramaic 'Son of God' Document from Qumran." Pp. 163–78 in *Methods of Investigation of the Dead Sea Scrolls and the Khirbet Qumran Site: Present Realities and Future Prospects*. Edited by M. O. Wise et al. Annals of the New York Academy of Sciences 722. New York: New York Academy of Sciences, 1994.

————. "4Q246: The 'Son of God' Document from Qumran." *Biblica* 74 (1993): 153–74.

————. *The Gospel according to Luke*. 2 vols. Anchor Bible. New York: Doubleday, 1983–85.

————. *The One Who Is to Come*. Grand Rapids: Eerdmans, 2007.

————. "The Palestinian Background of 'Son of God' as a Title for Jesus." Pp. 567–77 in *Texts and Contexts: Biblical Texts in Their Textual and Situational Contexts*. Edited by T. Fornberg and D. Hellholm. Festschrift for L. Hartman. Oslo: Scandinavian University Press, 1995.

————. *A Wandering Aramean: Collected Aramaic Essays*. Society of Biblical Literature Monograph Series 25. Missoula, MT: Scholars Press, 1979.

Fletcher-Louis, C. H. T. "Jesus as the High Priestly Messiah: Part 1." *Journal for the Study of the Historical Jesus* 4 (2006): 155–75

————. "Jesus as the High Priestly Messiah: Part 2." *Journal for the Study of the Historical Jesus* 5 (2007): 57–79.

Flusser, D., with R. S. Nutley. *The Sage from Galilee: Rediscovering Jesus' Genius.* Grand Rapids: Eerdmans, 2007.

France, R. T. *The Gospel of Mark.* New International Greek Testament Commentary. Grand Rapids: Eerdmans, 2002.

Fredriksen, P. *Jesus of Nazareth, King of the Jews.* New York: Vintage, 1999.

Freyne, S. "A Galilean Messiah?" *Studia theologica* 55 (2001): 198–218.

Fuller, R. H. *The Foundations of New Testament Christology.* New York: Scribner, 1965.

———. *The Mission and Achievement of Jesus: An Examination of the Presuppositions of New Testament Christology.* Studies in Biblical Theology 12. London: SCM, 1954.

Funk, R. W., and R. W. Hoover. *The Five Gospels: The Search for the Authentic Words of Jesus.* San Francisco: HarperCollins, 1997.

García Martínez, F. "Messianische Erwartungen in den Qumranschriften." *Jahrbuch für biblische Theologie* 8 (1993): 171–208.

Gathercole, S. J. *The Pre-existent Son: Recovering the Christologies of Matthew, Mark, and Luke.* Grand Rapids: Eerdmans, 2006.

Georgi, D. *The Opponents of Paul in Second Corinthians.* Philadelphia: Fortress, 1986.

Gese, H. *Zur biblischen Theologie.* Munich: Kaiser, 1977.

Gnilka, J. *Jesus of Nazareth: Message and History.* Translated by S. S. Schatzmann. Peabody, MA: Hendrickson, 1997.

Goulder, M. "Psalm 8 and the Son of Man." *New Testament Studies* 48 (2002): 18–28.

Grimm, W. *Weil ich dich liebe: Die Verkündigung Jesu und Deuterojesaja.* Bern: Herbert Lang, 1976.

Gruenwald, I., et al., eds. *Messiah and Christos: Studies in the Jewish Origins of Christianity.* Festschrift for David Flusser. Texte und Studien zum antiken Judentum 32. Tübingen: Mohr Siebeck, 1992.

Grundmann, W. "Χριστός." Pp. 527–80 in vol. 9 of *Theological Dictionary of the New Testament.* Edited by G. Kittel and G. Friedrich. Translated by G. W. Bromiley. 10 vols. Grand Rapids: Eerdmans, 1964–76.

Gundry, R. H. *Mark: A Commentary on His Apology for the Cross.* Grand Rapids: Eerdmans, 1993.

Hahn, F. "Χριστός." Pp. 478–86 in vol. 3 of *Exegetical Dictionary of the New Testament.* Edited by H. Balz and G. Schneider. 3 vols. Grand Rapids: Eerdmans, 1990–93.

———. *The Titles of Jesus in Christology: Their History in Early Christianity.* Translated by J. Knight and G. Ogg. New York: World, 1969.

Hampel, V. *Menschensohn und historischer Jesu: Ein Rätselwort als Schlüssel zum messianischen Selbstverständnis Jesu*. Neukirchen-Vluyn: Neukirchener Verlag, 1990.

Hanson, P. D. "Messiahs and Messianic Figures in Proto-apocalyptic Judaism." Pp. 67–75 in *The Messiah: Developments in Earliest Judaism and Christianity*. Edited by J. H. Charlesworth. Minneapolis: Fortress, 1992.

Hare, D. A. *The Son of Man Tradition*. Philadelphia: Fortress, 1990.

Harnack, A. von. " 'Ich bin gekommen': Die ausdrücklichen Selbstzeugnisse Jesu über den Zweck seiner Sendung und seines Kommens." *Zeitschrift für Theologie und Kirche* 22 (1912): 1–30.

————. *The Mission and Expansion of Christianity in the First Three Centuries*. Translated by James Moffatt. 2 vols. 1904–5. Reprint, New York: Harper & Brothers, 1961.

Hay, D. M. *Glory at the Right Hand: Psalm 110 in Early Christianity*. Nashville: Abingdon, 1973.

Hay, L. S. "Mark's Use of the Messianic Secret." *Journal of the American Academy of Religion* 35 (1967): 16–27.

Head, P. M. "A Text-Critical Study of Mark 1.1: 'The Beginning of the Gospel of Jesus Christ.' " *New Testament Studies* 37 (1991): 621–29.

Heid, S. "Frühjüdische Messianologie in Justins 'Dialog.' " *Jahrbuch für biblische Theologie* 8 (1993): 219–38.

Heintz, J.-G. "Royal Traits and Messianic Figures: A Thematic and Iconographical Approach." Pp. 52–66 in *The Messiah: Developments in Earliest Judaism and Christianity*. Edited by J. H. Charlesworth. Minneapolis: Fortress, 1992.

Hengel, M. *Acts and the History of Earliest Christianity*. Philadelphia: Fortress, 1980.

————. "The Effective History of Isaiah 53 in the Pre-Christian Period." Pp. 75–146 in *The Suffering Servant: Isaiah 53 in Jewish and Christian Sources*. Edited by B. Janowski and P. Stuhlmacher. Grand Rapids: Eerdmans, 2004.

————. "Das früheste Christentum als eine jüdische messianische und universalistische Bewegung." Pp. 200–218 in *Judaica, Hellenistica et Christiana: Kleine Schriften 2*. Wissenschaftliche Untersuchungen zum Neuen Testament 109. Tübingen: Mohr Siebeck, 1999.

————. "Jesus, the Messiah of Israel." Pp. 1–72 in *Studies in Early Christology*. London: SCM, 1995.

————. "Jesus, the Messiah of Israel: The Debate about the 'Messianic Mission' of Jesus." Pp. 323–49 in *Authenticating the Activities of Jesus*. Edited by B. D. Chilton and C. A. Evans. Leiden: Brill, 1999.

————. " 'Setz dich zu meiner Rechten!' Die Inthronisation Christi zur Rechten Gottes und Psalm 110,1." Pp. 108–94 in *Le trône de Dieu*. Edited by M. Philonenko. Tübingen: Mohr Siebeck, 1993.

————. *The Zealots*. Edinburgh: T&T Clark, 1989.

Hengel, M., and A. M. Schwemer. *Paul between Damascus and Antioch*. Translated by John Bowden. London: SCM, 1997.

Hess, R. S., and M. Daniel Carroll R., eds. *Israel's Messiah in the Bible and the Dead Sea Scrolls*. Grand Rapids: Baker Academic, 2003.

Hofius, O. "Ist Jesus der Messias? Thesen." *Jahrbuch für biblische Theologie* 8 (1993): 103–29.

Holtzmann, H. J. *Lehrbuch der neutestamentlichen Theologie*. Edited by D. A. Jülicher and W. Bauer. 2nd ed. 2 vols. Tübingen: Mohr, 1911.

Hooker, M. D. "Is the Son of Man Problem Really Insoluble?" Pp. 155–68 in *Text and Interpretation*. Edited by E. Best and R. McL. Wilson. Festschrift for Matthew Black. Cambridge: Cambridge University Press, 1979.

Horbury, W. "Jewish Messianism and Early Christology." Pp. 3–24 in *Contours of Christology in the New Testament*. Edited by R. N. Longenecker. Grand Rapids: Eerdmans, 2005.

————. *Jewish Messianism and the Cult of Christ*. London: SCM, 1998.

————. "The Messianic Associations of 'the Son of Man.' " *Journal of Theological Studies* 36 (1985): 34–55.

————. *Messianism among Jews and Christians: Twelve Biblical and Historical Studies*. London: Continuum/T&T Clark, 2003.

Horsley, R. A. " 'Messianic' Figures and Movements in First-Century Palestine." Pp. 276–95 in *The Messiah*. Edited by J. H. Charlesworth. Minneapolis: Fortress, 1992.

Horsley, R. A., and J. Hanson. *Bandits, Prophets and Messiahs: Popular Movements at the Time of Jesus*. San Francisco: Harper & Row, 1986.

Hurst, L. D. "Did Qumran Expect Two Messiahs?" *Bulletin for Biblical Research* 9 (1999): 157–80.

Hurtado, L. W. "Christ." Pp. 106–17 in *Dictionary of Jesus and the Gospels*. Edited by J. B. Green, S. McKnight, and I. H. Marshall. Downers Grove, IL: InterVarsity, 1992.

————. *Lord Jesus Christ: Devotion to Jesus in Earliest Christianity*. Grand Rapid: Eerdmans, 2003.

Ingolfsland, D. "Kloppenborg's Stratification of Q and Its Significance for Historical Jesus Studies." *Journal of the Evangelical Theological Society* 46 (2003): 217–32.

Jeremias, J. *New Testament Theology: The Proclamation of Jesus*. Translated by J. Bowden. London: SCM, 1971.

Jonge, H. J. de. "The Historical Jesus' View of Himself and of His Mission." Pp. 21–37 in *From Jesus to John: Essays on Jesus and New Testament Christology in Honour of Marinus de Jonge*. Edited by M. C. de Boer. Sheffield: JSOT Press, 1993.

Jonge, M. de. "Christ." Pp. 914–21 in vol. 1 of *Anchor Bible Dictionary*. Edited by D. N. Freedman. 6 vols. Anchor Bible Reference Library. New York: Doubleday, 1992.

———. *God's Final Envoy: Early Christology and Jesus' Own View of His Mission*. Grand Rapids: Eerdmans, 1998.

———. *Jesus, the Servant-Messiah*. New Haven: Yale University Press, 1991.

———. "Messiah." Pp. 777–78 in vol. 4 of *Anchor Bible Dictionary*. Edited by D. N. Freedman. 6 vols. Anchor Bible Reference Library. New York: Doubleday, 1992.

———. "The Use of the Word 'Anointed' in the Time of Jesus." *Novum Testamentum* 8 (1966): 132–48.

Jossa, G. *Jews or Christians?* Translated by Molly Rogers. Wissenschaftliche Untersuchungen zum Neuen Testament 202. Tübingen: Mohr Siebeck, 2006.

Judge, E. A. "Judaism and the Rise of Christianity: A Roman Perspective." *Tyndale Bulletin* 45 (1994): 355–68.

Juel, D. H. "The Origin of Mark's Christology." Pp. 449–60 in *The Messiah*. Edited by James H. Charlesworth. Minneapolis: Fortress, 1992.

Käsemann, E. "The Problem of the Historical Jesus." Pp. 15–47 in *Essays on New Testament Themes*. Translated by W. J. Montague. Studies in Biblical Theology 41. London: SCM, 1964.

Keck, L. E. *Who Is Jesus? History in Perfect Tense*. Columbia: University of South Carolina, 2000.

Kee, H. C. *The Beginnings of Christianity: An Introduction to the New Testament*. New York: T&T Clark, 1995.

———. "Christology in Mark's Gospel." Pp. 187–208 in *Judaisms and Their Messiahs at the Turn of the Christian Era*. Edited by J. Neusner, W. S. Green, and E. Frerichs. Cambridge: Cambridge University Press, 1987.

———. *What Can We Know about Jesus?* New York: Cambridge University Press, 1990.

Kim, S. *The "Son of Man" as the Son of God*. Wissenschaftliche Untersuchungen zum Neuen Testament 30. Tübingen: Mohr Siebeck, 1983.

Kingsbury, J. D. "The Significance of the Cross within Mark's Story." Pp. 95–105 in *Gospel Interpretation: Narrative-Critical and Social-Scientific Approaches*. Edited by J. D. Kingsbury. Harrisburg, PA: Trinity, 1997.

Kinman, B. "Jesus' Royal Entry into Jerusalem." *Bulletin for Biblical Research* 15 (2005): 223–60.

Klausner, J. *Jesus of Nazareth: His Life, Times, and Teaching.* Translated by Herbert Danby. London: Allen & Unwin, 1929.

———. *The Messianic Idea in Israel from Its Beginning to the Completion of the Mishnah.* New York: Macmillan, 1955.

Kloppenborg, J. S. "As One Unknown, without a Name? Co-opting the Apocalyptic Jesus." Pp. 1–23 in *Apocalypticism, Anti-Semitism and the Historical Jesus: Subtexts in Criticism.* Edited by J. S. Kloppenborg and J. W. Marshall. Journal for the Study of the New Testament: Supplement Series 275. London: T&T Clark/Continuum, 2005.

———. *The Formation of Q: Trajectories in Ancient Wisdom Collections.* Philadelphia: Fortress, 1987.

Knight, J. *Jesus: An Historical and Theological Investigation.* Understanding the Bible and Its World. London: T&T Clark, 2004.

Knohl, I. *The Messiah before Jesus: The Suffering Servant and the Dead Sea Scrolls.* Translated by D. Maisel. Berkeley: University of California, 2000.

Koch, K. "Heilandserwartungen im Judäa der Zeitenwende." Pp. 107–35 in *Die Schriftrollen von Qumran: Zur aufregenden Geschichte ihrer Erforschung und Deutung.* Edited by S. Talmon. Regensburg: Pustet, 1998.

———. "Messias und Menschensohn: Die zweistufige messianologie der jüngeren Apocalyptic." *Jahrbuch für biblische Theologie* 8 (1993): 73–102.

Koester, H. *Ancient Christian Gospels: Their History and Development.* London, SCM, 1990.

———. "The Historical Jesus and the Cult of the Kyrios Christos." *Harvard Divinity Bulletin* 24 (1995): 13–18.

———. *Introduction to the New Testament.* 2 vols. Philadelphia: Fortress, 1982.

Kuhn, H.-W. "Röm 1,3f und der davidische Messias als Gottessohn in den Qumrantexten." Pp. 103–12 in *Lese-Zeichen für Annelies Findeiss zum 65. Geburtstag am 15. März 1984.* Edited by C. Burchard and G. Theissen. Dielheimer Blätter zum Alten Testament Beihefte 3. Heidelberg: Carl Winter, 1984.

Kuhn, K. A. "The 'One Like a Son of Man' Becomes the 'Son of God.'" *Catholic Biblical Quarterly* 69 (2007): 22–42.

Kümmel, W. G. "Jesu Antwort an Johannes den Täufer: Ein Beispiel zum Methodenproblem in der Jesusforschung." Pp. 177–200 in vol. 2 of *Heilsgeschehen und Geschichte: Gesammelte Aufsätze 1965–1977.* Edited by E. Grässer, O. Merk, and A. Fritz. 2 vols. Marburg: Elwert, 1965–78.

Laato, A. *A Star Is Rising: The Historical Development of the Old Testament Royal Ideology and the Rise of the Jewish Messianic Expectations.* Atlanta: Scholars Press, 1997.

Labahn, M. "The Significance of Signs in Luke 7:22–23 in Light of Isaiah 61 and the Messianic Apocalypse." Pp. 146–68 in *From Prophecy to Testament.* Edited by C. A. Evans. Peabody, MA: Hendrickson, 2004.

Lagrange, M.-J. "La prophétie des soixante-dix semaines de Daniel (Dan. ix,24–27)." *Revue biblique* 39 (1930): 179–98.

Lattke, M. "Psalms of Solomon." Pp. 853–57 in *Dictionary of New Testament Background.* Edited by C. A. Evans and S. E. Porter. Downers Grove, IL: InterVarsity, 2000.

Lee, A. H. I. *From Messiah to Preexistent Son: Jesus' Self-Consciousness and Early Christian Exegesis of the Messianic Psalms.* Wissenschaftliche Untersuchungen zum Neuen Testament 2.192. Tübingen: Mohr Siebeck, 2005.

Leske, A. "Context and Meaning of Zechariah 9:9." *Catholic Biblical Quarterly* 62 (2000): 663–68.

Levine, A-J. *The Misunderstood Jew: The Church and the Scandal of the Jewish Jesus.* San Francisco: HarperSanFrancisco, 2006.

Lindars, B. *Jesus, Son of Man: A Fresh Examination of the Son of Man Sayings in the Gospels in the Light of Recent Research.* Grand Rapids: Eerdmans, 1983.

Longenecker, R. N. "The Messianic Secret in the Light of Recent Discoveries." *Evangelical Quarterly* 41 (1969): 207–15.

Longman, Tremper, III. "The Messiah: Explorations in the Law and Writings." Pp. 13–34 in *The Messiah in the Old and New Testaments.* Edited by S. E. Porter. Grand Rapids: Eerdmans, 2007.

Lüdemann, G. *Early Christianity according to the Traditions in Acts: A Commentary.* Translated by John Bowden. London: SCM, 1989.

———. *Jesus after 2000 Years.* Translated by John Bowden. London: SCM, 2000.

Luz, U. "Das Geheimnismotiv und die markinische Christologie." *Zeitschrift für die neutestamentliche Wissenschaft* 56 (1965): 9–30.

Mack, B. L. "The Christ and Jewish Wisdom." Pp. 192–221 in *The Messiah.* Edited by J. H. Charlesworth. Minneapolis: Fortress, 1992.

Manson, T. W. *The Sayings of Jesus.* London: SCM, 1949.

———. *The Servant Messiah.* Cambridge: Cambridge University Press, 1961.

Manson, W. *Jesus the Messiah: The Synoptic Tradition of the Revelation of God in Christ, with Special Reference to Form-Criticism.* London: Hodder & Stoughton, 1943.

Marcus, J. "Are You the 'Messiah-Son-of-God?' " *Novum Testamentum* 31 (1989): 125–41.

Marshall, I. H. "Jesus as Messiah in Mark and Matthew." Pp. 117–43 in *The Messiah in the Old and New Testaments*. Edited by S. E. Porter. Grand Rapids: Eerdmans, 2007.

Martin-Achard, R. *A Light to the Nations: A Study of the Old Testament Concept of Israel's Mission to the World*. Translated by J. P. Smith. Edinburgh: Oliver & Boyd, 1962.

McConville, J. G. "Messianic Interpretation of the Old Testament in Modern Context." Pp. 1–17 in *The Lord's Anointed: Interpretation of Old Testament Messianic Texts*. Edited by P. E. Satterthwaite, R. S. Hess, and G. J. Wenham. Carlisle, UK: Paternoster, 1995.

McDonald, L. M., and S. E. Porter. *Early Christianity and Its Sacred Literature*. Peabody, MA: Hendrickson, 2001.

McKnight, S. *Jesus and His Death: Historiography, the Historical Jesus, and Atonement Theory*. Waco: Baylor University Press, 2005.

———. *A New Vision for Israel: The Teachings of Jesus in National Context*. Grand Rapids: Eerdmans, 1999.

Meadors, E. P. *Jesus the Messianic Herald of Salvation*. Peabody, MA: Hendrickson, 1997.

———. "The 'Messianic' Implications of the Q Material." *Journal of Biblical Literature* 118 (1999): 253–77.

Mearns, C. L. "Parables, Secrecy and Eschatology in Mark's Gospel." *Scottish Journal of Theology* 44 (1991): 423–42.

Meeks, W. A., and R. L. Wilken. *Jews and Christians in Antioch in the First Four Centuries of the Common Era*. Society of Biblical Literature Dissertation Series 13. Missoula, MT: Scholars Press, 1978.

Meier, J. P. *A Marginal Jew*. 3 vols. Anchor Bible Reference Library. New York: Doubleday, 1991–2001.

Metzdorf, C. *Die Tempelaktion Jesu: Patristische und historisch-kritische Exegese im Vergleich*. Wissenschaftliche Untersuchungen zum Neuen Testament 2.168. Tübingen: Mohr Siebeck, 2003.

Meyer, B. F. *The Aims of Jesus*. London: SCM, 1979.

Meyer, P. W. "The Problem of the Messianic Self-Consciousness of Jesus." *Novum Testamentum* 4 (1960): 122–38.

Minette de Tillesse, G. *Le secret messianique dans l'Évangile de Marc*. Paris: Cerf, 1968.

Montgomery, J. A. *A Critical and Exegetical Commentary on the Book of Daniel*. International Critical Commentary. Edinburgh: T&T Clark, 1927.

Moo, D. J. *The Epistle to the Romans*. New International Commentary on the New Testament. Grand Rapids: Eerdmans, 1996.

Morton, R. "Son of Man." Pp. 593–98 in *Encyclopedia of the Historical Jesus*. Edited by C. A. Evans. New York: Routledge, 2008.

Moule, C. F. D. *The Origins of Christology*. Cambridge: Cambridge University Press, 1977.

Mowinckel, S. *He That Cometh*. Nashville: Abingdon, 1954.

Müller, K. "Menschensohn und Messias." *Biblische Zeitschrift* 16 (1972): 161–87; 17 (1973): 52–66.

Müller, M. *The Expression "Son of Man" and the Development of Christology: A History of Interpretation*. Copenhagen International Seminar. London: Equinox, 2007.

Müller, U. B. *Messias und Menschensohn in jüdischen Apokalypsen und der Offenbarung des Johannes*. Gütersloh: Mohn, 1972.

Mundle, W. "Die Geschichtlichkeit des messianischen Bewusstseins Jesu." *Zeitschrift für die neutestamentliche Wissenschaft* 21 (1922): 299–311.

Neusner, J. *Rabbinic Judaism: Structure and System*. Minneapolis: Fortress, 1995.

———. "Varieties of Judaism in the Formative Age." Pp. 171–97 in *Jewish Spirituality*. Edited by A. Green. London: SCM, 1989.

Neusner, J., W. S. Green, and E. Frerichs, eds. *Judaisms and Their Messiahs at the Turn of the Christian Era*. Cambridge: Cambridge University Press, 1987.

Nickelsburg, G. W. E. *Ancient Judaism and Christian Origins: Diversity, Continuity, and Transformation*. Minneapolis: Fortress, 2003.

Novakovic, L. *Messiah, the Healer of the Sick: A Study of Jesus as the Son of David in the Gospel of Matthew*. Wissenschaftliche Untersuchungen zum Neuen Testament 2.170. Tübingen: Mohr Siebeck, 2003.

Oegema, G. S. *The Anointed and His People: Messianic Expectations from the Maccabees to Bar Kochba*. Journal for the Study of the Pseudepigrapha: Supplement Series 27. Sheffield: Sheffield Academic Press, 1998.

———. "Messiah/Christ." Pp. 399–404 in *Encyclopedia of the Historical Jesus*. Edited by C. A. Evans. New York: Routledge, 2008.

Oesterley, W. O. E. *The Evolution of the Messianic Idea: A Study in Comparative Religion*. London: Pitman, 1908.

O'Neil, J. C. *Messiah: Six Lectures on the Ministry of Jesus*. Cambridge: Cochrane, 1980.

———. *Who Did Jesus Think He Was?* Leiden: Brill, 1995.

Pannenberg, W. *Jesus, God and Man*. Translated by L. L. Wilkins and D. A. Priebe. London: SCM, 1968.

Pao, D. W., and E. J. Schnabel. "Luke." Pp. 251–414 in *Commentary on the New Testament Use of the Old Testament*. Edited by G. K. Beale and D. A. Carson. Grand Rapids: Baker Academic, 2007.

Pearson, B. W. R. "The Book of the Twelve, Aqiba's Messianic Interpretations, and the Refuge of Caves of the Second Jewish War." Pp. 221–39 in *The Scrolls and the Scriptures: Qumran Fifty Years After*. Edited by S. E. Porter and C. A. Evans. Sheffield: Sheffield Academic Press, 1997.

Perrin, N. *Rediscovering the Teaching of Jesus*. London: SCM, 1967.

———. "The Wredestrasse Becomes the Hauptstrasse." *Journal of Religion* 46 (1966): 296–300.

Perry, J. M. *Exploring the Messianic Secret in Mark's Gospel*. Kansas City: Sheed & Ward, 1997.

Pesch, R. *Das Markusevangelium*. 2 vols. Herders theologischer Kommentar zum Neuen Testament. Freiburg: Basel, 1976–77.

Pitre, B. *Jesus, the Tribulation, and the End of the Exile*. Wissenschaftliche Untersuchungen zum Neuen Testament 2.204. Tübingen: Mohr Siebeck, 2005.

Pomykala, K. *The Davidic Dynasty Tradition in Early Judaism: Its History and Significance for Messianism*. Atlanta: Scholars Press, 1995.

Porter, S. E. "The Messiah in Luke and Acts: Forgiveness for the Captives." Pp. 144–64 in *The Messiah in the Old and New Testaments*. Edited by S. E. Porter. Grand Rapids: Eerdmans, 2007.

———. *Studies in the Greek New Testament*. New York: Lang, 1996.

Puech, E. "Les manuscrits de la mer Morte et le Nouveau Testament." *Le Monde de la Bible* 86 (1994): 34–41.

Räisänen, H. *The "Messianic Secret" in Mark's Gospel*. Edinburgh: T&T Clark, 1990.

Reinhartz, A. "Rabbinic Perceptions of Simeon Bar Kosiba." *Journal for the Study of Judaism* 20 (1989): 171–94.

Rengstorf, K. "Jesus Christ." Pp. 330–48 in vol. 2 of *New International Dictionary of New Testament Theology*. Edited by C. Brown. 4 vols. Grand Rapids: Zondervan, 1975–85.

Riesner, R. *Paul's Early Period: Chronology, Mission Strategy, Theology*. Translated by D. Scott. Grand Rapids: Eerdmans, 1998.

Ringgren, H. *The Messiah in the Old Testament*. Studies in Biblical Theology 18. London: SCM, 1956.

Roberts, J. J. M. "The Old Testament's Contribution to Messianic Expectations." Pp. 39–51 in *The Messiah: Developments in Earliest Judaism and Christianity*. Edited by J. H. Charlesworth. Minneapolis: Fortress, 1992.

Robinson, J. M. *Jesus according to the Earliest Witness*. Minneapolis: Fortress, 2007.

Rosenberg, R. A. "The Slain Messiah in the Old Testament." *Zeitschrift für die alttestamentliche Wissenschaft* 99 (1987): 259–61.

Rowe, R. D. "Is Daniel's Son of Man Messianic?" Pp. 71–96 in *Christ the Lord: Studies in Christology Presented to Donald Guthrie*. London: InterVarsity, 1982.

Rowland, C. *Christian Origins*. London: SCM, 1985.

Rowley, H. H. "The Suffering Servant and the Davidic Messiah." Pp. 63–93 in *The Servant of the Lord and Other Essays on the Old Testament*. Edited by H. H. Rowley. Oxford: Blackwell, 1963.

Sanders, E. P. *The Historical Figure of Jesus*. London: SCM, 1993.

———. *Jesus and Judaism*. London: SCM, 1985.

———. *Judaism: Practice and Belief 63 BCE–66 CE*. London: SCM, 1992.

Schnabel, E. J. *Early Christian Mission*. 2 vols. 2002. Reprint, Downers Grove, IL: InterVarsity, 2004.

Schnackenburg, R. "Die Messiasfrage im Johannesevangelium." Pp. 240–64 in *Neutestamentliche Aufsätze: Festschrift für Prof. Josef Schmid zum 70. Geburtstag*. Edited by J. Blinzler, O. Kuss, and F. Mussner. Regensburg: Friedrich Pustet, 1963.

Schreiber, S. *Gesalbter und König: Titel und Konzeptionen der königlichen Gesalbtenerwartung in frühjudischen und urchristlichen Schriften*. Beihefte zur Zeitschrift für die alttestamentliche Wissenschaft 105. Berlin: de Gruyter, 2000.

Schröter, J. *Jesus und die Anfänge der Christologie: Methodische und exegetische Studien zu den Ursprüng des christlichen Glauben*. Biblisch-theologische Studien 47. Neukirchen-Vluyn: Neukirchener Verlag, 2001.

Schürer, E. *The History of the Jewish People in the Age of Jesus Christ*. Revised and edited by G. Vermes, F. Millar, and M. Black. 3 vols. Edinburgh: T&T Clark, 1973–87.

Schweitzer, A. *The Quest of the Historical Jesus*. Edited by John Bowden. 6th ed. London: SCM, 2000.

Schweizer, E. *Jesus*. Translated by D. E. Green. London: SCM, 1971.

Schwemer, A. M. "Jesus Christus als Prophet, König und Priester. Das *munus triplex* und die frühe Christologie." Pp. 165–230 in *Der messianische Anspruch Jesu und die Anfänge der Christologie: Vier Studien*. Edited by M. Hengel and A. M. Schwemer. Wissenschaftliche Untersuchungen zum Neuen Testament 138. Tübingen: Mohr Siebeck, 2001.

Shepherd, M. B. "Daniel 7:13 and the New Testament Son of Man." *Westminster Theological Journal* 68 (2007): 99–111.

Silver, A. H. *A History of Messianic Speculation in Israel from the First through the Seventeenth Centuries*. 1927. Reprint, Boston: Beacon, 1959.

Stein, R. *Jesus the Messiah*. Downers Grove, IL: InterVarsity, 1996.

Strecker, G. "Zur Messiasgeheimnistheorie im Markusevangelium." *Studia theologica* 3 (1964): 87–104.

Stuckenbruck, L. T. "Messianic Ideas in the Apocalyptic and Related Literature of Early Judaism." Pp. 90–113 in *The Messiah in the Old and New Testaments*. Edited by S. E. Porter. Grand Rapids: Eerdmans, 2007.

Stuhlmacher, P. *Jesus of Nazareth, Christ of Faith*. Translated by S. Schatzmann. Peabody, MA: Hendrickson, 1988.

Talmon, S. "The Concepts of Māšîaḥ and Messianism in Early Judaism." Pp. 79–115 in *The Messiah: Developments in Earliest Judaism and Christianity*. Edited by J. H. Charlesworth. Minneapolis: Fortress, 1992.

———. "Waiting for the Messiah: The Spiritual Universe of the Qumran Covenanters." Pp. 111–37 in *Judaisms and Their Messiahs at the Turn of the Christian Era*. Edited by J. Neusner, W. S. Green, and E. S. Frerichs. Cambridge: Cambridge University Press, 1987.

Taylor, V. *The Gospel according to St. Mark*. London: Macmillan, 1952.

Theisohn, J. *Der auserwählte Richter*. Göttingen: Vandenhoeck & Ruprecht, 1975.

Theissen, G., and A. Merz. *The Historical Jesus: A Comprehensive Guide*. Translated by J. Bowden. Minneapolis: Fortress, 1998.

Tooley, W. "The Shepherd and the Sheep Image in the Teaching of Jesus." *Novum Testamentum* 7 (1964–65): 15–25.

Tuckett, C., ed. *Christology and the New Testament: Jesus and His Earliest Followers*. Louisville: Westminster John Knox, 2001.

———. *The Messianic Secret*. London: SPCK, 1983.

———. "The Son of Man and Daniel 7: Inclusive Aspects of Early Christologies." Pp. 164–89 in *Christian Origins: Worship, Belief and Society*. Edited by K. J. O'Mahoney. Journal for the Study of the New Testament: Supplement Series 241. Sheffield: Sheffield Academic Press, 2003.

Twelftree, G. H. *Jesus the Exorcist: A Contribution to the Study of the Historical Jesus*. Peabody, MA: Hendrickson, 1993.

Unnik, W. C. van. "Jesus the Christ." *New Testament Studies* 8 (1962): 101–16.

Vanhoozer, K. J. *Is There a Meaning in This Text? The Bible, the Reader, and the Morality of Literary Knowledge*. Grand Rapids: Zondervan, 1998.

Vermes, G. *The Authentic Gospel of Jesus*. London: Penguin, 2004.

———. *The Religion of Jesus the Jew*. London: SCM, 1973.

Vielhauer, P. "Gottesreich und Menschensohn in der Verkündigung Jesu." Pp. 51–79 in *Festschrift für Günther Dehn*. Edited by W. Schneemelcher. Neukirchen: Erziehungsverein, 1957.

Walck, L. W. "The Son of Man in the Parables of Enoch and the Gospels." Pp. 299–337 in *Enoch and the Messiah Son of Man: Revisiting the Book of Parables*. Edited by G. Boccaccini. Grand Rapids: Eerdmans, 2007.

Waldensperger, W. *Das Selbstbewusstsein Jesu im Lichte der messianischen Hoffnungen seiner Zeit*. 2nd ed. Strassburg: Heitz, 1892.

Watson, D. F. "The 'Messianic Secret': Demythologizing a Non-existent Markan Theme." *Journal of Theology* 110 (2006): 33–44.

Watson, F. "The Social Function of Mark's Secrecy Theme." *Journal for the Study of the New Testament* 24 (1985): 49–69.

Wedderburn, A. J. M. *A History of the First Christians*. Understanding the Bible and Its World. London: T&T Clark, 2004.

Weiss, J. *Earliest Christianity: A History of the Period A.D. 30 to 150*. 2 vols. New York: Harper, 1959.

———. "Das Problem der Entstehung des Christentums." *Archiv für Religionswissenschaft* 16 (1913): 423–515.

———. *Das Urchristentum*. Göttingen: Vandenhoeck & Ruprecht, 1917.

Wellhausen, J. *Einleitung in die drei ersten Evangelien*. Berlin: Georg Reimer, 1905.

Westfall, C. L. "Messianic Themes of Temple, Enthronement, and Victory in Hebrews and the General Epistles." Pp. 210–29 in *The Messiah in the Old and New Testaments*. Edited by S. E. Porter. Grand Rapids: Eerdmans, 2007.

Whealey, A. "The Testimonium Flavianum in Syriac and Arabic." *New Testament Studies* 54 (2008): 573–90.

Wilckens, U. *Resurrection*. Atlanta: John Knox, 1977.

Williams, J. T. "What Kind of Messiah Was Jesus?" *Expository Times* 115 (2004): 195, 197.

Willitts, J. "Matthew's Messianic Shepherd-King: In Search of 'the Lost Sheep of the House of Israel.'" *Hervormde Teologiese Studies* 63 (2007): 365–82.

Wise, M. O. *The First Messiah: Investigating the Savior before Christ*. San Francisco: HarperCollins, 1999.

Wise, M. O., and J. Tabor. "Messiah at Qumran." *Biblical Archaeology Review* 18, no. 6 (1992): 60–65.

Witherington, B. *The Christology of Jesus*. Minneapolis: Fortress, 1990.

Wrede, W. *The Messianic Secret*. Translated by J. C. G. Greig. Cambridge: James Clark, 1971.

Wright, N. T. *The Climax of the Covenant*. Edinburgh: T&T Clark, 1991.

———. *Jesus and the Victory of God*. Vol. 2 of *Christian Origins and the Question of God*. London: SPCK, 1996.

———. *The New Testament and the People of God*. Vol. 1 of *Christian Origins and the Question of God*. Minneapolis: Fortress, 1992.

———. "The Paul of History and the Apostle of Faith." *Tyndale Bulletin* 29 (1978): 61–88.

———. *The Resurrection of the Son of God*. Vol. 3 of *Christian Origins and the Question of God*. Minneapolis: Fortress, 2003.

Wright, R. B. "Psalms of Solomon." Pp. 639–70 in vol. 2 of *Old Testament Pseudepigrapha*. Edited by J. H. Charlesworth. Anchor Bible Reference Library. New York: Doubleday, 1983–85.

Zacharias, D. "4Q521 (*Messianic Apocalypse*)." Pp. 138–39 in *Encyclopedia of the Historical Jesus*. Edited by C. A. Evans. New York: Routledge, 2008.

Zetterholm, M., ed. *The Messiah: In Early Judaism and Christianity*. Minneapolis: Fortress, 2007.

Zimmerman, J. *Messianische Texte aus Qumran: Königliche, priesterliche und prophetische Messiasvorstellungen in den Schriftfunden von Qumran*. Wissenschaftliche Untersuchungen zum Neuen Testament 104. Tübingen: Mohr Siebeck, 1998.

———. "Observations on 4Q246—the 'Son of God.' " Pp. 175–90 in *Qumran-Messianism: Studies on the Messianic Expectations in the Dead Sea Scrolls*. Edited by J. H. Charlesworth, H. Lichtenberger, and G. S. Oegema. Tübingen: Mohr Siebeck, 1998.

Zingg, P. *Das Wachsen der Kirche: Beiträge zur Frage der lukanischen Redaktion und Theologie*. Göttingen: Vandenhoeck & Ruprecht, 1974.

Index of Subjects

Index of Authors

Index of Scripture
and Other Ancient Sources

Tertullian

Apology
3.6 156n158

Classical Writers

Dio Cassius

Roman History
68.32 51n53
69.12–13 51n53
69.12–14 51n55

Dio Chrysostom

Orations
1.13–28 133n72
2.6 133n72
3.41 133n72
4.43–44 133n72
8.5 111

Homer

Iliad
2.75–109 133n72

Odyssey
3.156 133n72

Lucian

*Alexander the
False Prophet*
25 155n150
39 155n150

*Passing of
Peregrinus*
11–13 155n15

Pliny

Epistles
10.96.1–5 155n150

Plutarch

Moralia
230F 111

Suetonius

Claudius
25.4 74

Nero
16.2 155n150

Vespasian
4.5 156

Tacitus

Annals
15.44 155n150,
156n158

Histories
5.13 156

**Papyri and
Inscriptions**

Fayyum Fragment

in toto 134n78

Oxyrhynchus

1.6 100, 108

Sefire

3.14–17 81